Building Character through Multicultural Literature

A Guide for Middle School Readers

Rosann Jweid
Margaret Rizzo

The Scarecrow Press, Inc.
Lanham, Maryland • Toronto • Oxford
2004

SCARECROW PRESS, INC.

Published in the United States of America
by Scarecrow Press, Inc.
A wholly owned subsidiary of
The Rowman & Littlefield Publishing Group, Inc.
4501 Forbes Boulevard, Suite 200, Lanham, Maryland 20706
www.scarecrowpress.com

PO Box 317
Oxford
OX2 9RU, UK

British Library Cataloguing in Publication Information Available

Library of Congress Cataloging-in-Publication Data

Jweid, Rosann, 1933–
  Building character through multicultural literature : a guide for middle school
readers / Rosann Jweid, Margaret Rizzo.
    p. cm.
  Includes bibliographical references and index.
  ISBN 0-8108-5042-7 (pbk. : alk. paper)
  1. Children's literature—Bibliography. 2. Middle school students—Books and
reading. 3. Pluralism (Social sciences) in literature—Bibliography. 4. Ethnic
groups in literature—Bibliography. 5. Minorities in literature—Bibliography. 6.
Multicultural education—Activity programs. I. Rizzo, Margaret. II. Title.
Z1037.J935 2004
011.62—dc22
                                    2004006581

Contents

Preface

Global events of the past few years accentuate the need for understanding people of cultures different from our own. The attack on the World Trade Center in New York City, ongoing conflict in the Middle East, and violations of human rights in places like Africa, Europe, and Latin America have bred fear and distrust among peoples of different cultures, religions, and ethnicity. This distrust is present among nations of the world and even among people of different races and cultures living in the same country. The need to promote understanding and tolerance between races, religions, and cultures is essential to create peace among nations and individuals.

Our previous book *Building Character through Literature: A Guide for Middle School Readers* aimed at assisting educators and parents in using literature to educate children about the positive personal values essential to a healthy society. The primary purpose of this book was to introduce novels that showed strength of character with guidance for discussions that could raise character issues. Our intention was that the reader would be able to identify with the character issues that appeared in the book and develop the ability to evaluate them, determining those worthy of emulation. Our secondary purpose was to encourage a love of reading and of quality literature through a greater understanding of the relevance of literature to our everyday lives. Writers of literature for children and young adults have often concerned themselves with these same purposes: catching the interest of the reader, expanding awareness and knowledge of the world, and helping the reader to grow and develop into a thoughtful, caring adult.

We decided, due to the increasing hostility and violence around he world, to follow with a book in similar format but one that stresses multicultural understanding and acceptance. Our main criterion in selecting the fifty novels was to include books of varied cultures and nations in which the characters exemplify strong positive character traits. We hoped that the reader would be able to identify and evaluate character traits and decide which should be emulated. Though we gave preference to novels written by authors with a body of critically acclaimed work and novels that had been awarded literary prizes, we also included lesser-known authors whose work fulfilled our primary criterion. Our secondary purpose was to include novels with engaging plots, dynamic characters, and strong themes that would capture the imagination of the reader and foster an appreciation of good literature. We hope that this book will be useful for librarians working with individuals and groups, for teachers leading class discussions, and for librarians and teachers working together. Parents who educate their children at home and parents who read with their children will also find the information useful and stimulating.

Literature can be a powerful tool in promoting understanding, acceptance, and friendship. When children read about characters that share their dreams and problems, even though they are in different countries or cultures, they begin to realize the oneness of the human race. This knowledge is the foundation for acceptance. Through educating the children of today, we can hopefully avoid the hostility of the past and help to create peace in the future.

Introduction

Building Character through Multicultural Literature: A Guide for Middle School Readers is designed to assist the library teacher, classroom teacher, and parent in selecting novels, guiding students, and discussing books that explore the various cultures of the world and also demonstrate character building.

In the first section, the fifty novels chosen for inclusion are appropriate for students in grades four through eight, and are arranged alphabetically by title. The same format has been used to discuss each novel:

> Awards
> Characters
> Character Traits
> Setting
> Plot
> Questions for Discussion
> Projects
> Vocabulary
> About the Author
> From the Author

Specifically, the Awards section includes major literary honors given to the book. The sections titled Character, Setting, and Plot, taken together, provide an overview of what happens in the book to assist in evaluating the appropriateness of the novel for the reader. Under Character Traits are listed those qualities most obvious in the novels. Questions for Discussion stimulate children to think about both the unique qualities of a culture and the characters, their actions, words, motives, and character traits. They test the reader's comprehension of the novel's meaning and encourage a critical appreciation of literature and a love of reading. These questions may be used by class groups or individual students. Ideas given in the Projects section appeal to a broad range of interest and ability levels, and can be used for library research, curriculum correlation, and parental involvement. Vocabulary is given in direct quotations. The About the Author section provides brief information about the author and his or her motivations to guide the user in promoting the novel. Whenever possible, authors were contacted about their motivations for writing the books and their feelings about the finished works. These comments are included in the From the Author section.

The rest of the book includes the following:

> Titles Arranged by Genres and Themes
> Character Traits in the Novels
> Useful Websites for Young Adult Literature
> Bibliography of Novels
> Bibliography of Useful References

NOVELS

Adem's Cross
Author: Alice Mead
Publication date: 1996

Awards
ALA Best Books for Young Adults

Characters
Adem
Fatmira and Pranvera, his sisters
Besim, his cousin
Milos
Gregor
Fikel

Character Traits
Citizenship
Courage
Helpfulness
Kindness
Loyalty
Optimism
Patience
Perseverance
Resilience
Self-control
Tolerance
Trustworthiness

Setting
1993—Kosovo

Plot
Fourteen-year-old Adem is an ethnic Albanian boy living in Kosovo, a poor
province in Yugoslavia, occupied by the Serbs. Here, Slobodan Milosevic, the
leader of Serbia, had instigated fear and distrust among the Albanians and Serbs
who had lived together for many years. Now, the police, controlled by Milosevic, are guilty of extensive human rights abuses, and the Albanians live in
poverty and fear.

Adem's life has dramatically changed. His cousin Besim has come to live
with his family, and Adem is sure his father likes Besim better than him. Albanians are not allowed to play organized sports, so Adem plays invisible soccer

with his friends and misses the games with his Serb friend Milos. Tear gassing and violence always mark the beginning of the school year, in a building with no heat, lights, chairs, or books. His sister Fatmira promises him that things will be different this year. She tells him that she has joined a group of young activists in Prizren.

Fatmira asks Adem and Besim to go to Prizren with her where she and four other girls will be reading poetry, each standing on a bridge built by the Ottomans in an effort to prevent the Serbs from blowing up the river in order to change its course. As the girls read, the crowd becomes larger. The Serb police open fire, and Fatmira is killed.

Having died in this way, she becomes a heroine, but Adem believes he is responsible for her death because he did not tell anyone of her intention to protest. The police focus on Adem's family for particularly cruel treatment. They ruin their house searching for weapons, beat Adem's father, and take him prisoner. After he is released, Adem's father is a dispirited shadow of his former self. When the soldiers take possession of the bake shop in their house operated by Adem's grandmother, Adem's parents just accept this and Adem is frustrated with their attitude. Hearing the soldiers through the walls and seeing the passivity of his family, Adem is overwhelmed with hatred until a conversation with a Serb soldier Gregor makes him realize that they are people, too. After the soldiers catch him with their belongings in the bake shop, Adem decides to leave home. He is later attacked by Serbian soldiers who carve the Serb cross on his chest. His father contacted the Democratic Alliance because of this abuse, but Adem is reluctant to help the Alliance out of fear for his family. He decides that to protect his family, he must run away immediately. He contacts the Gypsy Fikel to help him over the border into Albania. When Fikel is killed by the border patrol, Adem is left to complete the journey. But, inspired by Fatmira and Fikel, he has a new calmness and knows he will some day return to Kosovo.

Questions for Discussion

1. Under what conditions are the Albanians living in Kosovo? How are they treated by the Serbs?
2. What are Adem's feelings about having his cousin Besim live with them? Why does he feel this way? Are Adem's feelings understandable to you?
3. Fatmira tells Adem that he doesn't consider others, and he agrees with her that he is angry, jealous, and impatient. Other boys call him a cynic. Do you agree with these descriptions of Adem? What does his decision to leave home tell you about him? What other positive and negative traits does he display? Would you like Adem for a friend?
4. What inspires Fatmira to join the resistance movement? Do you think she is foolish to engage in the poetry reading, or do you admire her? What character traits does she exhibit?
5. How does Adem feel when he learns that his sister has joined the resistance? Do you think he should have told someone she was going to do this? Is he right in feeling guilty for her death? What would you have done in Adem's place?

6. Adem and Milos were friends and soccer teammates. What has happened to their friendship? Do you think that either of them has feelings of friendship remaining toward the other?

7. Adam and his friends cannot play soccer, but they play invisible soccer. Describe the game as you visualize it. How does this game represent more to them than entertainment or sport?

8. What do you learn about the culture of Albania from this novel? What are the roles of women and children in an Albanian family? Why was the beating Adem's father endured especially painful?

9. Why does Adem's mother want to have a party? What does this tell you about her?

10. How is Adem's father affected by his imprisonment? Why does Adem disagree with his father on the action they should take against the Serbs? When and why does Adem change his opinion to agree with his father? What is your opinion about fighting back versus not fighting back?

11. What is life like for the Gypsies? How are they treated by others? Why does Adem trust Fikel? Do know of any group in your own country who are treated in a similar way?

12. How does Adem react to the Serbian soldier Gregor and the Serbian driver who helps him out of Kosovo? What does he learn from his associations with these "enemies."

13. Adem knows that each school year will start with tear gassing and violence. How does Adem handle the beginning of school? How do you think you would handle going to school in a situation like this?

14. Why is the book titled *Adem's Cross*? How is the carving of the cross pivotal to Adem and the plot of the novel?

Projects

1. Draw a map of the region in which Adem lives as its borders are today.

2. Use the Internet or online databases to find information on the status of Kosovo today. Organize your information into a news story.

3. Fatmira has written a poem based upon the myth of Demeter and Persephone. Write your own poem based upon this myth or another myth of your choice.

4. Locate recipes for the food of Albania and the Baltic region. Select a recipe to share with your class.

5. Go to the website of an organization that exists to document and eliminate human rights violations, such as Amnesty International or Human Rights Watch. Create a *PowerPoint* presentation that describes these organizations and the areas in the world where human rights are in danger.

6. The Serbian cross is carved into Adem's chest. Use an encyclopedia, design book, or the Internet to locate pictures of different versions of the cross, such as the Serbian, the Celtic, the Maltese, and the Latin. Create a poster including several of these, labeling each.

Vocabulary

Each of the following quotations chosen from *Adem's Cross* includes one or more vocabulary words in **bold print**.

1. "The other kids in the back of the room, including me, **snickered** nervously."
2. "Mr. Gashi stepped carefully through the crowd of kids sitting **wedged** in tightly on the floor."
3. "I wanted to do something **rash** and **impulsive**."
4. "But while I rested on one of the living room sofas, I **fretted** about my conversation with Fatmira."
5. "They knew we played **invisible** soccer out of **defiance**."
6. "I threw myself on her and shook her to try to **rouse** her, but she wouldn't wake up."
7. "My grandmother **restrained** her as best she could."
8. "I **clenched** my fists and dug my fingernails into my palms."
9. "He ate **ravenously**."
10. "Without her, shoveling the mounds would be pure **drudgery**."
11. "The bread was baked very early by women in the village and then sold for a **pittance**."
12. "It seemed that Albanian families were **destined** to be forced apart."
13. "It came on without warning, without **premonition**, and it followed me everywhere."
14. "Stiff with **indignation**, my grandfather got up and left the house."
15. "A few minutes later, the bear sat down and refused to **budge**."

About the Author

Alice Mead was born in Portchester, New York, and received Bachelor's Degrees from Bryn Mawr College and the University of Southern Maine, and a Master's Degree from Southern Connecticut State University. She has been an art teacher and a preschool teacher. She often writes about young people living in difficult situations and has actively worked for the welfare of Kosovo children, bringing nine Albanian teenagers to Maine for high school and organizing a toy drive for the children of Kosovo. She relaxes by playing the flute, gardening, painting, and taking photographs.

Alone at Ninety Foot
Author: Katherine Holubitsky
Publication date: 1999

Awards
Canadian Library Association Young Adult Best Book of the Year
IODE Violet Downey Book Award
ALA Best Books for Young Adults
American Booksellers "Pick of the Lists"
NYPL Books for the Teen Age
Teacher Librarian Magazine Best Books for Young Adults
Canadian Children's Book Centre Our Choice

Characters
Pamela Collins
Mr. Collins
Joanne Robertson
Danielle Higgins
Matt Leighton
Jennifer Reid
Nana Jean

Character Traits
Compassion
Kindness
Optimism
Resilience
Respect
Respect for the environment
Self-control
Self-respect

Setting
Present day—Vancouver, British Columbia, Canada

Plot
Pamela Collins likes to spend time in Lynn Canyon Park; here, a pool called Ninety Foot is surrounded by rock walls that extend ninety feet up, and a suspension bridge crosses a gorge. Fourteen-year-old Pam has come here for years with her mother, but here also her mother took her own life a year before, jumping from the bridge because she was depressed after the death of her baby from Sudden Infant Death Syndrome.

Pam misses talking to her mom about her life, her friends, and the physical changes she is experiencing. Her mother taught her how to make wreaths and how to bead, and also instilled in Pam a love of nature. In fact, one of Pam's hobbies is to collect pieces of nature, such as stones, flowers, water, and soil, from places she has visited. Dealing with her mother's death is a difficult process for Pam who lives with her father. When her father meets Jennifer Reid, Pam finds a new friend who is sensitive to Pam's feelings and who Pam can tease about the old-fashioned clichés of her vocabulary.

Pam doesn't think of herself as having many friends; she doesn't want to be cool if it means that she has to sacrifice her self-respect and values. When her friend Joanne wants to be part of the popular crowd led by Danielle, she steals a shirt and puts it in Pam's bag. Pam is caught and horrified at this experience. Joanne finally stops hanging around with Danielle, who is obnoxious and cruel. When Joanne encourages Pam to go to a graduation party commemorating their completion of eighth grade, Danielle becomes furious when her boyfriend Matt starts talking to Pam. She begins a tirade about the suicide of Pam's mother, and, while Pam effectively stops her by calling her one of Jennifer's old-fashioned names, "dweeb," she still runs out of the party in tears. This unfortunate incident does, however, precipitate a discussion with her father about her mother's death. He reassures Pam that her mother did not choose to be with the baby instead of Pam, that her mother thought that Pam and her father would be better off if she were not around, and that Pam shares her mother's sense of humor and love of life; her mother would always be part of her life. This discussion, along with a vivid dream in which she talks with her mother, helps Pam to accept her mother's death and begin to move to the future with hope.

Questions for Discussion

1. Pam doesn't want to be part of the in-crowd if it means she has to compromise her values. What does this tell you about Pam? What values does she possess?
2. Pam doesn't mind being alone, but she doesn't like to be lonely, and she can be lonely even in a crowd. Have you ever shared these feelings? Why do you think Pam feels alone when she is among others?
3. How does Pam deal with the death of her mother at the beginning of the novel? Why is spending time at Ninety Foot important to her? What does she mean when she says she is getting the intangibles back? Why is the conversation that Pam has with her father important in helping her to come to terms with her mother's death? What is the importance of Pam's dream about her mother? How would you describe her acceptance by the end of the novel?
4. How do others treat Pam after her mother's death? Have you ever had a friend who experienced the loss of someone close? How did you treat this person? After reading Pam's story, what have you learned about how to interact with a bereaved person?

5. What is Pam's relationship with her father? Why doesn't he like Pam going to walk in the canyon? How does he react when his prize car is destroyed? What does this tell you about him?
6. Why doesn't Pam tell anyone that she has been attacked? How could she have benefited from talking to someone? Who could she have talked to?
7. What kind of friend is Joanne? Why does she want to be Danielle's friend? Why doesn't Joanne apologize to Pam after the shirt incident? What do you think of the way Pam reacted to Joanne? Do you think theirs is a stronger friendship after this incident?
8. What do you think of Danielle? Do you agree with Pam that she doesn't really have any friends? What actions of Danielle do you find to be particularly loathsome? Why does Danielle act the way she does? Do you think Pam's reaction to her at the party was effective? Why?
9. What qualities does Jennifer have that make Pam and Nana like her? Why do Pam and Jennifer become friends? Are you surprised that Pam accepts her so easily? What does this tell you about Pam?
10. Why does the author include the incident of the child lost in the canyon? What does this add to the novel?
11. Why is the setting important to this novel? How would the novel be different if it were not set at Ninety Foot? Can you think of another setting that could be effective for this novel?

Projects

1. Pam likes the paintings of Emily Carr. Use the Internet to locate information on this Canadian painter, and find copies of her work. Create a *PowerPoint* presentation including information on her life and her style and copies of some of her pictures that you download from the Internet.
2. Pam's baby sister died of SIDS. Locate information on this condition, including its causes and prevention. Organize your data into an informational pamphlet that babysitters your own age would find useful.
3. Pam's hobbies of beading and collecting pieces of nature tell something about her background and her interests. What hobbies do you have that tell something about you? Share these with your class including how you got involved in the hobbies and who might have influenced you.
4. Locate information on the dangers of smoking, and make a poster aimed at teaching your peers the dangers of smoking.
5. Pam is amused by Jennifer's use of outdated words. Interview your parents, grandparents, and elderly friends and neighbors asking them for words and phrases that they commonly used in their youth. Also make a list of words and expressions that you and your friends use. Make a mini-dictionary including both lists of expressions and their definitions.

Vocabulary

Each of the following quotations chosen from *Alone at Ninety Foot* includes one or more vocabulary words in **bold print**.

1. "I used to feel sort of **invincible** swaying in the air above it."

2. "Like seeds popping open and leaves **unfurling** and insects **burrowing** under the soil."
3. "In fact, I thought it was quite a beautiful plant and didn't think it deserved such an **offensive** name."
4. "He has this **pompous, affected** way of reading to us."
5. "And then he stands **smugly**, waiting for a reaction."
6. "His **scraggy** beard and bug eyes give me the creeps."
7. "They glared at me **accusingly**."
8. "I felt as **loathsome** as a twelve-inch slug."
9. "She **interrogated** anyone who came close to talk to me, demanding their motives before they could speak."
10. "But it doesn't surprise me that that attempt **fizzled** out."
11. "With this **inquisitive** look, he glanced around trying to find it."
12. "Tony continues to **prod** at a mass of sticks and moss caught in the bank by the creek."
13. "She made him believe it was his parental duty to **harass** me."
14. "What if I **inadvertently** offend her?"
15. "With no content to speak of, but with some **intricately** drawn, far-out title page."
16. "Linda was, like, totally **oblivious** to Mrs. Robertson."
17. "The things I keep discovering are **intangible**. I can't touch or see them or even put any kind of label on them."
18. "For Joanne, being stuck in her room was truly **traumatic**."

About the Author

Katherine Holubitsky was born in Toronto, Ontario, Canada. She attended Simon Fraser University and graduated from Grant MacEwan College. She began to write seriously when she reached her thirties, and she enjoys writing about adolescents with the dual goals of providing entertaining reading and showing teens that their emotions are normal. She lives in Edmonton, Alberta, Canada, with her husband, children, Clumber spaniel, and Siamese cats.

Ashes of Roses
Author: Mary Jane Auch
Publication date: 2002

Characters
Margaret Rose Nolen
Mr. and Mrs. Nolen, her parents
Maureen and Bridget, her sisters, and Joseph, her brother
Patrick Nolen, her uncle
Elsa
Mr. Garoff
Gussella Garoff
Rose Klein
Rose Bellini

Character Traits
Citizenship
Compassion
Cooperation
Courage
Dependability
Helpfulness
Loyalty
Optimism
Perseverance
Resilience
Resourcefulness
Responsibility
Self-control

Setting
1911—New York City

Plot
Margaret Rose and her family come to America from Ireland. Their journey is a difficult one. When they get to Ellis Island, the baby Joseph is turned away because of an eye infection, and Margaret's father decides that he will take the baby back to Ireland and return to America later, while his wife and other children will stay with his brother in New York City.

Ma, Margaret, who now prefers to be called by her middle name Rose, Maureen, and Bridget appear at Uncle Patrick's apartment where he welcomes them, but his wife and her daughters are anything but welcoming. Ma is furious that Uncle Patrick has abandoned Catholicism in favor of his wife's Lutheranism. Tensions rise and Rose decides that her only recourse is to find a job to earn money for them to have a place of their own. She gets a job making paper flowers, but Mr. Moscovitz takes advantage of the girls in his shop and tries to take physical advantage of Rose. At home, things are worse, and after a big fight, Ma decides to return to Ireland. Rose refuses to go, and Maureen wants to stay with her.

Rose and Maureen rent a room from Mr. Garoff and his daughter Gussela. Gussie finds Rose a job in the Triangle Shirtwaist Company where she works. Gussie is involved with making the conditions at the factory better for the workers and has little room in her life for fun. Soon Rose meets two other Roses, Rose Klein and Rose Bellini, who introduce her to the moving pictures and dime novels. Rose has promised her mother that Maureen will continue in school, but one day Maureen appears at the factory. After a knock-down-drag-out fight, Maureen convinces Rose that she should work and save all her money for her family to return to America.

When fire breaks out at the factory, the girls cannot exit because the doors are locked. Many jump to their deaths, including the other Roses. Rose, who has refused to take the elevator, escapes by riding down on the top of the elevator. Rose cannot find either Gussie, who has gone back to help someone, or Maureen. Maureen has escaped with the help of university students who lay a ladder across rooftops. The sisters go with Mr. Garoff to the morgue where they find Gussie's body.

Rose and Maureen agree that their parents will never come back to America, but they will stay. Rose knows that the same courage that saved her from dying in the fire will be needed, but she is determined that her friends will not be forgotten and conditions at the factory will be exposed.

Questions for Discussion

1. When she lands in America, Rose says she is overcome with both hope and fear. Explain how she can be experiencing both of these emotions. Have you ever been in a situation like this when you felt many emotions at one time?
2. Describe Rose's parents and their strengths of character. Why does Da decide that he should be the one to return to Ireland? What difficulties does Ma face staying in America? Do you understand why she decides she must return to Ireland?
3. What do you think about the way that Elsa and her daughters treat Rose and her family? Why don't they welcome the newcomers? Could Uncle Patrick have done anything to make the situation better? Could Ma have done anything to make the situation better? What does Rose mean when she says that her arguments with the sisters are changing her into another person?
4. What does Rose learn about the world of work from her first job making flowers? How does Rose taking work home affect the rest of the girls? What are her feelings when she starts her job at the Triangle? Have you ever

experienced similar feelings when you started something new? How did you handle your fears?

5. Describe the strengths and weaknesses displayed by Rose. Why does she want to be known as Rose? What qualities does she have that would make her a good friend?

6. What are the character strengths and weaknesses of Maureen? What qualities does she show when they live with Uncle Patrick's family, when she insists on staying in America, and when she gets a job in the factory? What do you learn about her after the fire? Describe the bond that exists between Maureen and Rose.

7. What qualities does Gussie exhibit? Why is she so passionate about gaining rights for workers? Why is this work important? Would you like Gussie for a friend? Why or why not?

8. What kinds of things does Rose enjoy doing with the friends she meets at the factory? What conflicting emotions does she feel in regard to Gussie? Have you ever had feelings like this when you made new friends?

9. In what ways does the fire change Rose? Why does she feel guilty about Maureen, her friends, and Gussie after the fire? Why does Rose lash out at the curiosity seekers who came to look at the devastation and those trying to capitalize on the fire? She vows to make sure that those who died are not forgotten. What can she do to keep their memories alive?

10. The author powerfully depicts the fire at the factory. How does the author make the reader aware of its horror? What images made the biggest impression on you?

11. Why do Rose and Maureen decide to stay in America? What does this tell you about them? Do you think their parents will ever return to America?

12. Explain the significance of the novel's title.

Projects

1. Information on the entry of immigrants into the United States can be found on the Internet at many websites, for example, www.ellisisland.com/ and www.historychannel.com/ellisisland/gateway/index.html. Locate information on the medical exams and other tests that immigrants had to take. Create a poster or a *PowerPoint* presentation through which you present this information.

2. Did your ancestors leave their homeland and settle in another country? When did they emigrate? Interview a relative, and supplement the information they give you by research. Find out why they and others left their country of origin. Assume the persona of one of your ancestors, and write a series of diary entries or letters that document this individual's journey to a new home.

3. Locate information on the fire at the Triangle Waist Company. Organize the information into a news story for a city paper.

4. Find out about the union movement in the garment industry at the beginning of the twentieth century. How are conditions today different from the conditions in which Rose worked?

5. Rose and her friends are interested in nice clothes. Draw a series of sketches of clothing of the early twentieth century.
6. Project the lives of Rose and Maureen ten years into the future. Write a series of letters from one of the girls to family back in Ireland. Be sure that the qualities displayed by the girl in the novel is reflected in the letters.

Vocabulary

Each of the following quotations chosen from *Ashes of Roses* includes one or more vocabulary words in **bold print**.

1. "I'd be glad to get off the ship so I wouldn't have to **endure** the comments of our fellow passengers, who were gettin' less patient with Joseph by the day."
2. "it made it harder to push through the people with the **cumbersome** feather bed."
3. "There was a young man with a rackin' cough who didn't seem **destined** to become an American, either."
4. "A whole new world was stretchin' out before me, and I wanted a chance to **savor** it before I was weighed down with babies like Ma."
5. "We **huddled** together in the registry room, tryin' to comfort Ma, though she was near **inconsolable**."
6. "the ferry landed and we were **spewed** down the gangplank with the other passengers."
7. "Ma was so excited she ate the sauerkraut without noticin' **what an abomination** it was."
8. "But if I could find some work, we could leave here with our **dignity intact**."
9. "After all, it must get **tedious** doin' the same thing over and over."
10. "I didn't want to do anything to hurt him, even though I **despised** his family."
11. "At first she **jutted** out her chin and started to say somethin', but then she thought better of it and joined him."
12. "We finally arrived at the front, leavin' a path of **irate** people in our wake."
13. "I asked, hopin' to **distract** them from Maureen's rudeness."
14. "followed by a **raspy** sound from all around me, as if hundreds of bumblebees the size of cats had flown in and settled on the tables."
15. "I knew Gussie had little interest in what she called **frivolous** things, but it wouldn't hurt her to spend more time on her appearance."

About the Author

Mary Jane Auch was born in Mineola, New York, and received a B.A. in art from Skidmore College. Because she did not enjoy working as a graphic artist, she received a degree in occupational therapy from Columbia University and worked as a therapist in a children's hospital. After raising her children, she attended a workshop on writing for children and decided that this was what she should do. Auch has written and illustrated picture books and has written novels. She lives in Rochester, New York.

The Bamboo Flute
Author: Garry Disher
Publication date: 1993

Awards
Australian Book Council Children's Book of the Year
Shortlisted for New South Wales Premier Award
Publisher's Weekly Best Books of the Year

Characters
Paul
Paul's mother and father
Eric the Red
Margaret
Mr. Riggs

Character Traits
Compassion
Courage
Dependability
Generosity
Kindness
Perseverance
Responsibility

Setting
1932—A rural community in South Australia

Plot
The Great Depression that swept the world in the 1930s is felt even in the vast farmlands of South Australia has changed the lifestyle of Paul and his mother and father. The music that used to be mainstay of the family has vanished. The piano that Paul's mother always played has been sold to cover expenses, and now she is sad and his father is bitter. There is too much work and too little time. After his father returned from the war in 1919, Paul's parents married, started the farm, and the house was filled with his father's "warbling whistling and his mother's rippling piano." Now they are poor, in danger of losing the farm, and itinerant men tramp the roads.

Paul gets up every morning, does his chores, and then walks one hour to school. Often, he falls asleep or gets lost in musical daydreams and is chastised by Mr. Riggs, his teacher, for not paying attention. A country boy, Paul envies Margaret and her secret society of town kids and yearns to a part of the group. It is when he is watching for Margaret to come to school that he first glimpses Eric the Red, the swagman, who plays such an important role in his life. At school, Mr. Riggs discusses the gold that has been found at the Granites and the route that many of the miners will take to get there. The children are warned not to talk to the men passing through the area.

Paul dreams of gold bringing music back into his life, sets out on Saturday to pan the nearby stream, and again encounters Eric the Red. Though Paul knows he should not be talking to him and knows the lamb he is eating is from their farm, he is fascinated, especially by Eric's flute. After showing him the rudiments of playing, Eric says that the stand of bamboo will produce a piece for a perfect flute and shows Paul how to make one.

Paul starts his first attempt, but it is taken away by Mr. Riggs who thinks this is playing with a stick rather than paying attention. His second attempt is improved by Eric the Red, and soon Paul discovers his natural gift. He plays for his mother and then for Mr. Riggs who asks him to perform at the school concert. Even Margaret and the town kids are impressed and finally, most of all, his father who drops some of his worries and allows music back into the family.

Questions for Discussion

1. The Great Depression causes many people to be out of work, with many of them drifting around the country homeless. How differently do Paul's mother and his father react to these men? Why do you think this is so? Do you think that the roles of men and women in this time have anything to do with the way they behave? What does this tell you about each of them?

2. Tales soon spread of strange men lurking in the area, animals being killed, and food being stolen. How does the community react to these rumors? How would your community react in similar circumstances? What do you think could be done to alleviate the problem? Are there agencies in your community that work toward this goal?

3. Paul is frequently distracted or asleep in class and cannot answer Mr. Riggs's questions. How does Mr. Riggs treat Paul's inattention? Has this ever happened to you in school? How did you feel at the time? Why do you think Mr. Riggs treats Paul in this manner?

4. Paul's father is always morose. Why do you think this is so? How would you feel if you were constantly worried about being able to feed and house your family? Do you think many fathers in today's world carry the same burden? Why do you think this is so? What can you do to help the situation?

5. Why do you think that Margaret and her friends do not accept Paul? Do you have groups in your school that do not befriend individuals? Are you a member of such a group? What can be done about your attitude and the attitude of others?

6. What is Constable Bailey's advice to children at school about the swagmen? Have you have previously heard the advice? Why is it wise for you to follow these words? Why do you think Paul ignores the advice? Was it smart for him to do so?

7. How does Paul's music on the bamboo flute change his relationships with Mr. Riggs, Margaret, his mother, and his father? Why do you think these changes occur? How does the music help Paul and his family?

Projects
1. Paul's home is located in Tralee near Adelaide, Australia. Create an imaginary home page for the local Chamber of Commerce. The purpose of the home page is to encourage tourism by highlighting the unusual and interesting features of the area.
2. Collect a piece of bamboo and attempt to make a flute similar to the one Paul made. Ask the instrumental teacher in your school for assistance in locating the holes and positioning the lips and the hands for playing.
3. In Australia, the out-of-work men roaming the roads were called swagmen. Research and report on The Great Depression in your country; see if there were men similar to the swagmen. Discover what programs were developed to alleviate the poverty and the unemployment, and evaluate their success.
4. Paul counts his way through town. Select a location in your community to which you can walk; create a map showing how many steps it is to each site on your route.
5. Draw a picture of Paul's classroom as you would imagine it looks with the young ones practicing the alphabet, the middle kids doing diction, and the older ones doing arithmetic.
6. Write a journal for Mr. Riggs, describing his activities and feelings during one day at school.

Vocabulary
Each of the following quotations chosen from *The Bamboo Flute* includes one or more vocabulary words in **bold print.**
1. "It's **exasperation**."
2. "He opens the gate and I follow him into the **paddock**."
3. "These days, I rarely hear his **warbling** whistle, the one that **coils** and dips like water over stones or magpies in a gum tree."
4. "Instant **pandemonium**."
5. "The clock on the **rickety** dresser **whirrs** and clangs."
6. "The **corrugated**-iron roof is fringed with rust."
7. "He has a **phlegmy** voice that makes you want to cough for him."
8. "I feel more **confident** now."
9. "He's **indicating** a stand of bamboo stalks clumped together like **quarreling, tattered** feather dusters."
10. Dust **motes** blaze in the bands of the sunlight."
11. "Then I trail my fingers over the **calcified** deposit left by years of **seepage**."
12. "But when he sees I'm a kid his face grows **cunning**."
13. "Then the **eruption**."
14. "My movements are so slight and **inoffensive**, surely I am **invisible**."
15. "The entire district is gripped by the **exploits** Eric the Red."
16. "The notes **emerge** like the songs of **raucous** birds far away."

17. "He **glowers** at us."
18. "He answers all the **idiotic** questions about crimes you'd need a whole army of thieves for."
19. "He is returning to his **briskness** and **severity**, so I pick up my knapsack to go."
20. "through the **shimmering mirages** that disappear before I ever reach them."

About the Author
Garry Disher, a native of South Australia has lived in many parts of the world but, now makes his home in Melbourne. His writings have one won many major awards, including the Stanford University Writing Fellowship, National Short Story Award, and Children's Book Council Book of the Year. Mr. Disher writes in several genres for adults and children and feels they are equal in worth.

Bearstone
Author: Will Hobbs
Publication date: 1989

Awards
ALA Best Book for Young Adults
ALA Books for the Reluctant Reader
National Council for the Social Studies/Children's Book Council Notable
    Children's Book in the Field of Social Studies
NYPL Books for the Teenage
IRA Teachers' Choice
Western Writers of America Spur Award
American Booksellers "Pick of the Lists"

Characters
Cloyd Atcitty
Walter Landis
Susan Jones
Rusty
Grandmother

Character Traits
Compassion
Courage
Dependability
Generosity
Kindness
Loyalty
Perseverance
Respect for the environment
Trustworthiness

Setting
Present day—Colorado

Plot
Bearstone is the story of two people, Cloyd and Walter Landis. Cloyd is a four-teen-year-old Ute Indian who has pretty much run wild for the last four years. Living with his grandmother, he has attended no school, spending his time tend-ing her goats in the remote canyons of Utah. Finally, the tribe sends him to a group home in Durango, Colorado. Failing at school and disappointed that he will not be going home for the summer, he runs away to find his father, soon

returning with no satisfaction. Walter is an old rancher who was a gold miner in his younger days. Since losing his wife and his joy in living, he has let the ranch or farm, as he calls it, deteriorate, caring only for his wife's beloved peach trees.

Susan Jones, Cloyd's house mother brings Cloyd to the farm for the summer, hoping that the two would be good for each other. On his first day at the ranch, Cloyd finds a burial of the Ancient Ones and in it a blue stone shaped like a bear. From his grandmother, Cloyd knows that the bear is a very important animal to the Ute nation, so he keeps the stone for good luck and even gives himself the secret name, Lone Bear. When Walter speaks of going to the mountains to his gold mine, Cloyd is thrilled. He sets to work with zeal until Rusty, a friend of Walter's and a bear hunter, comes through Walter's land with a dead bear. Feeling anger and betrayal, he destroys Walter's beautiful peach trees. At first outraged, Walter begins to understand Cloyd's motivation and fulfills his promise to take Cloyd to the mountains. There, Cloyd encounters a bear and foolishly divulges its location to the bear hunter. While Cloyd is off in a futile attempt to save the bear, Walter is seriously injured, and Cloyd's first priority is to bring him to safety. The act brings him the realization that he has found the father for whom he was searching.

Questions for Discussion
1. Why do you think Cloyd is such a failure at school? What happens when Cloyd finds his father? Do you understand his feelings?
2. Why does Cloyd take the name "Lone Bear"? Do you agree with his assumption? What would you tell Cloyd about the need for someone?
3. What happens when Cloyd attempts to earn the mountains? Does this tell you something very important about setting goals? Why does Cloyd become angry when Walter offers to help him read? Have you ever acted with hostility to cover your shortcomings? What would be a wiser thing to do?
4. Due to his Ute heritage, Cloyd develops a close affinity to bears. How does he feel when Rusty, Walter's friend, returns with a dead bear? How does Walter react to Cloyd's vengeance? What makes him change his mind? What would you do in Cloyd or Walter's place?
5. How does Walter assess his life when he returns home alone from Utah? How does Cloyd's arrival change his outlook? What does Walter say about the hurt he felt? Have you seen the truth of this in your own life?
6. What does it tell you about their relationship when Cloyd shares his secret name with Walter? How does Walter feel about the name Cloyd has chosen?
7. When Cloyd is hurt in the mountains, he is helped by a stranger. What does he say to Cloyd about his actions? Do you agree with his assessment that it was no big deal, or is kindness and caring for your fellow man a very big deal?
8. What happens to Walter when he begins to work in the gold mine? What does his decision to send Cloyd into the mountains tell you about him?

9. Why does Cloyd tell Rusty about sighting the bear? Has he let pride color his better judgment? Do you sometimes act unwisely to impress someone else? What should Cloyd have done?
10. How does Cloyd feel when Rusty kills the bear? What is Rusty's reaction when he realizes the bear is a grizzly? Why doesn't Cloyd report him to the game warden? What does he learn about revenge? Do you think this is a good life lesson?
11. How does Cloyd save Walter from dying after his injury? What has he gained from his time with Walter? What has Walter gained?
12. List the good and bad characteristic traits exhibited by Cloyd. Do the same for Walter. Identify a time in the novel when each tried to overcome his shortcomings.

Projects

1. Who are the Ancient Ones revered by Cloyd? Research their culture and draw or build a model of their dwellings.
2. The grizzly is an endangered species protected by the Fish and Wildlife Bureau. Select an endangered animal in the United States, and write a letter to the editor of a newspaper proposing what should be done to protect it.
3. Pointing with your lips is a Ute custom. Find out everything you can about the Ute history and culture, and prepare a written report on the results of your search. There are several websites concerning the Ute nation that would be helpful in your research.
4. Imagine that you are a prospector searching for gold. Prepare a list of the gear and supplies you would need. Tell the purpose of each.
5. Using a topographical map of the Weminuche Wilderness, follow Cloyd and Walter from the ranch to the Rio Grande Pyramid and the Window. Calculate the distances and the elevations they covered.

Vocabulary

Each of the following quotations chosen from *Bearstone* includes one or more vocabulary words in **bold print**.

1. "through the **miserable** days in school, he had looked forward to going home for the summer."
2. "The old man grinned **mischievously**."
3. "He was **astonished**."
4. "The old man had that **impish** grin on his face again."
5. "Arms spread wide, fingers **splayed** on the sandstone."
6. "the tendons in his heels began to **quiver**."
7. "behave carefully, treat the buried one with the **utmost** respect, and don't make any mistakes."
8. "he saw the **silhouette** of a piece of pottery."
9. "Cloyd put the smooth stone in his pocket and started back across the **precipice**."
10. "but he couldn't **concentrate** for worrying about the teenager."

11. "Cloyd's large, round face was **devoid** of expression, unless it was the mouth turning **dourly** down at the corners."
12. "He pointed with his lips to the **meager** haystack."
13. "His blister healed, his hands grew **callused**."
14. "standing in the hot sun all day long and **tediously** moving dirt and routing water."
15. "dragged them into the **arroyos**."
16. "A **revelation** was **forging** itself in his mind."
17. "and Walter had that **claustrophobic** feeling."
18. "More and more, Walter **begrudged** himself the time it took to eat and sleep."
19. "A **stratagem** came to mind."
20. "It **deviated** a **substantial margin** from the truth."

About the Author

Born in Pittsburgh, Pennsylvania, in 1947, Will Hobbs has a bachelor of arts and a master of arts from Stanford University. Mr. Hobbs's interests include hiking, archaeology, and natural history, themes that frequently appear in his novels. As he addresses the problems of choice and the struggle for identity in young people, he places them in an environment dealing with wildlife and wild places in hopes that this will increase the awareness of his readers concerning the natural world.

From the Author

"I believe there's a part of the human heart that longs for wild places. That part of my heart is filled with the forests, the alpine tundra, and the snowclad peaks of the Weminuche Wilderness in the San Juan Mountains of southwestern Colorado. . . .

Years before I ever thought of writing *Beardance*, I was gathering the knowledge and experiences that would lead to this story. In 1973, soon after my wife and I came to live in southwestern Colorado, we found teaching jobs in the little town of Pagosa Springs. I was lucky enough to be able to start a class called 'Living in the Southwest.' Along with my students, I was interviewing local oldtimers, exploring the library, learning about the human history and the natural history of the San Juans. We learned about the legend of the Lost Mine of the Window and the ways of old sheepherders, and we learned about our neighbors the Utes who still dance the Bear Dance every spring to help bring the bears out of hibernation.

What got me started writing *Beardance*, my first novel, was the surprising news that a grizzly had been killed in the San Juan Mountains, not far from where we were living, in 1979. . . . The idea I began my story with was that of a Ute boy meeting the last grizzly in Colorado. This being fiction, I got to make up how it would all happen. The boy became Cloyd, with Walter and Rusty soon joining the story.

After that 1979 incident, the experts once again agreed that the grizzlies were all gone. They were extinct in Colorado. I would never have the heart to invent the idea for *Beardance* if there hadn't been reason to hope there might still be some after all. It was a 1990 sighting of a mother grizzly and three cubs by a rancher on horseback that gave me that hope. In the summers following the sighting, bear biologists tested hair samples and other evidence found in the area, and now believe that these remote mountains of southwestern Colorado may indeed be home to a few surviving grizzlies.

Now I could begin to imagine Cloyd returning to the mountains and meeting the mate and cubs of the bear that had been killed in *Bearstone*. After reading for months, learning all I could about grizzlies and the traditions of the native people across the continent regarding bears. I began work on the novel. I found myself struggling with the early chapters, trying to get the story to come to life, so I decided to take a break from my desk and hike back up to the Window, that spectacular notch in the continental divide which I saw as the geographical focus of the story,

Standing in the Window, I could imagine I saw Cloyd and Walter camping down on the East Ute Creek far below. I could almost see the entrance to the lost gold mine on the ridge above the creek. And I could imagine Cloyd with the two grizzly cubs, Brownie and Cocoa, as the snow was starting to fall. I practically ran home, my head bursting with ideas for my story. I poured all my love of the mountains and of the bears into the writing, as well as my deep respect for native traditions.

I found my fingers flying all day and into the night. In writing, as in reading, you're imagining what it's like to be someone else, and I was fully imaging being Cloyd Atcitty, at 11,800 feet with winter coming on, risking his life for those grizzly cubs. I completed the novel in sort of trance, much like his, in a little less than a month. It was a wonderful experience, and I don't know if one like it will ever come again."

Before We Were Free
Author: Julia Alvarez
Publication date: 2002

Awards
> ALA Notable Children's Books
> ALA Best Books for Young Adults

Characters
> Anita de la Torre
> Mami
> Papi
> Lucinda
> Mundín
> Chucha
> Mr. Washburn, his wife, and children, Sammy and Susie
> Lorena
> Mr. Smith, aka El Jefe, and General Trujillo
> Mancini family

Character Traits
> Citizenship
> Cooperation
> Courage
> Helpfulness
> Loyalty
> Optimism
> Patience
> Perseverance
> Resourcefulness
> Trustworthiness

Setting
> 1961—Dominican Republic

Plot

Twelve-year-old Anita de la Torre and her family live in the Dominican Republic that is ruled by the dictator General Trujillo. Under his regime, all mail is inspected by censors. Anita's family is under suspicion since her uncle was arrested for participating in a plot against the regime. SIM, the secret police, searches the de la Torre house for relatives who have escaped to New York.

Anita's parents will not leave the country; they want to work for freedom there, but when Trujillo makes romantic overtures to her fifteen-year-old sister Lucinda, they decide to send her to the United States. After Lucinda leaves and her school is closed, Anita virtually stops talking. Overhearing the conversations of her father with the men he is working with against the government makes her fear even worse. She repeatedly cannot think of the right words or articulate them.

The coup, which her parents and others are planning, fails. Anita's father and uncle are arrested, and Anita, her mother, and brother are hidden—her brother Mundín at the embassy, and she and her mother with the Mancini family. They live in a closet off the master bedroom, can only come out when the bedroom door is locked, and must flee to a crawl space when anything suspicious occurs. To keep her sanity, Anita writes in her diary, reads, and adheres to a schedule. She finds herself talking more since she is writing. After almost two months in this captivity, they are airlifted out and brought to the United States

They ultimately learn the her father and uncle have both been killed. They settle in New York, and Anita realizes that she is free both outside and inside. She is able to fly like a butterfly, exactly as her father wished for her.

Questions for Discussion

1. Describe Anita's extended family and their relationship with each other. Are they able to retain their relationship when some of them move away? How important are the bonds among extended family members?

2. How does Anita's relationship with her parents change as the novel progresses? What is her relationship with her sister? How does she feel and react when her sister moves away? How do you think you would feel if your sister or brother had to be separated as Lucinda did?

3. Chucha and Lorena are both servants of the family. Contrast their loyalty to the de la Torre family. What special powers does Chucha possess?

4. Anita's father calls her "strong and brave." Do you agree? In what ways does Anita demonstrate these qualities? Does she change as the novel progresses? Do you know of any children in the world today who are experiencing adversity similar to that experienced by Anita? How does this affect their childhood? Does it make them stronger or weaker?

5. How do Anita and her family demonstrate their reliance on their faith? How does religion help them?

6. Describe Anita's life in hiding. How does she try to amuse herself? How important is her diary to her? Why is it important for her to think positively? How would you have reacted if you lived in this situation? How would you have amused yourself?

7. Anita asks in her diary if an evil person like Trujillo could be changed. What world leaders today resemble him and act in ways similar to him? Do you think any of them can be changed? What can other nations do to bring about change in them?

8. How does Anita adjust to life in New York? Does she face any special problems? If Anita moved to your school, how would you help her adjust to her new surroundings?

9. Together in New York, Anita's family reminisces about her father and other family members. How does this help them adjust to the changes in their lives? How does your family share its memories?

10. Anita's father wants her to spread her wings and fly away. When they part, Chucha tells her, "Fly, fly free!" What is the meaning of these wishes that the adults have for Anita? What does Anita mean when she says, "After all, as Chucha herself would say, what good is it to escape captivity only to be imprisoned in your own misery?" By the end of the novel, does Anita have this freedom?

Projects

1. Anita's sister comes here on a visa. Visit the website for the United States of America Immigration Services, www.usaid.org to learn about the different types of visas for which immigrants could apply. Compile your information into a *PowerPoint* presentation.

2. When her cousins leave the Dominican Republic, they can only take one special thing with them. If you had to leave almost everything behind, what one special thing from your possessions would you take with you? Draw a picture of this item, and write a haiku poem about it.

3. Find information on General Trujillo and his regime. Using this information, write a news story.

4. Anita depends on her diary to keep her sane. In some ways, this is similar to the longer *Diary of Anne Frank*. Read Anne Frank's words, and write a review of this book for your school newspaper, mentioning the importance of the diary to Anne.

5. Draw a map of the Dominican Republic and the countries surrounding it.

Vocabulary

Each of the following quotations chosen from *Before We Were Free* includes one or more vocabulary words in **bold print**.

1. "For the rest of the afternoon, I **mope** around the house, until Mami sends me over to help Chucha move in."

2. "Mami smiles **wanly**, trying to show she has nothing to hide."

3. "Her eyes **stray** up to my hair."

4. "Lucinda loves parties and talking on the phone, and she hates being **cooped** up."

5. "A few months ago, he and his friends were involved in a plot to get rid of our **dictator**."

6. "He calls me in from the hallway, where I've been trying to be **invisible** so no one will ask me to leave."

7. "One time when he's up in the air, he catches sight of me **lurking** behind the hedge."

8. "The next day, Sam and I are exploring down by Tía Mimí's orchid shed, where the orchids have grown **straggly** since Porfirio left."
9. "But even after everything is laid out, I feel **apprehensive** about going back."
10. "Lucinda closes her eyes until she **regains** her patience with me."
11. "Sometimes Papi pauses as he walks by, the reddish light **illuminating** his **tense** face."
12. "Wiping my tears from the page, I **smudge** the writing so badly, I won't have to erase a thing tonight."
13. "Voices **drift** over from the neighboring yard, **punctuated** every now and then by the report of firecrackers going off in different parts of the city in honor of Independence Day."
14. "It's no secret to any of us that Lorena is really **superstitious** and **squeamish**."
15. Not even the thought of falling in love with Sam is a **consolation** anymore."
16. "I promise not to **divulge** her secrets, but for the first time, I ask her to return the favor."
17. "This saint has long hair and wears a red tunic and sandals and **wields** a huge sword above a disgusting-looking dragon with a tiny human face."
18. "Out in the hall, Mami and Mundín are racing to the door as the men come trooping in, **brandishing** guns."

About the Author

Soon after she was born in New York City in 1950, Julia Alvarez moved with her family to the Dominican Republic. In 1960, she moved back to the United States after her father was involved in a failed attempt to overthrow the dictatorship of Trujillo. She decided that she wanted to be a writer when she was in high school. She graduated summa cum laude from Middlebury College in 1971 and received her M.F.A. from Syracuse University in 1975. She has been a Poet-in-the-Schools in Kentucky, Delaware, and North Carolina and a professor at Phillips Andover Academy, the University of Vermont, and the University of Illinois. Since 1988, Alvarez has been a professor of English at Middlebury College.

Beyond Safe Boundaries
Author: Margaret Sacks
Publication date: 1989

Characters
- Elizabeth Levin
- Evie Levin
- Lydia Levin
- Dr. Abie Levin
- Willem Coetzee

Character Traits
- Cooperation
- Courage
- Helpfulness
- Integrity
- Kindness
- Perseverance
- Respect
- Tolerance

Setting
1950s and early 1960s—South Africa

Plot
Elizabeth Levin is a thirteen-year-old growing up in the highly volatile world of South Africa in the late 1950s and the early 1960s. Dr. Verwoerd, an Afrikaner, is Prime Minister, and apartheid is the law of the land. The Levin's are affluent, living in a house on a golf course—one that Dr. Levin can play as a guest but cannot be a member of because he is Jewish. Elizabeth and her older sister, Evie, live a privileged life in a household surrounded by servants, who because they are black must have a passbook to travel in the countryside. Dr. Levin brings a new mother into their home. Lydia is welcomed joyfully by Elizabeth but is resented by Evie who is used to being the woman of the family. A dentist, Dr. Levin, has a Colored man, Popeye Coetzee, working clandestinely for him. As a Colored man, the descendent of a white settler and a native woman, Mr. Coetzee speaks Afrikaans like his forbears, but is only permitted to do menial work. When South Kloof, a community of Coloreds, Indians, and Chinese, is declared for whites only, Mr. Coetzee divorces his wife so that she and their son, Willem, may continue to live in their home.

Evie leaves home to attend Witwatersrand University in Johannesburg and soon is a political activist. On her visits home, she is often heard arguing her liberal views with her father. At the University, she moves into a house shared by Saraswathi Khanni, an Indian student, and becomes involved with Willem, who is a leader in the Movement. The Movement is a multiracial group opposed to the apartheid policies of the white supremacist government. When Elizabeth visits Evie at the University, she witnesses Willem's dynamic leadership, Evie's devotion to him and the Movement, and a raid by the Special Forces triggered by a phone tap of Elizabeth's call home. At a rally for the Movement, Willem is arrested and held in solitary confinement while Evie, who was not at the rally is placed under house arrest. After Willem's supposed suicide in prison, Lydia arranges for Evie to be secretly smuggled to England. Elizabeth and her father mourn for South Africa whose children will leave the country of their birth.

Questions for Discussion

1. Why do you think Elizabeth willingly accepts Lydia as her new mother while Evie perceives her as an unwanted stepmother? Faced with this situation, how would you react? Why would you feel this way?

2. As a family, the Levin's are not allowed to join the golf club. Do you know of any such restrictions in your community or country? How do you feel about such discrimination? What can you do to change the situation?

3. Elizabeth is sure she will be picked for the school play, but she is not picked because her mother said it would be difficult to attend rehearsals. What is Elizabeth's reaction to this news? How would you feel toward your new mother? How does she feel when she learns the real reason? Why do you think Evie did such a mean thing?

4. What impressions do you get from the people who attend Lydia Levin's party? What do they have in common, and what is different about each of the parties? Why does Lydia invite the Van Zyl Smiths? Is her reason very admirable? What happens during the party that confirms her suspicions? What does Jeremy mean when he says there is no future in South Africa? What does Mr. Van mean when he agrees with him? With whose views do you agree?

5. How can you explain Mrs. Levin's ambivalent attitude about Beauty's pass book? What does this tell you about her?

6. Why do you think Dr. Levin forbids Evie to see Willem in their home? Why does he relent when she says she will go to Willem's home instead? What do this action and his treatment of Willem's father tell you about Dr. Levin and the time in which he lives? What do you admire about Dr. Levin? What do you not like about him?

7. Even though Willem has spent weeks helping Elizabeth prepare for the tennis tournament, she does not want him to come. How does this decision make you feel about Elizabeth? What causes her to change her mind?

8. The porter in the train is called a bedding boy even though he is a middle-aged Colored man. How do you think this makes the man feel? What do you think is the purpose of this ploy? Do you know of similar situations where this same technique has been used?

9. When Elizabeth visits Evie at the University, she is surprised to learn that she is sharing a house with Sara, an Indian girl. Why was Elizabeth dreading the moment when Evie would bring Sara over to meet Aunt Phoebe and Uncle Cy? What does Uncle Cy's remark about Sara tell you about him?

10. How does Elizabeth cause the raid on Evie's meeting? If you were Elizabeth, would you have any idea this would happen? What does this tell you about Elizabeth's home life?

11. When Willem is taken into solitary confinement and Evie is placed under house arrest, how do her parents react to this situation? Why do you think this is so? How does Evie know that Willem did not kill himself? What do Lydia's actions regarding Evie's house arrest tell you about her?

12. Dr. Levin has never had separate sterilizers for his black and white patients. Why does he install the separate sterilizer for whites in his surgery? Do you agree that he has something to fear?

13. Is *Beyond Safe Boundaries* a good title for this book? Why do you think this is true?

Projects

1. Write a journal for Evie revealing the early experiences at the University that bring about the change in her political awareness and zeal.

2. *Beyond Safe Boundaries* states that South Africa, especially the cities, is ethnically varied. Create a graph illustrating the demographics of the population as it is today.

3. Create a timeline showing the important historical dates affecting the South African policy of apartheid from the 1950s to the present day.

4. Write a press release announcing the awarding of the Nobel Peace Prize to Frederick Willem DeKlerk and Nelson Mandela. The article should contain the description of the prize and the reasons for awarding it to these two men.

5. Archbishop Desmond Tutu, Nelson Mandela, Hendrik Frensch Verwoerd, and Frederick Willem DeKlerk are all important figures in the history of South Africa in the later half of the twentieth century. Select one and do a report on your findings.

6. Draw a physical map of South Africa showing its geographic features.

7. Write a concluding chapter for this novel revealing whether Elizabeth remains in South Africa or leaves the country of her birth.

An excellent source for information about South Africa is CIA—The World Factbook—South Africa
www.umsl.edu/services/govdocs/wofact/96/2

Vocabulary

Each of the following quotations chosen from *Beyond Safe Boundaries* includes one or more vocabulary words in **bold print**.

1. "I had avoided discarding the notebook, but this time, without a **qualm**, I dropped it in the dustbin."

2. "quite **exotic** compared with my brown bread and jam that Mathilda, our cook, slapped together for me every morning."
3. "The heat came up off the pavement in front of our house where the ants **relentlessly** tried to drag a dead beetle into a too-narrow **crevice**."
4. "Although I made her promise not to tell anyone, the word *stepmother* was soon being **bandied** around at school."
5. "'Your neighbor is so **puerile**,' Delia said, **plaiting** a piece of hair that fell over her shoulder."
6. "the African township that my father must have been named by a **cynical** Englishman, considering the **impoverished** housing conditions."
7. "I barked like a dog to scare off any burglars who might be **lurking** there."
8. "I showed my mother the lounge, my least favorite room, with its **stodgy** formal furniture."
9. "My mother, who I discovered was equally **superstitious**, went one step further and exchanged the wardrobe, too."
10. "the idea of performing on the city hall stage **enthralled** me."
11. "She was a born actress and knew how to **manipulate** the teachers with her **dimpled** smile and perfect **diction**."
12. "I went and stood **forlornly** in my mother's darkened room."

About the Author
Though born in Port Elizabeth, South Africa, Margaret Sacks now lives in Memphis, Tennessee, with her family. She continues to write books for children.

From the Author
"At the time *Beyond Safe Boundaries* was written, no one would have dreamed that a peaceful change of government was possible in South Africa. But in spite of change to majority rule, the apartheid era, as portrayed in the book, has left its legacy. Black people, deprived of a solid education which would enable them to find jobs and economic security, have had to play 'catch-up' and many have taken to random violence against white property owners. It will take decades to create a stable, educated population.

I still live in the United States as do many who fled apartheid. The new South Africa is an exciting place to visit, a combination of sophistication and third world set against a landscape of great beauty."

Bloomability
Author: Sharon Creech
Publication date: 1998

Award
   Parenting Magazine Reading Magic Award

Characters
   Domenica Santolina Doone, or Dinnie
   Mr. and Mrs. Doone
   Crick, Dinnie's brother
   Stella, Dinnie's sister
   Aunt Sandy
   Uncle Max
   Guthrie
   Lila
   Keisuke
   Belen
   Mrs. Stirling

Character Traits
   Cooperation
   Helpfulness
   Kindness
   Optimism
   Patience
   Respect
   Respect for the Environment
   Self-control
   Self-respect
   Tolerance

Setting
   Present day—Switzerland

Plot
Dinnie has moved all over the country with her family as her father searched for
new and better opportunities. One day, with the cooperation of her mother, Dinnie is taken away by her aunt and uncle, Aunt Sandy and Uncle Max. Their plan
is to bring Dinnie to Lugano, Switzerland, where Uncle Max is going to be the
headmaster of an American school, founded and owned by Mrs. Stirling. Aunt
Sandy will teach there, and Dinnie will attend the school.

At first, Dinnie considers herself a kidnapping victim. She is worried she is being punished or sent off to make room for her sister's new baby. Her aunt and uncle are enthusiastic and treat Dinnie with kindness and love. Dinnie does what she is told while still planning to escape. On their first day in Switzerland, while her aunt and uncle rave about the scenery, she can only wish she was looking at her family. Finally, she reaches the point of being both happy in her new surroundings while still homesick for her family.

Dinnie overheard her mother telling her aunt that she was adaptable, and she does adapt and flourish in her new surroundings. The school provides opportunities for meeting students from all over the world, like the countries of Europe as well as Japan, China, and Saudi Arabia. Among her closest friends are two Americans, the exuberant and spontaneous Guthrie and the complaining and demanding Lila, Belen from Spain, and Keisuke from Japan. Dinnie isn't the only nomad in her school.

The students take excursions around the countryside. Dinnie and Guthrie go to the top of Mt. San Salvatore in a train called a funicolare. Dinnie learns to ski during ski term after Christmas in St. Moritz. On a ski trip to the Dolomites, Lila and Guthrie are caught in an avalanche; both survive but are injured. They also have unique experiences in the classroom, like Global Awareness Month and a month when the students' only homework assignment is to think. At the middle school ceremony at the end of the year, Guthrie talks about how they will always be part of each other's lives. Dinnie goes home for the summer. She may return to the school that has taught her that life has endless bloomabilities.

Questions for Discussion

1. What are Dinnie's feelings when she is taken away from her family? How do you think you would feel in Dinnie's position? Do you think her mother made the correct decision to send Dinnie with her sister Sandy?

2. How do Uncle Max and Aunt Sandy deal with Dinnie's fears and unhappiness? Do you think they should have done anything differently?

3. Dinnie's mother says that Dinnie is adaptable. Do you agree with her? In what ways does Dinnie display this trait? How is this a positive trait to possess? Do you think that you are adaptable?

4. What kind of girl is Lila? What do you think of her attitude toward students who are not American? Does this attitude change? Does her family life shed any light on Lila's behavior? Why does Dinnie consider Lila a friend even though she can be so difficult?

5. How does Dinnie view herself? How does she change and grow as the book progresses? How do you interpret Dinnie's feeling that she is in a bubble? When does her bubble disappear?

6. Dinnie keeps a notebook in which she records her dreams. These are also interspersed with her story. How do her dreams reflect what is going on in Dinnie's life? Do you have dreams that reflect your own life?

7. Dinnie reads a story about a character who struggles and is more interesting because of this. Afterward, she worries that she hasn't had to struggle enough for her new skis. Do you think it is important to struggle or work for

things? Have you ever had to struggle for something? Has this made you appreciate it more?

8. At an assembly. Uncle Max asks students to think about what they would do if they could be sure they wouldn't get caught for it. What would different answers to this question tell you about the responders?

9. How is the title of this novel significant? Can you think of another title that would be as effective?

10. What important lessons can students learn from going to a school like the one Dinnie attends? In what ways does your school offer opportunities for you to learn about other cultures? Why is this important?

11. How does Guthrie sum up the importance of their school experience in his speech?

12. Do you think Dinnie will return to the school in Switzerland? Would you return if you were Dinnie?

Projects

1. Locate information on traveling to Switzerland and, using this information, create a colorful and interesting travel brochure for the country. Include details on tourist sites, landmarks, and activities for tourists.

2. All the students in the school have to do four hours of community service a week. Using your telephone book and newspaper, create a directory of community service activities that you and your friends could participate in. Plan to share this directory with scout troops and school service organizations. If possible, organize a group of students to participate in a service project.

3. Dinnie takes her box of important things with her whenever she moves. What important things would you put into your own box? What could someone learn about you from this collection of objects?

4. Dinnie learns how the Swiss deal with avalanches. Locate information on this type of disaster. Create a poster which includes information on how a person could survive an avalanche.

5. Mark a map with the places Dinnie has lived. On the same map, mark the places you have lived.

6. Based on the descriptions of Switzerland, draw a scene from the novel.

7. During Global Awareness Month, students study natural and man-made disasters. Pay attention to news reports of disease, environmental disasters, and natural disasters. Make a *PowerPoint* presentation that outlines these.

8. Guthrie chooses to read a poem by Robert Frost at the middle school ceremony. Read some of Frost's poems, and select one that you like. Write an essay discussing the meaning of this poem and your reason for liking it.

9. Dinnie, Guthrie, Lila, Keisuke, and Belen gather for a reunion ten years after the novel ends. Write an afterword to the novel or a one-act play about this reunion.

Vocabulary

Each of the following quotations chosen from *Bloomability* includes one or more vocabulary words in **bold print**.

1. "She was **bellowing** like a bull by this time."
2. "They **swooped** down on our little New Mexico hill town and stayed up all night talking to my mother."
3. "and you were **suspended** above it and you knew where you were."
4. "I felt as if I were trying to keep two little kids from **squabbling** with each other."
5. "Through the Alps the train rushed, as if on a mission, **urgent** and efficient."
6. "From the outside, the villa looked **dignified** and **sturdy** and **vast** and frightening."
7. "Later I would be able to look at this view and to see it and appreciate it, and it would **affect** me **profoundly**."
8. "It was odd how the mountain seemed to **loom** there."
9. "Two girls **accosted** me on my way home. . . ."
10. "This was her uniform, **altered** only occasionally and only slightly, with the exchange, say, of spiked red heels for the spiked black ones."
11. "Mrs. Stirling drove a blue Volvo and was known for **careening** around curves and challenging the speed limits."
12. "He looked a bit **intimidated** by that."
13. "We wound all through the woods like this, up and down hills, along cliffs and then **veering** back into the trees."
14. "a flood of affection for my own parents with their **zany** style, their **nomadic** existence, and even their **quirky** forgetfulness."

About the Author

Sharon Creech was born in Cleveland and received a Bachelor's Degree from Hiram College and a Master's Degree from George Mason University. As a child, she loved to read and write. She taught literature to American and international students in England and in Switzerland. She makes her home in New Jersey.

From the Author

"Before I left Europe, after eighteen years there, I wanted to capture the international school experience, and that was the impetus for writing *Bloomability*. For nearly fifteen years I taught in American/international schools (TASIS) in England and Switzerland. I learned as much from my students (perhaps more) as they learned from me!

The founder of these schools was fond of saying, 'Every child needs and deserves beauty,' and I agree with her. The influence of natural beauty is a central motif in this book, and I've since realized it appears in others of my books as well (*Walk Two Moons, Chasing Redbird*, and *Ruby Holler*.)"

The Breadwinner
Author: Deborah Ellis
Publication date: 2000

Awards

Red Maple Reading Award shortlist

Characters

Parvana
Parvana's parents
Nooria, Maryam, and Ali, Parvana's siblings
Mrs. Weera
Shauzia

Character Traits

Cooperation
Courage
Optimism
Perseverance
Resilience
Resourcefulness
Responsibility

Setting

Present day—Afghanistan

Plot

When the Taliban takes over Afghanistan, the everyday lives of the people radically change. For example, females must stay inside, girls cannot go to school, and women cannot shop. Eleven-year-old Parvana and her family have endured major changes in their lives. Both of her parents were university educated, but her mother, a writer for a radio station, has lost her job. Her father has been a teacher but now goes to the marketplace each day in hopes of earning money by reading and writing for others. Having lived in a big house with servants, a courtyard, and modern conveniences, her family now lives in a single room.

Parvana's father is arrested by Taliban soldiers who burst into their apartment and accuse him of holding foreign ideas. As he is taken away, he tells Parvana to take care of the family. Because her mother is depressed and incapable of taking care of the family and Nooria is afraid to go outside, Parvana goes to the market to buy food. There she is accosted by a Taliban and runs away. At the marketplace, she meets Mrs. Weera, who has been part of the Afghan Women's Union with Parvana's mother. Like the physical education teacher she was before the Taliban removed her from her position, she optimistically rallies the family like a team and helps mother. Mrs. Weera moves in and, with Parvana's mother, starts a magazine. She, Parvana's mother, and Nooria decide that Parvana will be turned into a boy so she can go to the marketplace. Her hair cut, wearing her dead brother's clothes, she goes to the market with her father's writing implements to earn some money.

Parvana is shocked when she meets a tea boy who actually is a girl, Shauzia, from her school. Shauzia has a plan for them to make a lot of money, by digging up bones. Parvana and Shauzia go to a cemetery where explosions have disturbed the graves so that bones are sticking out; they sell the bones they collect to a bone broker. The girls want to earn enough money to buy trays and the items on them that they could sell at the market.

Although Parvana and Nooria have regularly squabbled, Parvana plays the devil's advocate when Nooria decides to marry a man she hasn't seen since they were children. Nooria explains that she wants to get away from Kabul and, living in Mazar-e-Sharif, she will be away from the Taliban and able to go to school and go out in public. Parvana does not accompany the family when they go to Mazar; she cannot leave Kabul with her father in prison. Finally, part of her hopes are realized when her father is released from prison. Her father learns that many people fleeing Mazar have fled to refugee camps, and he and Parvana will go to find the rest of their family. Parvana and Shauzia pledge to meet on the top of the Eiffel Tower in Paris on the first day of spring in twenty years.

Through her time at the marketplace, Parvana notices movement behind a blacked-out window above her. A piece of embroidered cloth, a handkerchief, a wooden bead, and candy are some of the small gifts that land on Parvana's blanket from the person she refers to as the Window Woman. One day she hears an angry man shouting and a woman crying. When a tiny beaded camel hits her on the head, she knows the Window Woman is all right. Before she leaves to find her mother, Parvana plants wildflowers where her blanket usually lay as a present for her unseen friend.

Questions for Discussion

1. What kind of changes do Parvana and her family experience after the Taliban takes over? How well do they adjust to the changes in their lives? What strengths do they exhibit? Have you ever experienced major changes like this? How have you coped?

2. Parvana has known war and its devastation her whole life. How do you think children are affected by living in war-torn areas? What positive and negative character traits might they develop because of their environment?

3. What responsibilities does Parvana have in the family? Why is she both proud and resentful of being the only one who can get the water? How does her father rely on her?

4. Why didn't Parvana's mother leave the house after the Taliban took over? How does she react to the beating at the prison? How is Mrs. Weera different from her? What affect does Mrs. Weera have on their household?

5. What is Nooria like? Describe her relationship with Parvana. Why does she decide to marry and leave Kabul? Do you think that she is making a wise decision?
6. Why do her mother and Mrs. Weera decide that Parvana should masquerade as a boy? Why does it help her to be allowed to decide for herself whether to cut her hair? What qualities does Parvana exhibit when she goes into the marketplace?
7. What kind of girl is Shauzia? What is her plan for earning more money? Why won't the girls turn over all their money to their families? Why does Parvana say they will have to remember the day they dug bones to earn money for their families? How does her mother feel about this way of earning money?
8. What do Parvana and Shauzia witness in the sports stadium? Do you think it is natural that Parvana needs to stay home for a few days after this experience? Why does she go back to work soon? What does this tell you about her?
9. What do Shauzia and Parvana want for their futures? Can you understand Parvana's wish to have her ordinary life back? What ordinary aspects of your own life would you miss if they were taken from you? Mrs. Weera does not think Shauzia is right to want to leave the country. Do you think Shauzia has a right to go and leave her family in Afghanistan?
10. How does Parvana exhibit caring and compassion for others in need?
11. What is Parvana's reaction to the news that Mazar is in the hands of the Taliban? What does this mean for her family? What encourages Parvana to keep going?
12. How is the contact between the Window Woman and Parvana important to each of them? Why does Parvana want to plant flowers that the Window Woman can see?

Projects

1. Draw a map of Afghanistan including the places mentioned in the novel—Kabul and Mazar-e-Sharif and surrounding countries.
2. Using print periodical indexes or online databases, locate information from magazines and newspapers on the life of Afghan women today, in the areas of health, education, and jobs. Create a *PowerPoint* presentation detailing their plight and any improvements since the fall of the Taliban.
3. Parvana and Shauzia are afraid that they will step on a land mine. Visit the website of the International Campaign to Ban Landmines, www.icbl.org, to find out how a person could sponsor a mine-detection dog. Create a poster to encourage involvement by sponsoring a dog.
4. Parvana and Shauzia agree to meet on the first day on spring, in twenty years, at the top of the Eiffel Tower. Write a feature story for your local newspaper about the meeting of these two old friends. Include what happened to them in the intervening years and what they are currently doing. Be sure that your sequel logically complements the original novel.

Vocabulary
Each of the following quotations chosen from *The Breadwinner* includes one or
more vocabulary words in **bold print**.

1. "They even **forbade** girls to go to school."
2. "Parvana would **slump** down further on the blanket and try to make herself look smaller."
3. "Men shopped for their families, and peddlers **hawked** their goods and services."
4. "Tea boys ran back and forth into the **labyrinth** of the marketplace,"
5. "He offered such a good price that Father eventually **relented**."
6. "Since the Taliban **decreed** that women must stay inside, many husbands took their wives' false legs away."
7. "Parvana knew she had to **fetch** the water because there was nobody else in the family who could do it."
8. "The **vibrant** red cloth caught Parvana's eye."
9. "She ran her fingers over the **intricate** embroidery."
10. "The creases were **imbedded** in the paper."
11. "She walked as though she were rounding up children who were **dawdling** after class."
12. "There wasn't a single **intact** building in the whole area, just piles of bricks, dust and **rubble**."
13. "The two girls were a little **intimidated** by so many people and stayed next to each other as they went up into the bleachers to sell their wares."
14. "Parvana **rummaged** around on her tray until she found a box of the matches she sold with the cigarettes."

About the Author
Deborah Ellis was born in Ontario, Canada. During the months she spent interviewing women and girls in Afghan refugee camps, she met relatives of a girl just like Parvana who cut her hair, dressed as a boy, and sold items in the marketplace to earn money for her family. All the royalties from the sale of this novel will be donated to Women for Women in Afghanistan, an organization that works to educate Afghan girls in Pakistani refugee camps. Ms. Ellis resides in Ontario.

Bronx Masquerade
Author: Nikki Grimes
Publication date: 2002

Awards
Coretta Scott King Award

Characters
Mr. Ward and the eighteen students in his English class

Character Traits
Compassion
Courage
Helpfulness
Integrity
Loyalty
Resilience
Resourcefulness
Self-respect
Tolerance

Setting
Present day—Bronx, New York

Plot
Mr. Ward's eleventh grade English class in the Bronx had spent a month study-ing the poets of the Harlem Renaissance when he assigned them to write an es-say on the subject. Wesley Boone, whose ambition is to become a songwriter, creates a poem about Langston Hughes instead. After he reads it to the class, others shout out that they have a poem that they would like to read as well. This begins "Open Mike," a once-a-week class devoted to the reading of poems cre-ated by the class members. Though there is little ethnic diversity in the class, the students' interests, backgrounds, and aspirations for the future are varied. Through the weekly poetry readings, they expose their inner selves and reach an understanding of each other, and, more important, of their own inadequacies and strengths. Through the poems, we learn of Raynard's dyslexia, Diondra's will-ingness to pursue her artistic talent, Steve's advice to pack your dreams for they are portable, and the secret emotions of the each of the students. Weekly, they examine their lives and express their fears and dreams in the poems. As they read the poetry, we see a layers of protective façade peeled away, revealing the real person behind the masquerade. Tyrone's observations about many of the

readings show how the students are growing in understanding each other, realizing that each person should be judged not by appearances but by what is in their heads and hearts. At the end-of-the-year assembly, Tyrone best sums the message of *Bronx Masquerade* by saying, "'. . . even though the people in our class are all different colors and some of you speak a different language and everything, I feel like we connected. I feel like I know you now. You know what I'm saying? I feel like we're not as different as I thought.' "

Questions for Discussion

1. Tyrone worries about reaching the age of twenty because of the neighborhood in which he lives. What do you think it is like to live with this fear? How would you feel if your father had been killed in a drive-by shooting? What would you do in Tyrone's place?

2. What does Chankara's poem, "Bruised Love" tell you about her sister and how Chankara feels about her? Why do you think some people allow others to abuse them? Do you think Chankara has learned from watching her sister? What can you learn from her poem? Explain what Tyrone means when he calls abusers, "'Little Men' "?

3. What do you think Raul wishes to accomplish with his painting? Do you think he is trying to eradicate stereotypes of his people?

4. Devon is a talented basketball player, but he knows he is something more. Why do you think he has to sneak to the library and lie about his destination? Do you think we often put people in categories that limit their potential? Do you? Why do you think this happens? How does Devon express his change in the poem, "Bronx Masquerade"? Why do you think this poem was chosen as the title of this book?

5. Why does Lupe envy Gloria? What does she think a baby can give her that she does not have? Why does Gloria envy Lupe? How does Gloria feel about having a baby while she is still in high school? What qualities do you admire in each of the girls?

6. Janelle worries that people see her only as an obese girl. What would she like people to see about her? Do you know anyone like Janelle? What can you do to show that you understand?

7. Do you agree with Leslie that the scariest thing is being alone in the world? Why does Leslie feel so alone? How would you feel if you were different from everyone around you and had no family or friends to care about you? What does Lupe mean by being alone together? How does this help?

8. Why does Sterling's behavior toward Leon frighten him more than physical violence would have? Why does Sterling wish to become a teacher? Why is having direction important to a young person's life? Do you feel your life has direction; if not, how can you rectify the problem?

9. Diondra ends her poem, "High Dive," with the words, "to be continued." What does she mean by this? Is this attitude one that should be part of your outlook on life? Why?

10. Amy is jealous of the love between Mr. Ward and his daughter and of the friendships of her classmates. How does she respond to Sterling's advice?

Can you understand her fear? Why does she want to be a stone? How would you help her?

11. Why does Sheila wish to change her name? What does Tyrone think of her decision? Do you agree with his estimation?

12. Does the attitude of the Gamberoni family reflect that of many members of society toward ethnic groups different from their own? Is Tyrone's attitude toward white people so different from the Gamberoni's toward Blacks? What does this tell you about discrimination? What does *Bronx Masquerade* offer as the solution to this problem? What would your solution be?

Projects

1. The Internet offers several valuable sites for learning about the Harlem Renaissance. Using it or other resources, create a *PowerPoint* presentation depicting some of the leading characters and their contributions to the movement. Remember the Renaissance included members of the performing arts as well as poets, novelists, and dramatists.

2. The Apollo Theatre on 125th Street in Manhattan launched the careers of many black performers. Create a poster advertising the appearance of one these stars.

3. Write the poem that you think Mai Tren might create.

4. Locate the Spanish words used in the text, and create a dictionary translating Spanish to English; supply illustrations where possible.

5. Research the learning disability, dyslexia; write a research paper showing your findings.

6. Several authors connected with the Harlem Renaissance are mentioned in this novel. Research one of them, read some of his or her writings, and report your findings orally to the class.

7. Imagine that you are a member of Mr. Ward's class. Select one of your eighteen classmates and through an analysis of his or her poetry, show how he or she has changed and grown through the year.

8. List the eighteen students in Mr. Ward's class, and talk about one characteristic that you liked about them.

Vocabulary

Each of the following quotations chosen from *Bronx Masquerade* includes one or more vocabulary words in **bold print**.

1. "It's me, Tyrone, up here all alone **rapping** into a **microphone** 'cause I've got something to say."

2. "It's the **fabrications** that take a lot of time."

3. "Lunch is a memory of **indigestion**."

4. "We kind of have our own little **clique** now."

5. "That's why I've got to show it off, wear clothes that **accentuate** the positive."

6. "and dream about the great **transformation** I'm going to make someday."

7. "I spun around, more **aggravated** than angry . . ."

8. "I am **notorious** for turning in library books late."

9. "We talked about **superficial** judgments . . ."
10. "reminded that my plans for the future do not include **fisticuffs** or **expulsion.**"
11. "They are only trying to prove that the peace of God is **nonexistent**."
12. "Apparently, I had **appendicitis**."
13. "When my mom left, I was suddenly out of **orbit**."
14. "I'll show you how to take a **shellacking**."
15. "The only one who doesn't think they're all lazy and **shiftless**."
16. "Never mind that they've been **discriminated** against and shoved to the bottom of the **economic** rung since they've been here."
17. "for wanting to go into social work to help **minorities**."
18. "It popped up at the most **inconvenient** times, **effervesced** in all my rhymes."
19. "but after seeing those **brochures**, he looked like he needed a **transfusion**."

About the Author

Born and raised in New York City, Nikki Grimes now lives in Corona, California. A noted author, poet, and lecturer, Ms. Grimes has written over two dozen books for children celebrating the themes of friendship, family, and community relationships. She has stated that writing is her first love and poetry her greatest pleasure. Her previous books received several awards and were placed on the list of Notable Books by the American Library Association.

Cat Herself
Author: Mollie Hunter
Publication date: 1985

Awards
> ALA Best Books for Young Adults
> *School Library Journal* Best Book

Characters
> Catriona McPhie "Cat"
> Charlie Drummond
> Jim and Ilse McPhie, Cat's parents
> Old Nan, Cat's grandmother
> Rhona
> Alec
> Dr. Ballantyne

Character Traits
> Compassion
> Cooperation
> Courage
> Generosity
> Kindness
> Resourcefulness
> Self-respect

Setting
> 1970s—Scotland

Plot
Eleven-year-old Catriona "Cat" McPhie is a Traveller, one of the semi-nomadic people who roam throughout Scotland and other parts of the United Kingdom. They live their lives as others before them have lived for centuries, roaming the countryside, camping in vacant areas that are fast disappearing, and surviving by doing odd jobs. We first meet Cat when she is being chased by the police for stealing pheasant eggs. Though she is innocent, her whole group is made to leave its camping ground by a prejudiced police sergeant. Forced to leave her friends, Charlie, Rhona, and Alec, Cat travels with her family north to the special places of her mother and her grandmother. As they travel, Cat and her mother, Ilse, sell her father's willow baskets, and her father, Jim, entertains the tourists, by playing his bagpipes by the side of the road. They encounter the fear and distrust of many people to their kind. In the north, Cat learns of "the hills of

home" from Old Nan, her grandmother, and of her mother's sorrow for the children she has lost. Since he has no sons to teach, Cat begins to learn her father's skills of poaching and pearling though this defies the strict definition of women's roles among her people and leaves her open to ridicule.

As Cat matures, she makes a determination for herself that she will live life on her own terms, ignoring the prejudices within and without her society. When she is fifteen, marriageable age among her people, a terrible tragedy occurs. Youths set fire to the campers in which the Travellers live, killing Rhona and Alec's small baby. The tragedy points out the good and bad attributes of people in general and strengthens Cat's resolve to marry and live her life with Charlie, according to the old ways of her people.

Questions for Discussion

1. Why does the sergeant immediately believe that Cat has stolen the pheasant eggs? Does he have a preconceived picture of all Travellers? Why does Cat lie about her name? Why does she run away instead of showing the sergeant her stones? Can you understand her fear?

2. How does Cat react when the youths laugh at her? Why does she feel superior to them? Can you understand her attitude? What do you think of her attitude?

   "How does Charlie feel about Traveller men having the right to beat their wives? How does his attitude change when Cat asks to go pearling with him? Can you identify the ambivalence in his attitudes? Why do you think this is so?

3. What does Old Nan mean by the term "the hills of home?" Do you have a special place that has this meaning to you?

4. Why is Cat opposed to learning her father's skills? Have you ever felt this type of peer pressure? How does her father change her attitude? Can you apply this lesson when dealing with unfavorable peer pressure? What does Old Nan say about friendship? Have you learned the wisdom of her advice and applied the knowledge in your own friendships?

5. How does Cat's father rationalize the breaking of the law by poaching game and fish? Is his argument justified? Is it possible for society to abide by his reasoning? Why?

6. How does learning her father's skills change Cat's estimation of herself? Do you think this is something you should try to emulate? Why?

7. Cat and her mother have the ability to see the future. Do you think this would be a pleasant or frightening ability? How would you react if the future was known to you?

8. Mr. Brownlee permits the Travellers to camp on his land during the winter so that the children may have their 100 days of compulsory education. What does his discussion with Sergeant Mac Kendrick about the situation tell you about the two men? Who would you rather have for a friend?

9. What school subject causes problems for Rhona and Cat? Is this a problem that arises in your school community? How is it handled? How was it han-

dled in the book? How does Dr. Ballantyne help the Travellers solve the problem? What have you learned about Dr. Ballantyne?

10. What is happening to the traditional resting sites for the travelling people? How do you think this will affect their way of life? Do you know of other instances where this has occurred?

11. How does Mr. McPhie explain the conduct of the boys who burn the camp and kill Rhona's baby? Do you agree with his opinion? Do you think you would feel this way toward people who had caused so much harm?

12. Jim McPhie and Dr. Ballantyne are described as remarkable men. What have they done during this novel to make you agree with this opinion? List some of the exemplary character traits possessed by both men.

13. What obstacles face Cat and Charlie concerning their marriage? Do you agree with Cat's position? How do you feel about Charlie's position? How do they reach a solution? Do you think that they may have future problems in their marriage? Why?

Projects

1. Several interesting sites for information about the Travellers can be found by entering "the travelling people of Scotland" into a search engine on the Internet. Using these and other information sources of your choosing, write a report on the topic.

2. A particular problem facing "the travelling people" is this disappearance of their traditional resting places due to the encroachment of civilization into the countryside in the way of malls and tourist motels. Find what the government is trying to do to solve this problem. Write an editorial essay either supporting or criticizing the government position.

3. Electroconvulsive therapy, ECT, also known as "shock treatment" is a controversial method of treatment for mental disorders. Prepare a *PowerPoint* presentation of the pros and cons of the treatment.

4. Draw a map of Scotland showing the McPhie's route north.

5. The "gift" that Cat and her mother share is called precognition. Research the scientific studies that have been done on this extrasensory perception, and deliver your findings in a written report.

Vocabulary

Each of the following quotations chosen from *Cat Herself* includes one or more vocabulary words in **bold print**.

1. "Happily, unaware that the garnet-bearing **schist** she carried was a common worthless find."

2. "And you said that tinkers were good to their bairns, whatever else they were!"

3. "Pale-blue eyes, **bulbous** and bright with **hostility**."

4. "The sergeant's lip curled **satirically**."

5. "and felt a swift, returning stab of the **exhilaration** that had been hers when she and Shuffler had run off together."

6. "she was **overwhelmed** by it."

7. "**Desperately** Cat tugged at her father's jacket...."
8. "With both of his hands covering her **frantic** ones, her father calmed the **babble** of **denial**; but the sergeant's vice sounded above this **reassurance**."
9. "fifty-four years of being **harassed** from pillar to post by big voices from big men in blue uniforms...."
10. "Her step grew **buoyant**."
11. "Afraid of the day they never saw, she thought **contemptuously**."
12. "The bene hante woman's puzzled look changed suddenly to one of cool and **haughty** displeasure."
13. "she had given the same **coquettish** toss of her head, and the same **provocative** glint of the eyes."
14. "And now she was looking for something to prolong the moment of **preening** herself on the men's laughter."
15. "The **mockery** in the words was so clear that Cat felt an immediate sense of outrage."
16. "it was really Jim's responsibility to take up the **cudgels**."
17. "the pipes **caterwauling** at their loudest."
18. "The eyes that had been closed in **ecstasy languidly** opened."
19. "Cat ate **voraciously**...."
20. "Charlie's brow **furrowed** with concentration."

About the Author

Mollie Hunter is an extraordinary storyteller, chronicling the history and the people of her native Scotland. With her great ability to describe place and atmosphere, she has written realistic novels for young teens, historical novels, and great fantasy adventure stories. Her books stress the values of loyalty, creativity, and sympathy for the poor and downtrodden. Her heroines embody the desires and pleasures of her own youth, the desire for freedom, and the enjoyment of the sights and smells of the countryside.

The Circuit
Author: Francisco Jiménez
Publication date: 1997

Awards

Boston Globe/Horn Book Award
Booklist Editors' Choice
Américas Award for Children's and Young Adult Literature
Jane Addams Children's Honor Book
California Library Association's John and Patricia Beatty Award
NYPL Books for the Teen Age
ALA Best Books for Young Adults
Los Angeles Public Library System FOCAL Award
University of San Francisco Reading the World Award

Characters

Francisco
Papá
Mamá
Roberto, Trampita, Torito, and Rubén, Francisco's brothers
Rorra, Francisco's sister
Mr. Lema
Curtis
Carlos
Carl

Character Traits

Cooperation
Courage
Dependability
Integrity
Perseverance
Resourcefulness
Respect

Setting

1940s and 1950s—California

Plot

Subtitled "Stories from the Life of a Migrant Child," *The Circuit* is the semi-autobiographical account of Francisco's life in a family of migrant workers in California. As a small child, he and his family steal across the border from Mexico into California in search of a better life. They move from farm to farm, harvesting the seasonal crops, such as lettuce, grapes, carrots, strawberries, and cotton. They move their personal possessions and make their homes in such places as tents, garages, and barracks.

Through all his family's moves, Francisco treasures his days in school. When he is enrolled in the first grade, he knows no English. He enjoys drawing, and his picture of a butterfly wins a blue ribbon. Francisco gives the winning drawing to Curtis, a classmate with whom he has had a fight. He enters sixth grade in November because he has had to wait until the grape season is over to go to school. He spends his lunchtimes with his teacher, Mr. Lema, who helps him with English. Before the year is out, however, they are moving again. On his last day of seventh grade, he counts the days until he can go to school again. Francisco is so diligent about learning that he carries a notepad in his shirt pocket in which he has written words to know, spelling, and math and grammar rules. He is devastated when his first notepad burns in a fire in their home.

Francisco's other interest is collecting pennies, which he keeps in a small cardboard box. He is unwilling to give his little sister a penny, and she takes two with which she buys gum. He is devastated until his mother reminds him that people are more important than things. The migrant workers live in fear of the border patrol who regularly come to the fields and tent cities in search of undocumented workers. Papá warns them not to trust anyone and not to tell anyone they were born in Mexico. In the end, an immigration officer comes up to Francisco while he is sitting in his eighth grade classroom.

Questions for Discussion

1. Francisco is not happy to be left babysitting his brother while the rest of the family picks cotton. What does he do? Why is his father unhappy with him? What lesson does he teach Francisco?

2. Do you think Curtis was right to fight with Francisco over the jacket? How did Francisco feel after the fight? What was the reaction of Francisco's parents over the fight? What does this tell you about the values his parents think are important? Francisco gives his winning drawing to Curtis who likes it very much. What does this tell you about Francisco?

3. A young couple tries to sell personal items to Francisco's parents because they are in need of money, but Francisco's parents are poor, too. How does Papá help the couple and show his love for Mamá at the same time? What does this tell you about Papá?

4. Francisco wants a ball for Christmas, but he and his brothers all receive bags of candy. What intangible gifts does Francisco receive during his childhood that are more important than the ball? As you look back on birthdays and holidays you have celebrated, what relationships, feelings, and memories are more longlasting than toys and other presents that you received?

5. Why does Papá attack the parrot? Is his action understandable? Why does Francisco pray for both the parrot and his father?

6. Francisco never seems to stay in any school long enough to make friends and get settled. What are the advantages and disadvantages of moving a lot like he does? Have you ever moved? What feelings did you have at this time? In your opinion, how does Francisco adjust to his lifestyle?

7. Francisco has two very different friends. Carlos needs to organize everything and order everyone around. How would you describe Carlos? Do you know any children like him? How does Francisco stand up to him? What do you think of this tactic? What special qualities does Carlos have? Why is Francisco reluctant to bring Carlos home? Are his feelings understandable?

8. How does Francisco feel when his little sister takes his pennies? Would you feel the same way? How does Mamá try to make him feel better?

9. One of Francisco's assignments is to learn part of the Declaration of Independence by heart. How are the words that he learns important for him and for all of us?

10. How do Francisco's teachers influence him? How are their actions admirable? How have teachers positively influenced you? What other careers offer opportunities to affect the lives of others? Would you like to pursue any of these careers? Why?

Projects

1. cbp.customs.gov is the website for the U. S. Border Patrol. At the site, click on Border Patrol. What is its history and mission? How much land do they protect, and where is it? How many people work for the Border Patrol? What are some of the methods they use to detect illegal aliens? Compile your information into a *PowerPoint* presentation.

2. Pretend that you have a new student in your class who does not speak a word of English. Create a mini-dictionary for your new friend with words and phrases that you think are important for this person to learn. Illustrate your booklet with drawings, clip art, or illustrations from magazines.

3. When his brother is ill, Francisco's family prays to the Virgen de Guadalupe. Using Google, search for the Virgin of Guadalupe. Locate information on the history of this saint, and find out why she is worshiped. Organize your information on a bookmark. If possible, draw a picture or print a picture from the website for the reverse side.

4. Francisco has a penny collection. A popular hobby today is collecting quarters from each of the 50 states of the United States. Collect as many different quarters as you can. Find out the significance of the illustration for each state. Organize your information into a poster.

Vocabulary

Each of the following quotations chosen from *The Circuit* includes one or more vocabulary words in **bold print**.

1. "**Spewing** black smoke, it passed behind the camp, traveling much faster than the train we had taken from Guadalajara."

2. "We ran **straddling** the rails or walked on them as fast as we could to see how far we could go without falling off."

3. "The **furrows** that came up to the two-lane road looked like giant legs running alongside us."

4. "Aiming his head directly at me, and pulling his arms straight back with his hands **clenched**, he **stomped** up to me and started yelling."

5. "Her skin was **ruddy** and **pockmarked**, and her eyes were deep set and light green."

6. "Torito is a little better, but we can't bring him home until tomorrow,' she said, teary-eyed and with a **feigned** smile."

7. "Then, days later, when the clouds disappeared and the sun **emerged**, the lake began to split into hundreds of small puddles throughout the labor camp."

8. "The mud was **suffocating** them."

9. "Papá felt **obligated** to stay until the rancher's cotton had been all picked, even though other farmers had better crops."

10. "We **huddled** together and covered ourselves with army blankets we had bought at a secondhand store."

11. "*El Perico* wandered around freely in the **dilapidated** garage where we lived while harvesting Mr. Jacobson's vineyards."

About the Author

Francisco Jiménez was born in Mexico and immigrated to California with his family as a young boy. He graduated from Santa Clara University and received Master's and Doctorate degrees in Latin American literature from Columbia University under a Woodrow Wilson Fellowship. He is the director of the Ethnic Studies Program and the Fay Boyle Professor in the Department of Modern Languages and Literatures at Santa Clara University. He wrote *The Circuit* during a year's sabbatical when he interviewed family members, studied family documents and photographs, and visited sites where he had lived with his family in migrant labor camps. Finding little information about migrant farm workers during this time, he became even more convinced that he should write this book. He lives in Santa Clara with his wife and children.

From the Author

"The concern for the common good, and the pursuit for social justice informs and guides much of my own writing. For example, I write *The Circuit: Stories from the Life of a Migrant Child* to chronicle part of my family's history but, more importantly, to voice the experiences of a large sector of our society that has been frequently ignored. Through my writing I hope to give readers an insight into the lives of migrant farm workers and their children whose backbreaking labor of picking fruits and vegetables, for very low wages, puts food on our tables. Their courage and struggles, hopes and dreams for a better life for their children and their children's children give meaning to the term 'American dream.' Their story is the American story. It is your story."

The Clay Marble
Author: Minfong Ho
Publication date: 1991

Awards
National Council for the Social Studies/Children's Book Council Notable
Children's Book in the Field of Social Studies
Parents Magazine Best Books selection
American Booksellers Association "Pick of the Lists"
The National Council of Teachers of English Notable Children's Trade
Books in the Language Arts
Hungry Mind Review Children's Book of Distinction

Characters
Dara
Dara's mother
Sarun, Dara's brother
Nea
Bou Kem, Nea's grandfather
Jantu
Chnay
Duoic

Character Traits
Citizenship
Compassion
Cooperation
Courage
Helpfulness
Kindness
Optimism
Perseverance
Resilience
Resourcefulness
Respect
Responsibility
Self-respect

Setting
1980—Cambodia

Plot

Dara looks back ten years to her life when she was twelve years old. At that time, the Cambodian village in which Dara, her mother, and her brother Sarun live is a desolate shadow of its former self. "Liberated" by the Communists and the Vietnamese, the people have nothing to eat, no rice seeds to plant, and nowhere to live. Dara's father was murdered. To save their family, Sarun devises a plan; the family should travel to a refugee camp on the border between Cambodia and Thailand, Nong Chan, where refugees are being given food, tools, and rice seed. When they arrive at the camp, they find it has the feeling of their village back home before it was destroyed. There they meet Nea who lives with her grandfather and two cousins; like others, their family has lost many members, but it is a family just the same.

Nea's cousin Jantu and Dara become friends and play by an old stone beam, the remnant of an ancient temple. Jantu is a clever girl and can make toys and objects out of virtually nothing. She makes a toy village out of clay with figures representing their families, but reminds her friend that these are only toys, and what really matters is what a person carries inside himself or herself. When the fighting reaches them, people pack their belongings on their oxcarts and head into Thailand. Dara and Jantu become separated from the rest of the family, Jantu's little brother is injured and has to be taken to a hospital, and Dara has to find their families. Jantu makes her a clay marble and tells Dara that if she believes in the magical power of the marble, it will help her find her family. When she finds them, she believes the magic marble is responsible.

She uses its powers again when she and Nea go to the hospital to find Jantu and her brother. Dara, Nea, Jantu, and her brother become lost on their way back to the camp, and Jantu is shot by a patrol in which Sarun is a soldier. Sarun surprises and disappoints Dara by his militant attitude and insistence that they wait to take her to the hospital until after a flag-raising ceremony. Jantu dies, but before she does, she tells Dara that the marble was magic because she believed it was, and the time had come for her to make her own marble. Dara does this and stands up to Sarun about going home. When she loses the marble Jantu had made for her, she realizes the magic is in her.

Questions for Discussion

1. Jantu tells Dara that theirs are not real families but are pieces of families. Why does Jantu say this? Do you agree with her? What different types of families have you been in contact with? How is each special?
2. What is the role of Sarun in the family? Why is he reluctant to take the food from Nea when they arrive at the camp? How does he change when he becomes involved with the military? Do you respect the way he acts and the decisions he makes? Why doesn't he want to go home?
3. Why is Dara's family hopeful that their lives will improve after they leave the camp? Why is it important to be hopeful?
4. What did Dara know about Chnay before she ever met him? What is his life like? How does he behave when Dara meets him? How does his behavior change? How does Dara feel when Chnay says that no one ever notices

him? Describe the friendship that develops between Dara and Chnay. What do you learn from the character of Chnay about the reasons for bullies acting the way they do and the ways their behavior could be changed?

5. What kind of girl is Dara? How does she change as the book progresses? What admirable qualities does she possess? Would you like her for a friend? Why?

6. What special qualities does Jantu have? What do you learn about her from the way she treats her brother? What do you learn about her by the way she deals with Duoic, the boy in the hospital?

7. Describe the friendship between Dara and Jantu. How does Jantu give Dara courage to find her family and later to go home? How does Dara show her love for her friend when Jantu is near death?

8. Dara does not want to leave their toy village, but Jantu says that it is what inside that really matters. What does Jantu mean? With which girl do you agree?

9. Dara recognizes that not all children live in the difficult conditions in which she lives. How would you feel about this if you were Dara? How do you think children change when they grow up in a world of turmoil? Are there other situations besides war that could make children's lives difficult?

10. How does the clay marble give Dara strength? Do you agree with Jantu that the strength is in the person? Why did it take time for Dara to agree with this?

11. This novel shows the effect of war on the ordinary lives of people. Dara wonders how people could "fight for peace." What is the irony of this comment? How can ordinary people work to make a peaceful world?

12. Dara's mother takes comfort from her prayers to Buddha, and Dara takes courage from the marble. Are there any actions or objects that give you comfort and courage? Why are these important?

Projects

1. Jantu can cleverly make toys and figures out of ordinary materials: tin cans and a stick into a truck, and pieces of plastic and newspaper into a kite. Using materials such as scraps of cloth, string, and wood, make a selection of toys and dolls like those Jantu makes.

2. Dara and Jantu play beside a beam that they think is part of the remains of an ancient Buddhist temple. Find out what an ancient temple would have looked like, and make a drawing of this structure.

3. Dara intends to lead her group back home to plant rice. Locate information on how this crop is grown and harvested. Prepare a *PowerPoint* presentation that would show a new farmer these processes.

4. Write a news story about what is happening in Cambodia now. Who is ruling the country? What is life like for the people?

5. When Dara and her family arrived there, 40,000 people were in the refugee camp at Nong Chan. In many places in the world, refugees are living in crisis. Go to a website like that of the U.S. Committee for Refugees, www.refugees.org, or that of the United Nations Refugee Agency,

www.unhcr.ch. Find information, for example, countries housing refugees, number of refugees worldwide, and conditions in which they live, that will help you organize an effort to raise awareness of the plight of refugees and help to improve their situations. Share your information with a school or civic organization that can assist you in the effort.

Vocabulary

Each of the following quotations chosen from *The Clay Marble* includes one or more vocabulary words in **bold print**.

1. "In the latest **spate** of fighting, the Khmer Rouge soldiers had even set fire to our houses . . ."
2. "Our little village was a peaceful and **prosperous** place then, the rice fields green and calm, the harvests plentiful."
3. "Kill the imperialists, they **exhorted** us, and kick out Prince Sihanouk."
4. "**Liberation** turned out to be a long nightmare of hunger and misery."
5. "One night my father was **roused** from his sleep and taken away by two soldiers."
6. "It seemed as if all the paths out of Cambodia were **converging** on this one spot on the Thai border."
7. "Yet, as we finally **emerged** from the forest, all we could see was a **vast barren** plain dotted with shrubs and scraggly trees, flat and **desolate**."
8. "Even though many people seemed to be only **fragments** of a family—a **frail** grandmother with several young toddlers, or a group of young boys **clustered** around a few old men—they were a family just the same."
9. "I folded up my sleeping mat and **stashed** it in our oxcart."
10. "**Deftly** she shaped it into four walls and put some leaves on top of it for a roof."
11. "Hard though we tried to **immerse** ourselves in this make-believe world, we could sense the growing tension in the real world around us."
12. "a shelter woven from plastic bags and cardboard, now **abandoned** and looking **forlorn**."

About the Author

Minfong Ho was born in Rangoon, Burma. She attended Tunghai University in Taiwan and received a B.A. degree with honors in history and economics and an M.F.A. degree in creative writing from Cornell University. She enjoys gardening, swimming, and hiking, and lives in Ithaca, New York, with her husband and children.

From the Author

"Writing the story *The Clay Marble* was not an easy process, but it was a slow, healing one. I started moulding it around the girl who gave me her clay marble, naming her Dara, and eventually she took over the whole story. At the time I was writing, I had not known the word *empowerment*, but looking back on it, I think that was what happened to Dara, and through her to myself."

Crispin
Author: Avi
Publication date: 2002

Awards
Newbery Medal
ALA Notable Children's Book

Characters
Crispin
Bear
John Aycliffe
Fr. Quinel
Widow Daventry

Character Traits
Compassion
Cooperation
Courage
Dependability
Helpfulness
Integrity
Kindness
Loyalty
Perseverance
Resilience
Resourcefulness
Self-respect

Setting
England—14th Century

Plot
The narrator of the story is a thirteen-year-old boy known only as "Asta's son." He and his mother are poor serfs, who work in the fields of Lord Furnival. They own no land and live in a rented one-room house, scorned and shunned by other villagers. He has never known his father who he believes died in the Plague. Soon after the novel begins, Asta dies, and the steward of the manor, Aycliffe, demands the boy's ox as death tax. The tiny cottage is burned, and after the boy is accused of stealing money from the manor house, he is declared a wolf's head; in other words, he is not considered human and can be killed by anyone.

Before he flees, he meets with Father Quinel who tells him he was baptized with the name Crispin, and that his mother could read and write. He gives Crispin the cross of lead, which his mother often used to pray and which had words on it written by her. Father Quinel promises to tell Crispin about his father the next day before he leaves, but the priest is found dead before he can give Crispin any more information.

Crispin comes upon a village ravaged by the plague, and in the village church, finds a huge man dressed like a jester, singing and playing a drum. Crispin is forced to tell him the truth about himself, and as someone who has unlawfully left his master, Crispin becomes the servant of this first free man who claims him, Orson Hrothgar, known as Bear. He tells Crispin that he before taking his final vows as a monk, he ran away with a band of mummers from whom he learned music and humor. Now he teaches Crispin to juggle, to sing, and to play the recorder. When they see Aycliffe still searching for Crispin, Bear asks him if he stole from the manor, and he believes Crispin when he tells him that he is innocent. Crispin shows him the cross of lead, and believes Bear learns something from the cross that he will not share. Through their travels, they perform together and earn money. They learn that Crispin is still being hunted and is now accused of killing Father Quinel. Caring and trust grow between Crispin and Bear.

Things are happening in medieval England, and, besides entertaining, Bear is gathering information from his travels that he shares with the group trying to bring about change. When they reach Great Wexly, Bear meets with these compatriots. They learn that Lord Furnival has died and Aycliffe, a relative of Lady Furnival, is there. When he sees Crispin, he orders his men to attack the boy. Aycliffe and his men storm into a meeting of Bear and his friends, capturing Bear, who tells Crispin that it is Crispin and not himself whom they are after. The Widow Daventry tells Crispin what is written upon his cross of lead: "Crispin—son of Furnival." Aycliffe is after Crispin because he is a potential claimant to the estate. As Crispin suspected, Bear had shared this information with the Widow.

At this point, Crispin can begin to make sense of the mysteries of his life. But Bear has taught him about freedom, and he does not wish to claim his birthright because being the son of the lord is being part of the system that has oppressed others. He strikes a bargain with Aycliffe that he will give up the cross of lead and any claim to the house of Furnival in exchange for Bear's freedom. Aycliffe tries to renege on the bargain and is killed in a fight with Bear. Crispin still places the cross of lead on the bloody chest of the steward. Crispin and Bear will continue to travel and entertain as free men.

Questions for Discussion
1. What does the taunting and shunning that Crispin endured do to his self-image? What does this teach you about the young people among you who constantly are picked on and bullied?

2. Describe Crispin's reliance on his religion. How is religion part of the daily life of the people among whom he lived? How does Bear view religion?

3. What kind of person is Bear? He says that he has two sides to his nature. Do you agree that he is both gentle and fierce, good and bad?

4. Describe the relationship between Crispin and Bear. How does their relationship change from the time they meet until the end of the book?

5. What is your opinion of the various pieces of advice that Bear gives to Crispin, for example, a person should not trust or love another, everyone should be a master of himself, or the only person who can betray you is yourself. Do you think his advice is generally sound? Why is Crispin occasionally confused by his words?

6. What value does Bear put on humor? Do you agree with him? Can you think of any everyday situations when humor could be useful?

7. How does trust develop between Crispin and Bear? Do you agree with Bear that trust takes time to develop?

8. Bear tells Crispin that when he looks down, he resembles a servant, and that he should look directly at people. Why does Bear give him this advice? What reaction do you have when people do not look at you when they are speaking? What other expressions of body language are important when people interact with each other?

9. How does the concept of freedom develop for Crispin from the beginning of the novel when Father Quinel tells him to go away and be free?

10. Do you think Crispin is right in feeling responsible for Bear's capture? What does this tell you about Crispin? Would you have felt the same?

11. How does Crispin feel when he sees his own image on a picture with the Virgin? How does this image bring him to a realization of who he is and what he wants to be?

12. What bargain does Crispin make with Aycliffe to save Bear? Does it surprise you that he makes this bargain? What does this tell you about him, his feelings for Bear, and his sense of self? Is Aycliffe true to his nature in carrying out his end of the bargain? What is the significance of Crispin putting the cross of lead on Aycliffe's chest?

Projects

1. Crispin comes upon a town ravaged by the Plague. Locate information on this topic, and organize your information into a report.

2. Locate information on the feudal system, and organize your information into a *PowerPoint* presentation.

3. Using the descriptions in the book or other sources, make a model of either a medieval manor or a medieval town.

4. The novel contains a detailed description of Bear. Using a medium of your choice, create a picture of Bear from this description.

5. Write another chapter to this book continuing the story of Crispin and Bear as they travel the countryside one year after the novel ends.

Vocabulary
Each of the following quotations chosen from *Crispin* includes one or more vocabulary words in **bold print**.

1. "Stunned, I lay upon the decaying earth, fingers **clutching** rotting leaves, a cold rain **drenching** me."
2. "**Transfixed** by fear, I stood rooted to the spot."
3. "These confessions were **numerous**, since I had become convinced there was some sin **embedded** in me, a sin I was **desperate** to root out."
4. "He seemed **distraught**, as if the pain of the whole world had settled in his soul."
5. "Concerned that I had been observed, I stood still and **scrutinized** the place where I'd seen movement."
6. "But what I kept **pondering** endlessly were the priest's revelations about my mother."
7. "Gasping for breath, I **flailed** around until my feet touched bottom."
8. "Late that day, **besieged** by fears, very lonely and quite **famished**, I fell to my knees and prayed with deep-hearted, sobbing words."
9. "It was all I could do to **suppress** screams of **rage**."
10. "We had **trudged** on for I don't know how much longer when Bear stopped."
11. "He **rummaged** in it, producing more bread, which he tore and gave me half."
12. "He gazed at Bear with such **malevolence** I thought he might offer harm."
13. "But now the market town of Great Wexly **loomed** before us, as if it had sprung from the ground."
14. "Its brown stone walls were **immense**, stretching away for as far as I could see."
15. "Still, what **assaulted** my senses more than anything—aside from the **sheer** numbers of people of all ages and the **ensuing cacophony**—was the **stench** that filled the air . . ."
16. "a few small **tallow** candles had been stuck into **crannies** in the walls."
17. "a dim and smoky place that **reeked** of bad ale, stale bread, and sour wine."
18. "But the square was **dominated** by two buildings which stood at opposite sides."

About the Author
Avi, whose full name is Avi Wortis, was born in New York. He always loved to read and received a master's degree in Library Science from Columbia University. He decided in high school that he wanted to write and began to write for young people after his own children were born. He believes this is a special calling because young people do not automatically accept adults into their world.

Dragonwings
Author: Laurence Yep
Publication date: 1975

Awards
   Newbery Honor Book
   Children's Book Award
   IRA Award
   Carter A. Woodson Award
   National Council for the Social Studies/Children's Book Council Notable
       Children's Book in the Field of Social Studies
   Lewis Carroll Shelf Award
   Friend of Children and Literature Award

Characters
   Moon Shadow
   Windrider
   The Company
       Uncle Bright Star
       White Deer
       Hand Clap
       Lefty
   Black Dog
   Miss Whitlaw
   Robin

Character Traits
   Courage
   Generosity
   Loyalty
   Perseverance
   Resourcefulness

Setting
   1903—1909—San Francisco's Chinatown

Plot
Dragonwings is great historical fiction with just a touch of fantasy. For more than fifty years, Chinese immigrants have been coming to the Golden Mountain, the United States, from the Middle Kingdom, China, when Moon Shadow, an eight-year-old boy, joins his father in San Francisco. Windrider, Moon Shadow's father, works in the family laundry business but has a burning ambi-

tion to fly. On Moon Shadow's first night, Windrider tells him of waking on a strange beach and meeting the Imperial Dragon. The Dragon King informs Windrider that once he was not only a dragon, but also a phenomenal flyer and healer. Due to his many sins, especially trying to fan out the sun's fires, his head was cut off and he was reborn as a human. The Dragon King tells Windrider that he must live out his life as a human before he can hope to be a dragon again. Before returning Windrider to the mortal world, the dragon attaches wings to his back and shows him the wonders of the dragon kingdom. He tells Windrider that he must watch for the tests and hold to the dragon-ness within that softskin body. Though others in the Tang family believe this is a dream, Moon Shadow and his father believe that it truly happened.

As Moon Shadow adjusts to life in Chinatown, he learns of the cruelty of the San Franciscans to the immigrants, destroying their businesses and beating and even murdering them at times. The evil is not only on the side of the white demons, but also among the family. Black Dog, Uncle's son, a drug addict, beats Moon Shadow for the money he is collecting. When Windrider retaliates, he offends the Brotherhood, causing the two to leave Chinatown and live among the white demons. They meet Miss Whitlaw and Robin, learn of the success of the Wright Brothers, experience the 1906 earthquake, and forsake all for Windrider to build his own aeroplane. Through great sacrifice and the help of family and friends, Windrider, finally achieves his goal but realizes that his family is more important than flying.

Questions for Discussion
1. How does Grandmother describe the United States to Moon Shadow? Would her description make you want to go there? How did Moon Shadow react when he knew he could emigrate? Are his mother and grandmother's reactions the same as might occur in your family? What made him decide to go?
2. What happens to Moon Shadow when he first enters the United States? What do you think he feels about his new country? How would you, as an eight-year-old boy, have felt in this situation?
3. What are Moon Shadow's fears when he first meets his father? How does his father dispel his fears?
4. Black Dog, Uncle's son, resents coming to America where instead of living like a lord he must do menial labor. How does he show his resentment? What does his gift to Moon Shadow tell you about him?
5. On Moon Shadow's first night in America, there is a raid on the laundry. Why are the Americans resentful of the new immigrants? What does Uncle's statement about bad times mean? Do incidences like this still occur in America? Why?
6. What is the true story of Grandfather's death? What is a queue, and why was it important enough for Grandfather to die defending his right to wear it? How does the story of his courage help Moon Shadow? Does your family have someone whose memory they cherish? Is this important for families?

7. Windrider not only builds kites but is especially adept with machines. What does he do for Mr. Alger? Do you agree with his statement about the language of machines? Can you give an example of the truth of the statement?

8. As a result of Black Dog's treachery, Moon Shadow and Windrider must leave the safety of Chinatown. Where do they go and how do they live?

9. What does their first meeting with Mrs. Whitlaw and Robin tell you about their landlady? Is she someone you would like? What admirable qualities does she demonstrate in that encounter?

10. Windrider is fascinated by flying and is convinced that he can build a machine that will fly. How do Moon Shadow and Miss Whitlaw help him with this ambition? What is Windrider's first reaction? How does Miss Whitlaw help Moon Shadow understand his father? Why do you think Windrider changed his mind about the Wrights?

11. On Polk St., a gang of boys, led by Jack, terrorize Moon Shadow. What does Robin tell Moon Shadow about Jack? What does Moon Shadow do with this knowledge? What does Moon Shadow learn from this incident? Why does it give him confidence?

12. The earthquake of 1906 cost the lives of many and destroyed the homes of more including those of The Company in Chinatown and those on Polk St. How does this disaster affect the lives of Moon Shadow and Windrider? What good traits do they exhibit at this time? What is at least one good thing that resulted from this catastrophe?

13. What do Moon Shadow and Windrider do after the earthquake? Do you agree with Windrider's driving ambition? How does Moon Shadow help his father? How does Windrider finally accomplish his goal? What does this tell you about the value of friends and family? What does Windrider finally realize about his goal?

14. As you reflect on this book, do you have any thoughts about the nature of people revealed in this story? How can you apply this knowledge to your everyday life?

Projects

1. Learn what you can about the art of calligraphy. Design a poster that illustrates its history and shows examples of the Chinese art.

2. Design, build, and fly a kite.

3. Write a thoroughly researched report about the Boxer Rebellion. Attempt to show both the Chinese and the British sides in the conflict.

4. Research the Immigration Laws of the early 1900s. Compile statistics that illustrate how the laws varied for the different groups immigrating to the United States. Illustrate these with a graph.

5. Create a timeline of the history of the Chinese in the United States, showing their contributions and the persecutions they endured before becoming an integral part of the American population.

6. In his eighties, Uncle Bright Star owns a laundry in San Francisco's Chinatown, but in his years in the United States, he has participated in the California Gold Rush and in the building of the railroad. Check the authenticity

of this for a Chinese immigrant, list your verification sources, and then write a journal for Uncle's exploits.

7. Do an imaginary interview with Wilbur and Orville Wright in which they describe the building of their airplane, its first flight, and their subsequent contributions to aviation history.

8. Research the 1906 San Francisco earthquake. Create a television documentary on the quake and the resulting destruction to life and property.

9. Create examples of both the Chinese calendar and the one used in the Western world. Be prepared to explain the differences.

10. The novel mentions such interesting inventions as the stereopticon, crystal sets, cable cars, abacuses, and dirigibles. Select one and draw or build a model of it.

Vocabulary
Each of the following quotations chosen from *Dragonwings* includes one or more vocabulary words in **bold print**.

1. "Mother was never **stingy** about **incense** for father."
2. "but for a small fee, the village schoolmaster would read one of father's weekly letters to us or write a letter at our **dictation**."
3. "and his kites were often treasured by their owners like family **heirlooms**."
4. "to flush a sunbeam or a stray **phoenix** out of the clouds."
5. "I failed **miserably** the first times I tried to fly a kite."
6. "Through all this, Hand Clap sat **unperturbed**."
7. "And then hand Clap took me below to the hold to **rehearse** my story for the **custom** demons."
8. "His hands were **calloused** by mining the California streams for gold."
9. "Then the vendors had to dodge **nimbly** to avoid being trampled under the heavy hooves . . ."
10. "when the real president, McKinley, had been shot in a **provincial** city."
11. "Father **rumpled** my hair **affectionately**."
12. "he found himself doing the most **drudgelike** work."
13. "He worked during the day in an **offhand, insolent** manner."
14. "Suddenly my hands were as **transparent** as the finest glass."
15. "but now I saw how they shone **iridescently**."
16. "The object he had treated so **casually** was beautifully **meticulous**."
17. "wrestled the brake of his carriage free with a loud **ratchety** sound."
18. "he did not so much speak as make **proclamations**."
19. "Show Moon Shadow our **stereopticon**, Robin."
20. "Father grinned **sardonically**."

About the Author
A man of two worlds, Lawrence Yep grew up in San Francisco's Chinatown in the 1950s. As a youngster, he wanted nothing more than to be an All-American boy, and he rejected learning about his heritage, language, and customs. Later, he regretted this attitude when he wanted to know more about his roots with the

intention of writing about them. Schooled at Marquette and SUNY Buffalo, he has been a lecturer on Asian-American studies. His writings include science fiction, fantasy, historical fiction, tales of contemporary life in Chinatown, and retellings of Chinese folktales and legends. With more than fifty works of fiction, he has realistically chronicled the history and culture of the Chinese American in the United States.

Esperanza Rising
Author: Pam Muñoz Ryan
Publication date: 2000

Awards
Jane Addams Children's Book Award
Women's International League for Peace and Freedom, Excellence in a
    Work of Fiction Award
Judy Goddard/Libraries Limited Arizona Young Adult Author Award
ALA Best Books for Young Adults
Los Angeles Times Book Prize Finalist
NYPL 100 Titles for Reading and Sharing
Publisher's Weekly Best Books of the Year
Smithsonian Notable Books for Children
YALSA Best Books for Young Adults
Pura Belpre Award

Characters
Esperanza Ortega
Ramona and Sixto Ortega, her parents
Abuelita, her grandmother
Hortensia
Alfonso
Miguel
Tio Luis and Tio Marco
Carmen
Isabel

Character Traits
Cooperation
Courage
Helpfulness
Kindness
Perseverance
Resilience
Respect
Respect for the environment
Responsibility

Setting
1924–1937— Mexico and California

Plot

As a young child, Esperanza leads a privileged life on her parents' Mexican ranch where her father teaches her to love their land. The day before her thirteenth birthday, she pricks her finger on a thorn from a rose bush and has a premonition of bad luck. Her fear increases as her father does not return from working on the grasslands. Soon the family learns that he has been ambushed and killed by bandits. On her birthday, she opens a gift from her father, a porcelain doll, like the dolls he had given her on every other birthday of her life.

Soon Esperanza and her mother learn that, by the terms of her father's will, they will receive their house, its contents, and an income from the grapes. However, since women do not usually own land, their land has been willed to his older stepbrother Tio Luis. When Ramona refuses Luis' offer to buy their home, he proposes marriage. When she refuses that, Luis threatens to make their lives difficult.

For years, Hortensia and Alfonso have been trusted servants. Esperanza and their son Miguel have been playmates since they were babies, but her relationship with Miguel is damaged when she points out their different stations in life. Because they cannot work for the cruel and unfair uncles, Miguel and his family decide to move to the United States.

After the uncles burn down their house, Ramona tells Luis she will consider his proposal. However, she never intends to marry him and instead decides to go to the United States with Hortensia, Alfonso, and Miguel, who are no longer servants but now friends and saviors. They escape hidden in a wagonload of guavas and finish their journey riding in a locomotive into the United States. On the train, Esperanza's actions show arrogance and intolerance.

Nothing in her life to this point has prepared Esperanza for the difficulties she will be facing in the United States. She and her mother live in a two-room cabin in a migrant worker camp, with Hortensia and Alfonso, and Isabel, the daughter of Alfonso's brother. Esperanza is at first angry about the way they are living and unable to accept the changes in her life. She has to help in the family effort by learning to wash clothes, sweep, and take care of little children. Girls in the camp mock her lack of knowledge about simple things. When her mother becomes ill with valley fever, Esperanza, determined to earn the money to bring her grandmother to the United States, gets a job cutting potato eyes. Because she needs to care for her mother, she will not support a strike that migrant workers plan to protest poor working conditions and wages. Esperanza discovers that the money she has been saving to bring Abuelita to them is gone; in fact, Miguel has taken it and uses it to bring Esperanza's grandmother to them. At her next birthday, Esperanza shows how much she has grown and changed during the year.

Questions for Discussion

1. Describe Esperanza's life at the beginning of the story. Does she appreciate the privileges that she has?
2. After Esperanza points out the differences in their positions in life, Miguel acts differently toward her. How do you feel about what Esperanza said? Do you understand Miguel's feelings?

3. Why does Tio Luis propose to Ramona? Why does she tell him that she will consider his proposal? What motivates the uncles to threaten Ramona and to burn down their house?

4. As she leaves the ranch, Esperanza experiences both sadness and anger. Are her feelings understandable? What did her mother say to make her feel better?

5. What are Esperanza's feelings and fears when they board the train? Are her feelings understandable? Do you agree with her mother that Esperanza shows bad manners when the little girl wants to touch her doll?

6. What admirable qualities does Carmen have? Are you surprised that she and Ramona become friends? What do you think of Esperanza's attitude toward the generosity of Carmen?

7. Does Esperanza have an understandable reaction to their living arrangements in California? Does her mother deal correctly with Esperanza's feelings? Why is Isabel fascinated with Esperanza's past life?

8. What does Esperanza learn from Isabel? In what ways does Esperanza begin to behave differently? Why?

9. Alfonso and Miguel have carried pieces of their rose bushes from Mexico. Why did they do this? What do the rose bushes represent to Esperanza and her mother?

10. How are the Mexicans treated in contrast to Americans, such as people from Oklahoma? Do you know of other situations of discrimination against a group?

11. Why isn't Isabel chosen as "Queen of the May"? How does Esperanza try to make her feel better? What does this tell you about the ways in which Esperanza has changed?

12. Esperanza celebrated her next birthday in California. How is it different from her previous birthdays? Does Esperanza enjoy her birthday? What does this tell you about the ways in which she has changed?

13. Abuelita is always crocheting and teaches Esperanza to crochet in a pattern of mountains and valleys. She also tells Esperanza not to be afraid to start over when her pattern is not satisfactory. How does this crocheting parallel the theme of this book?

Projects

1. To enter the United States, Esperanza neeeds a visa, and papers are examined at the border. What is the process for a Mexican to enter this country legally today? Organize the data you gather into an informational pamphlet.

2. Abuelita often read the story of the phoenix to Esperanza. Read the myth, and draw your vision of the rebirth of the bird from its own ashes.

3. Locate information on the life of migrant workers today. Do any work in your area? What are the problems that they face? How could their lives be improved? Organize your information into a feature story for your local paper.

4. Some of the migrant workers in the novel organize a strike. They make signs that spell out their grievances. List the problems experienced by the

workers in this novel. Make the signs for the workers to carry, and write a speech for a strike leader that will encourage workers to join the strike.

5. Esperanza's mother suffers from valley fever and pneumonia. Find information on these two illnesses, and make a chart including symptoms and treatment.

6. Each chapter of this novel is titled with the name of a fruit or vegetable. Critically examine the novel in light of these titles. Explain why these titles are relevant and appropriate for the chapters.

7. In her note to the book, the author says that its inspiration was her grandmother, Esperanza Ortega, who led a privileged life in Mexico and then came here and worked in a farm camp. Interview an elderly relative or friend about his or her childhood experiences. Write your interview in the form of journal entries, and share these with the person you interviewed.

Vocabulary

Each of the following quotations chosen from *Esperanza Rising* includes one or more vocabulary words in **bold print**.

1. "She put the knife to it, and with a quick **swipe**, the heavy cluster of grapes dropped into her waiting hand."

2. "Esperanza loved her more for her **capricious** ways than for her **propriety**."

3. "**Distracted**, Mama **paced** at the window, each step making a hollow tapping sound on the tile floor."

4. "They tried to pass the time with small talk but their words **dwindled** into silence."

5. "Esperanza modeled Mama's **refined** manners, accepting Marisol's **condolences**."

6. "Her uncles' papers were **strewn** across the desk."

7. "A sudden breeze carried a familiar, **pungent** smell."

8. "Their overripe sweetness now **pervaded** the air with each breath of wind."

9. "He was **mesmerized** by the locomotive, watching it slowly pull in."

10. "The wagon **jostled** them now as it hit a hole in the road."

11. "For hours, Esperanza watched the **undulating** land pass in front of her."

12. "To **pacify** them, we let them try on the finished bangles."

13. "The song of the locomotive was **monotonous** as they traveled north, . . ."

14. "Finally, the train stopped moving and everyone **disembarked**. The land was dry and the **panorama** was **barren** except for date palms, cactus, and an occasional squirrel or roadrunner."

15. "When she checked the pot, they appeared to be **scorched** only on the bottom, so she poured in water and stirred them."

About the Author

Pam Muñoz Ryan was born and raised in California. As a child, she became an avid reader and lover of books. She wanted to be part of a profession in which books were important, so she became a teacher and administrator, and then began to write herself. Now, she devotes all her time to writing books for adults and children. She makes her home in California with her husband and four children.

From the Author

"My grandmother, Esperanza Ortega, was the inspiration for my book Esperanza Rising. . . .

It wasn't until I had children of my own that my grandmother told me about her life in Mexico, about a fairy-tale existence with servants, wealth, and grandeur, which preceded her life in the company farm camp. I wrote down some of her recollections from her childhood. . . . Eventually, I started to imagine a story based on the girl who might have been her."

First Apple
Author: Ching Yeung Russell
Publication date: 1994

Awards
> *Parents'* Choice Award
> NYS Reading Assn. Charlotte Award
> Charlie May Simon Book Master List citation
> Nene Award

Characters
> Ying Yeung
> Ah Mei
> Ah Pui
> Kee
> Ah Pau
> Ng Shing
> Dr. Tan

Character Traits
> Integrity
> Kindness
> Perseverance
> Resourcefulness

Setting
> Late 1940s—Chan Village, town of Tai Kong, China

Plot

At the age of five, Ying's parents go to Hong Kong, leaving her with her grandmother, Ah Pau. Now nine, Ying's life is happy and content, she is well-cared for by Ah Pau, and busy with school and play. In school, the children learn that apples are grown in northern China far from their tiny village and further learn that they taste "sweet and crunchy." Because apples are grown at such a distance from Chan Village, they are very rare and expensive.

When speaking with her seventy-year-old grandmother about her desire to taste an apple, she learns that Ah Pau has never tasted one either. This sparks her dream to purchase an apple, half for a birthday present for Ah Pau and the other half for her to taste. The price for one apple is exorbitant, but Ying works a deal with her cousin, Kee, for the junk he has been collecting. The sale of their combined junk brings in seventeen cents, enough to buy the apple. Her joy is short-lived for on her way home with her precious apple, she is beset by Ng Shing, the class bully. Intimidated, she gives him the smaller half but his try for the other half causes it to go down the storm drain. Ying is left with nothing for Ah Pau's birthday.

Still obsessed with her desire for an apple, she talks her friend Ah Mei into pulling up plantains growing wildly in a private garden. They plan to sell them to make herb medicine. Chased by the housekeeper, they escape, but Ying cannot live with her conscience. Her sincere confession to Dr. Tan, the owner of the plantains, so impresses him that he sends an apple to her house. She and Ah Pau find the apple "sweet and crunchy."

Questions for Discussion

1. What does Ah Pau answer when Ying asks her grandmother why she isn't afraid of catching her germs? What do you think is the real meaning of these words? What does this say about the relationship between Ah Pau and Ying?
2. Describe Ying's family unit. How does this differ from most family units in your community? What are some admirable qualities about this life style? What are some qualities that you see as less desirable?
3. Ng Shing is a bully who plagues the life of Ying. How does Ying react to his intimidation? Can you make any suggestions of how she could better deal with him? Is this how you deal with classroom bullies, or is it empty advice that you do not follow?
4. Ying is determined to purchase an apple for Ah Pau's birthday. What qualities does she exhibit in her pursuit of this goal? How would these traits assist you in pursuit of your goals?
5. What do the presents given to Ah Pau tell you about the givers and their feelings for Ah Pau? How do you think Ying felt as she watched? How would you have handled this situation?
6. Ying's determination to taste an apple causes her to perform an unethical act. How does this affect her? What good qualities does she display in handling the situation? Why does Dr. Tan give Ying an apple? What does this tell you about Dr. Tan?
7. Pick your favorite characters from *First Apple* and tell why they would be an asset to your family, school, and community.

Projects

1. Research the history of China following World War II. With this information, write a letter to Ying from her mother, explaining why they had to move to Hong Kong leaving Ying behind.
2. Collect pictures of the fruits that Ying priced in the fruit store. Go to a market near you and price the fruits Ying priced. Create an advertisement flyer for the market to sell these fruits.
3. Draw a poster-size map of China locating all the places mentioned in *First Apple*.
4. Collect the tools needed for true Chinese calligraphy. Demonstrate their use by illustrating several Chinese surnames.

Vocabulary

Each of the following quotations chosen from *First Apple* includes one or more vocabulary words in **bold print.**

1. "I walked to the end of the **plaza** and kept **advertising** our show."
2. "I was the one who could yell the loudest and **exaggerate** the best."
3. "Then I got a **calligraphy** brush . . ."
4. "while the kids in the **audience** sat on the clay tile floor...."
5. "Then I made my hands as **limber** as I could."
6. "Do you think apples are **expensive** in Canton, too?"
7. "I **envied** my landlord's daughter because she always had apples to eat."
8. "If my elbow **accidentally** crossed to his side. . . ."
9. "You are **disgusting**."
10. "I did it without my usual **stalling**."
11. "I didn't even mind that I had to be very **cautious** . . . "
12. "My voice was **hoarse**, and I was **exhausted**."
13. "After a full night's sleep, I would be as **energetic** as before."
14. "I had never seen **plantains** in a garden before."
15. "I **pretended** to **concentrate** on my homework."

About the Author

Born in a small village in China at the close of World War II, Ching Yeung Russell lived with her grandmother until rejoined with her parents in Hong Kong at the age of twelve. Her family, used to the crowded urban conditions of Hong Kong, loved to hear her stories of the freedom of small village living. It was not until her marriage to Philip Russell that she ever thought to write in English. Living now in South Carolina, her novels for children portray the rural life in China and the family-centered culture found there. She has been acclaimed for her contribution to multicultural literature.

From the Author

"When I was growing up in China, I had never heard of Christmas. Later, when I moved to Hong Kong, I learned about Christmas from my school's Christmas holiday and the Christmas decorations in department stores. I attended a few Christmas parties where we exchanged presents.

Then I moved to the United States and started my own family. At Christmas, our sons get a lot of Christmas presents from us, relatives, friends, and Santa. They always had more toys than they could play with.

When my older son, Jonathan, was about seven, one day he and his brother stayed in their room one afternoon. It looked like Jonathan was teaching Jeremy, which he often did. They stayed there for a long time. When they finally came out, both of them were holding long lists in their hands and they shouted, 'We want Santa to give this to us!' That's what they were doing! Jonathan was helping Jeremy write his Christmas list! I glanced at the lists. Whaah! Both of their Christmas wish lists were almost a foot long! Even though some of the words were spelled wrong, I could sound out every item, so I knew what they wanted.

At that moment, I did not know what to think. But not Phil, my husband. He beamed when he read their lists and offered to send them to Santa.

Phil often told me we had to watch our budget because he was a social worker, working for a nonprofit children's home. But now, he ran all over town during his lunch hour to buy the toys on the list. He was as excited as the boys, as if he were reliving his childhood. Whenever he got the toys home and hid them, he whispered to me with excitement, 'Remind me where I hid them, I don't want to miss any of them on Christmas day!'

I guessed that it was the American way that parents would buy whatever the children asked for at Christmas—to let their dreams come true. But I grew worried. My boys took their toys for granted. And I knew what would happen to the new toys, because after a couple of months, some of the toys would disappear and my sons probably wouldn't even notice, because they had so many to play with!

The incident reminded me of the first apple that I struggled to try in China. At once, I thought about how hard I worked on the pumpkin patch and how my cousin cheated me. I recalled how the class bully stole my hard-earned apple and how the old servant lady chased and hit me with a long bamboo pole. I remembered how scared I was whenever I jumped over the broken dam on my way back and forth to school to avoid seeing her; how nervous I was in class, fearing my teacher would find out my guilt; and how I hid in the bathroom during breaks fearing the servant lady would come to school and recognize me. I recall how relieved I was after I finally admitted my wrongdoing to old doctor. Those scenes appeared in front of me one incident after another. That is why I decided to write it all down for my sons—to let them know how many obstacles I had to go through to try something as simple as an apple.

So *First Apple* was dedicated to Jonathan and Jeremy, who gave me the inspiration to write it."

Ghost Boy
Author: Iain Lawrence
Publication date: 2000

Awards
> ALA Notable Book
> ALA Best Book for Young Adults
> *School Library Journal* Best Book
> *Publisher's Weekly* Best Books of the Year
> NYPL Books for the Teen Age

Characters
> Harold Kline, Harold the Ghost
> Mrs. Beesley, Harold's mother
> Thunder Wakes Him
> Samuel
> Tina or Princess Minikin
> The Gypsy Magda
> Cannibal King
> Flip Pharoah
> Roman

Character Traits
> Compassion
> Cooperation
> Dependability
> Kindness
> Perseverance
> Resilience
> Respect
> Respect for the environment
> Self-respect

Setting
> Post-World War II—American West

Plot

Fourteen-year-old Harold Kline leads a lonely and miserable life. Harold is an albino; his skin is pure white, and his vision is extremely poor. His father died in World War II; his brother, who protected him and who, with him, dreamed of going west to Oregon, is missing in action. His mother has remarried a man he doesn't like. He is the victim of verbal abuse from other kids and even from his mother. Harold feels he has no one who cares for him except his dog. He thinks of himself as an invisible ghost as he chants to himself, "*No one can see me, no one can hurt me. The words that they say cannot harm me.*" Hunter & Green's Traveling Circus comes through town on its trip west, and Harold sees a poster with a picture of the Cannibal King. Since this is the first time he has seen another person just like himself, an albino, Harold has to meet him.

Because of this desire and his unhappy life in Liberty, Harold leaves his precious dog, packs his baseball, glove, and bat and catches up to the circus troupe. Among the circus's performers are an old Indian, Thunder Wakes Him, the doll-sized Tina, and the huge, hair-covered Samuel. Tina and Samuel encircle Harold with affection, even giving him their huge hug, the "geezer-squeezer." He also meets the Gypsy Magda who bears the tattoos of Nazi persecution on her arms, and who tells fortunes and scares him with her prediction: "Beware of ones with unnatural charm. And beast that feeds with its tail."

Harold is fascinated by Flip, the beautiful horseback rider and the owner of the circus elephants. He gets a job helping her and suggests that he could teach the elephants to play baseball and, in the process, save the circus from financial ruin. He is thrilled and excited by Flip's attention; she wants him to spend time with her and the elephants and leave the company of the freaks. He is flattered and becomes ashamed of his old friends; when he sees them coming from the dining tent, he is happy not to be among the freaks any longer, yet ashamed of the way he feels. He increasingly pulls away, especially from Tina and Samuel, but he eventually learns that Flip cares more about his work with the elephants because their value will be increased if they can perform exceptional tricks, and she could even be recognized by the Barnum & Bailey Circus. Moreover, she finally tells Harold that she plans to marry Roman, a circus rigger who makes fun of Harold. When Harold finally meets the Cannibal King, he realizes he has met someone who shares his physical problems as well as the experiences of teasing and taunting.

In the meantime, the elephants do learn to play their version of baseball. Yet the elephant Conrad attacks Roman after he taunts Harold, and Flip blames Harold for making the elephant mean. Harold misses Samuel and Tina and, when he realizes how little Flip cares for him, he returns to his old friends. But when, in the midst of a baseball game, Tina playfully shoves and punches Harold, Conrad turns on her and kills her. In her crystal ball, the Gypsy Magda has seen an angry boy; Harold assumes this is Roman, but after Tina's death, the Gypsy Magda tells Harold that the boy she saw was Harold himself, full of anger.

Before she dies, Tina tells Harold to go back to his mother, and he does return home with a new attitude. He sees his mother the way she was years earlier, before his father died. He wants to revive his father's old store. He is willing to accept his stepfather.

Questions for Discussion

1. Harold is the victim of bullying and taunting by the kids in Liberty. Beyond the obvious reason that he looks different, why do they make fun of him? In your own experience, is there anyone who is victimized as Harold is? What can you do to stop this lack of respect and kindness?

2. How does Harold deal with the verbal abuse of which he is the victim? Are his methods effective? How would you handle Harold's situation if you were the victim?

3. What is your opinion of the way Harold is treated by his mother? Is there any excuse or explanation for the way she talks to him early in the novel? How do you think his home life contributes to Harold's leaving home? Does she change by the end of the novel? How does Harold see her in a different light?

4. How does Harold feel about himself? Why is he so happy when the farmer's wife dies his hair? Does he gain more self-respect as the novel progresses? Why is it important for a person to respect himself or herself?

5. What is life like for the circus freaks like Tina, Samuel, and the Gypsy Magda? What are the positive things about circus life for them? Do you think they are treated fairly in the circus?

6. Why is it important for Harold to meet the Cannibal King?

7. Why is it important for Harold to train the elephants to play baseball? What does he gain from working with them? Do you see any negative results from his success with them?

8. How does Harold feel about the freaks? How does his attitude toward them and his treatment of them change throughout the book? Why does he become ashamed of them? Do you admire the way his behavior toward them changes?

9. In what ways do Tina, Samuel, the Gypsy Magda, and the other freaks welcome Harold? How do Samuel and Tina react when Harold begins to pull away from them? How would you react in their places—like Tina or like Samuel? How do you feel about the way they treated Harold when he came back?

10. What kind of person is Flip? Why is she kind to Harold? Do you think she genuinely likes him? Why is Harold flattered by her attention?

11. Why does Roman treat Harold the way he does? When Conrad attacks Roman, Harold thinks of others who have made fun of him, yet he urges the elephant to free Roman. What does this tell you about Harold?

12. Flip tells Harold that he made the elephants mean. The Gypsy Magda tells him that he, not Roman, is the angry boy that she sees in her crystal ball. Do you agree that Harold is angry? If so, does he change by the end of the book? To what do you attribute this change?

13. The Cannibal King tells Harold that the freaks are fake outside, but not inside, while normal people are fakes inside. What does he mean? What examples from the novel support his position?

14. Why does the author have Tina die? Would the story have had the same impact if another character had died instead?

15. What lessons does Harold learn from his time with the circus and with the people he meets there?

Projects
1. Harold's albinism sets him apart from others and makes him feel like a freak. The National Organization for Albinism and Hypopigmentation sponsors an awareness program to educate doctors about albinism. Consult the organization's website, www.albinism.org, for information on this condition that you can use to educate your peers. Organize this information into a *PowerPoint* presentation that will promote understanding of the condition among young people.
2. Thunder Wakes Him tells Harold that Crazy Horse used to tell him legends; he tells Harold the legend of Buffalo Woman. Find and learn an authentic Native American legend. Tell the legend to your class or videotape your version of the story.
3. Locate information on either the history of the circus as a form of entertainment or circuses today. Reference sources or websites, like that of the Ringling Brothers Circus (www.ringling.com), or www.circusweb.com, will provide the information. Include illustrations like drawings or downloaded art, and organize your information into a circus album.
4. Harold's stepfather says there is nothing good about gypsies. Pretend that a group of gypsies comes into your town, and you are a reporter for the local paper covering the story. Locate information on gypsies, and write your feature story giving a balanced view of the group for readers like Harold's stepfather.
5. Harold teaches the elephants to play baseball. Conrad cries and also becomes violent. Locate information on elephants, their habitat, and especially their ability to learn and be trained. Organize your information on a poster.
6. The calliope creates joyful music that calls people to the circus. In your local library or bookstore, locate a recording of calliope music. Make a tape or burn a CD of your favorite calliope music.

Vocabulary
Each of the following quotations chosen from *Ghost Boy* includes one or more vocabulary words in **bold print**.
1. "They shuffled down Liberty's main street with puffs of dust **swirling** at their feet, as though the earth was so hot that it **smoldered**."
2. "Even his eyes were such a pale blue that they were almost clear, like raindrops or **quivering** dew."
3. "He picked through his jar and took another one out, hating to see the way it **slithered** and **thrashed** at the touch of the hook."
4. "He walked down a line of enormous old army trucks, some still in khaki and white stars, others **gaudily** painted, all **smeared** with the dust of the road."
5. "They **taunted** him with ghostly cries, looming up toward his face, swirling all around him in blurs of brown and gray."
6. "He **flexed** his toes in his thin black socks."
7. "Harold **squinted** at him through his round glasses."

8. "**Tattered** by the wind and rain, it curled across itself, a square of red and an arrow in the middle."
9. "The truck labored up the hills, its motor overheating, steam **wafting** from the hood."
10. "Windshield wipers **flailed** and squeaked, sweeping dust and bugs away."
11. "He stood on the tractor, black and **gaunt** against the clouds."
12. "And Harold felt his heart **plummet** to his stomach."
13. "The old Indian rode out from the assembly hall at a slow, **sedate** walk."
14. "And he saw the mountains in the distance, a **smudge** of blue against the sky."
15. "The tiny audience went out to a **deluge** that soaked them in an instant."

About the Author
Iain Lawrence was born in Ontario, Canada, and is still a resident of that country. He has always loved the circus and once had a job taking down a big top. He also worked on a fish farm and wrote for a newspaper.

Grab Hands and Run
Author: Frances Temple
Publication date: 1993

Awards
ALA Best Books for Young Adults
School Library Journal Best Books
National Council for the Social Studies/Children's Book Council Notable
Children's Book in the Field of Social Studies

Characters
Felipe Ramirez
Romelia Ramirez, "Romy"
Paloma Ramirez
Jacinto Ramirez
Carmen

Character Traits
Citizenship
Compassion
Courage
Generosity
Integrity
Kindness
Perseverance
Resourcefulness

Setting
Modern day—El Salvador, Guatemala, Mexico, United States

Plot
Jacinto Ramirez, father of twelve-year-old Felipe and eight-year-old Romy, is an
architect and a political activist in El Salvador. Therefore, he and his family are
in such danger from the government that Jacinto has left instructions that should
anything happen to him, the family should "grab hands and run" to Canada, one
of the few countries that admit Salvadoran émigrés. When the worst happens,
and Jacinto's motorcycle is found abandoned, Paloma gathers her resources and,
with Felipe and Romy, begins the trek to Canada. To reach Canada, they must
illegally pass the borders of Guatemala, Mexico, and the hardest of all, the
United States.

On the first phase if their journey, they travel on the roof of a bus where they
encounter the kindness of others and see firsthand the atrocities of the military.

Others along the route show them kindness by sharing food, lodging and, like Ines and Eusebio, help in crossing the borders. But, they also encounter the greed and deceit of people like the oarsman who carries them across Lago de Guija, the lake that separates El Salvador and Guatamala, but then demands twice the fare he quoted.

When they cross the border into the safety of the United States, they are picked up while hitchhiking and brought to a refugee detention center. There, they learn of Jacinto's death, proving that it is dangerous for them to be returned to El Salvador. While in the center, Carmen and the priest, Padre Jim, offer assistance and advice, which enables them to be legally admitted into Canada.

Questions for Discussion

1. What is Chuy's attitude toward Jacinto's activities? Since he is the father of Paloma and grandfather to Felipe and Romy, can you understand his attitude? Why do you think Jacinto pursues these activities even though it endangers him and his family? Do you admire Jacinto for his efforts?

2. Why does Abuela send Felipe away when they hear the mazingers? How would you feel if you had to fear being abducted into the army? Do you think twelve-year-olds should be involved in wars? Why do you think this is a common practice in many countries?

3. Describe the home life of the Ramirez family. What do you like about the family relations? Why do you think they are able to continue with some ordinary activities? Do you think you think your family would be as strong under similar circumstances?

4. Why is Felipe proud that he can make a joke about his pants? What does this tell you about him and his feelings for his mother?

5. Paloma creates four rules for traveling. Give the importance of each for the safety of the family. Which do you think would be the hardest for you to follow? How do Felipe's rules differ from his mother's rules? Why do you think these are good rules for him?

6. The Ramirez family is helped across three separate bodies of water by three men. How do the motivations of each man differ?

7. What are some things that Paloma does during the trek that are contrary to her nature? Why do these things both frighten and shame Felipe? Why do you think Paloma feels the need to act this way? Can you empathize with her reasons?

8. Think of the people who showed kindness to the family. What do you think prompted them to do so? What do you think you might have done to make the journey less arduous?

9. How do Carmen and Padre Jim help the family at the detention center? Do you think they would have been received asylum without the help of these two people? What positive attributes besides kindness did they demonstrate?

10. Felipe has said that Romy does not do well in school because she is a dreamer. How did this characteristic help the family in their journey north?

11. In the detention center, Felipe decides to return home. Why does he feel that this decision is important in his maturity? Do you agree that growing up takes courage? Would you like to have Felipe and Romy as friends? What do you think you could offer in the way of friendship?

12. Why does Paloma refuse to speak to groups in the United States? Do you think her anger is justifiable?

Projects

1. On a map of North America, trace the route probably taken by the Felipe and his family to reach Michigan.

2. Prepare a timeline depicting important dates in the history of El Salvador.

3. *Grab Hands and Run* deals with the effect of the civil war that raged in El Salvador during the 1980s. Write a newspaper article describing one incident that happened during this war.

4. Amnesty International is an organization dedicated to working to protect human rights. Prepare an informative video magazine describing the founding and some of the contributions of the group.

5. Check the website for Amnesty International. Write a report concerning one of the site's references to El Salvador.

6. Felipe is a dedicated soccer player. Write a pictorial biography of a Latin American whose name has been synonymous with the sport.

7. Research the Latin American holiday, Day of the Dead. With your classmates, celebrate the day as it is celebrated in Latin America.

8. Like Felipe, start a collection of memories. Record them in a journal explaining why you selected each memory.

Vocabulary

Each of the following quotations chosen from *Grab Hands and Run* includes one or more vocabulary words in **bold print.**

1. "The **maguey** fibers I'm floating on fluff around me like a nest."
2. "I **trumpet** through my cupped hands."
3. "I picture his **machete** hanging from his wrist, his digging stick over his shoulder."
4. "Sometimes he is so tired. He **lurches** like a drunk."
5. "We filled sixteen **bobbins**, each holding about twenty meters of **twine**."
6. "The **muchachos** are the **guerillas**."
7. "A **subversive** sounds like a pest, a mouse or mole or maybe a termite."
8. "In the **hamlet** and along the road that leads to the lagoon, everyone has dogs."
9. "The military must have a battery-powered **megaphone**."
10. "Corn **shriveled**, there was nothing to eat, and people began to starve."
11. "The next time he is attacked by melancholy, I have a cigar for him from Chuy."
12. "I think her name has **dignity**."
13. "At last the bus pulls into the **terminal**, and there he is."

14. "He has a cloth on the ground, and **valves** and **pistons** laid out on it in a neat row."
15. "I know that Jacinto hopes that my **ignorance** will be a protection against **torture**."
16. "He has on a leather hat and a gray **serape**."
17. "With his **gnarled**, fishy hand, he reaches out for Romy's chin."
18. "Paloma **mumbles** under her breath the **litany** of village names, priest names."
19. "The young men cheer the bus driver, who crosses himself, waves **jauntily**, and takes off at top speed toward the ledge."

About the Author
Daughter of a United States diplomat, Frances Temple spent her youthful years in Virginia, France, and Vietnam, and her later adult years in Geneva, New York. While in Vietnam, her school was bombed, and she spent the time while her school was being rebuilt helping in an orphanage. Though she started college at Wellesley, she interrupted her education for a tour in Sierra Leone with the Peace Corps, finishing at the University of North Carolina. She is the author of several award-winning books. The first of them, *Taste of Salt: A Tale of Modern Haiti*, won the prestigious Jane Addams Children's Book Award. In 1995, Ms. Temple suffered a fatal heart attack, cutting short her contributions to children's literature.

Habibi
Author: Naomi Shihab Nye
Publication date: 1997

Awards
> ALA Best Books for Young Adults
> ALA Notable Children's Book
> Jane Addams Book Award
> NYPL Books for the Teen Age
> American Booksellers "Pick of the Lists"

Characters
> Liyana Abboud
> Drand MrsKamal Abboud, Liyana's parents
> Rafik, brother
> Sitti
> Khaled
> Nadine
> Omer

Character Traits
> Generosity
> Integrity
> Respect
> Tolerance

Setting
> Modern day—Palestine

Plot

Liyana, a fourteen-year-old American girl, comes home after receiving her first kiss to learn that her father, a doctor and a naturalized American citizen, has decided to move his family back to his native land, Palestine or Israel, depending on who is speaking of it Within weeks, Liyana, her parents, and her brother, Rafik, have pulled up roots, leaving behind Liyana's "short shorts" and many of their American ways, for such dress and behavior would be unacceptable in this strange, new home. Landing at the airport in Jerusalem, they, as Palestinians, have their luggage scrutinized much more carefully than the Israelis arriving on the same flight.

Though only Poppy, Liyana'a father, speaks the language, they are soon surrounded by Poppy's Arabic relatives and begin to learn new ways from the extended familyLiyana wonders why Sitti, her grandmother, is much more attentive to her than Rafik, but Poppy explains that Sitti knows only womanly things and wishes to teach them to LiyanaWhen Poppy is not at the hospital working, he tours the countryside with his family but never goes to the West Bank, which he says he does not know.

Feeling more comfortable in her new city, Liyana begins to roam the shops during her school lunch hourIt is in one of these that she meets Omer, a Jewish boy, who like Liyana has no deep prejudicesThey soon become friends and explore part of the city togetherLiyana and Rafik make two other friends, Khaled and Nadine, Palestinians, who live in a refugee campThough this a time when peace has been agreed upon, the Israeli soldiers enter Sitti's house, destroying her possessions. Another time, the soldiers raid the refugee camp, shooting Khaled and arresting Poppy

A message of hope is reached in the novel when Omer visits Ramallah, Sitti's village, and is accepted by her even though he is Jewish.

Questions for Discussion

1. How does Liyana feel about leaving the home she has always known for her father's native land? What are some of the changes that she must come to expect? How would you feel in her situation?
2. Why are the Abboud's treated differently from the other travelers in the airport? Have you seen instances of this type of discrimination in your own country? Explain your answer.
3. What are the children's first reactions to their new home? Why does Poppy's reaction differ so much from his wife's and children's? How would you feel if you were suddenly placed in a completely unknown atmosphere?
4. How do you feel about Poppy's statement that the Arabs and Israelis are bonded together whether they like it or not? Do you see any solution to this enigma?
5. Why do you think Sitti remains devoted to the old ways of doing things? Can you understand her thinking? How does a knowledge of the old customs and methods of doing things help us to understand a different culture?
6. Reread Liyana's description of different types of angerWhat does her analysis mean to you? Which type of anger is present in Israel?
7. Why does Liyana feel totally alone? Have you ever felt this total isolation? What did you do to help yourself, and what do you suggest that Liyana do?
8. Why is it often necessary for Poppy to explain that his wife, his children, and even himself are Americans? Does this help his relatives and friends to better understand their idiosyncrasies?
9. Do you think immigrants to your country have the same problems? What advice would you offer them?
10. How do you feel about Liyana's question to Omer about the sufferings of the Jewish people making them more sensitive to the sufferings of others? How do you think most Jewish people would answer this question? How do you feel most Arabs would answer the same question? Can you identify other countries in the world where this same intolerance is present? What do you see as the solution?

11. What does Poppy mean when he says that fundamentalists talk louder than liberals? Do you agree with his answer to this situation? Why do you think this does not happen?
12. When the soldiers destroy Sitti's possessions, no explanation is given or found. How would you feel about the answer, "THERE IS NO WHY"? Does this suggest that there is also no solution?
13. How do you feel about the cycle of violence that takes place in Israel? What can ordinary people do to counteract the hostilities? What is the message of hope that is extended in the novel?
14. What do you think is the significance of the Arabic word for darling being used as the title of this novel?

Projects

1. Jerusalem is the site of many holy places for several religions. Select a religion and prepare a *PowerPoint* presentation showing the sites and explaining their relevance to the religion.
2. Many Arabic foods, such as falafel, baba ghonouj, hummus, katayef, and baklava, are mentioned in the text Using these and other foods, prepare a communal meal for your class.
3. The Bedouins are a nomadic people who are slowly becoming more stationary in their living habits. Research the history of these people and prepare a written report of your findings.
4. The Armenians are a small segment of the population in Jerusalem. Prepare a timeline of the events that have led to their emigration there.
5. *Habibi* describes Arab–Israeli relations as they were in the 1970s. Make a study of the relations as they are now, and compare them with those mentioned in the book

Vocabulary

Each of the following quotations chosen from *Habibi* includes one or more vocabulary words in **bold print**.

1. "His face cracked into a most **contagious** smile."
2. "she said **dubiously**."
3. "as the train of taxis, driving faster now, flew by into another **dimension**.
4. "Mom had **scurried** around StLouis buying these things before they left."
5. "A *muezzin* gave the last call to prayer."
6. "Liyana **mused**."
7. "I'm fairI'm **floundering**I'm lonesome."
8. "And his face looked as stony as the streets of the city—**chiseled** and sharply defined."
9. "remembering the **skeptical** way he lifted one eyebrow anytime she spoke."
10. "Two strong rays of light entered the **subterranean** restaurant."
11. "a term that made her father **flinch**."
12. "They passed a few lone houses sitting off by themselves under **gnarled** trees."
13. "the temperature in the stone houses **plummeted**."

14. "Rafik interrupted her **reverie** by screaming."
15. "They liked it when she **mimicked** popular songs from the radio in the schoolyard."
16. "Liyana, feeling suddenly **bereft** without her friend . . ."
17. "Poppy looked **dubious** even as he **translated**.
18. "Liyana felt a charge of **enthusiasm** as if the dopey conversation were **electrifying** her."
19. "smiling that **generic** mother smile."
20. "her skin felt **marinated** after ten minutes."

About the Author

Like Liyana in *Habibi*, Naomi Shihab Nye was born in StLouis, Missouri, to an American mother and a Palestinian father. In her fourteenth year, her family moved to Jerusalem for one year. Returning to the United States, the family moved to San Antonio, Texas, where she still resides. Noted most for her poetry, Ms. Nye has also written children's books, music, and poetic recordings. Her work often voices the ideas and perspectives of Arab Americans like herself as well as other minorities in America.

A Hand Full of Stars
Author: Rafik Schami
Publication date: 1990

Awards
> Mildred L. Batchelder Award
> ALA Notable Book
> ALA Best Book for Young Adults

Characters
> Author of the journal
> Uncle Salim
> Mr. and Mrs. Hanna, the author's parents
> Leila, the author's sister
> Nadia, the author's girl friend
> Malmud and Josef, the author's friends
> Habib

Character Traits
> Compassion
> Cooperation
> Courage
> Integrity
> Kindness
> Resilience
> Resourcefulness

Setting
> Modern day—Damascus, Syria

Plot

At age fourteen, a young Syrian boy decides he wants to be a writer, more specifically, a journalist, and begins by keeping a journal. His entries over the three years grow and mature as he does. The early entries are mundane reports of his everyday life, which introduce us to his friends and family and to the habits and cultures of the people of Damascus. Foremost is Uncle Salim who is the author's mentor and mainstay. With his fabulous stories, Salim encourages the author to see the world in a unique fashion, and offers sage advice and understanding when the boy is despairing of his future. We meet Mr. and Mrs. Hanna, the author's parents. The father sees no need for his son to continue his education, for as the son of a baker, the author is destined to be a baker as well. In his entire life, he has only taken off two days from the bakery: his wedding day and his son's baptism. His daughter's baptism did not merit a day off. The mother is a kind and loving woman who treasures her children and cares for her neighbors. The author's two best friends, Josef and Mahmud, enter into mischief with him but as they age, only one, Mahmud, one shares the author's interests. Nadia, his girlfriend and Leila, his sister, depict the realistic position of woman in the Middle Eastern society.

Through his words, we see the clay houses that melt and leak in the rain, the courtyard that serves as a meeting place for the neighbors, and the magnificent mosque with a marbled edifice that cuts off the air and light from the nearby clay structures. We go to the bazaar and watch his mother haggle with the shopkeepers over the cost of an item. Through his investigation of the words the madman has written, we learn that Damascus is a cosmopolitan city with a Greek auto mechanic, a Jewish greengrocer, a Spanish violin maker, a Shiite who reads Persian, and an Italian pastry chef.

In his second year of journal writing, the author meets Habib, a journalist who is embittered by the lack of freedom of the press in Syria. From Habib, the author begins to learn the process of newspaper writing. When Habib is released from jail where he was incarcerated for writing an article unfavorable to the government, the author, Mahmud, and Habib start to publish a secret newspaper that they disperse by stuffing it in cheap socks hawked on the streets. Though they invent other ingenious ways of distributing the paper, Habib is eventually arrested, and this time he will not be freed. Mahmud and the author answer the arrest the best way they can; they publish another edition.

Questions for Discussion
1. A newspaper article written early in Uncle Salim's career as a coach driver describes him as a "man ahead of his time." What does the phrase mean to you? Why do you think the journalist described Uncle Salim in this manner?
2. How does Mrs. Hanna respond when the police question her about a Palestinian youth? Why does she do this? What does this tell you about her? Do you think you would like her for your mother?
3. How does the author's father react to his being first in his class? Why do you think his father is not impressed by his achievement? What does this tell you about his father? How does the author feel about his father's reaction? How would you feel in this situation?
4. Mr. Hanna does not attend his daughter's baptism. What does this tell you about his attitude toward women and girls? Do you think this is a common attitude in the Middle East? What leads you to your opinion?
5. When tricked by Georg, the author questions how to assess friendship. How does Uncle Salim respond to the author? Do you agree with him? Can you apply it to your friendships?
6. Nadia's father is a member of the secret service. Why does the author fear and dislike him? Do you agree with his estimation of Nadia's father? Why?
7. When Mr. Hanna takes the author from school, Mr. Katib, the English teacher comes to see him. What does he mean when he talks of duty to Mr. Hanna? Can you explain Mr. Hanna's behavior?

8. In despair, the author tells Uncle Salim of his decision to run away. How does Salim show his true friendship for the author? Why do you think he counsels the author to stay? Is this advice something you could practice in difficult times?

9. What is Uncle Salim's advice about troubles? Do the pressures of the day often cause problems in your family? How do you think you could incorporate Salim's wisdom into your home situation?

10. It is often true that writers and artists, like Gibran, are not appreciated in their own country until they are recognized abroad. Why do you think this is so? What does this tell you about people?

11. What does Mahmud's play about the editor mean to you? Do you think that people can be swayed as easily as in this play? Do you believe that the evil of one person can destroy the goodness in another? Why do you think Mahmud feels this way? Do you think expressing his feelings in the play helped assuage his anger?

12. How does Mr. Hanna react to the publication of the author's poems? What does this tell you about him? How does the author respond to his achievement? How would you react?

13. Why is Habib so disillusioned about writing for the government newspaper? What happens when he finally rebels? How would you react if your government allowed no criticism from the press? Do you think this occurs in many countries today? Why do you think this occurs?

14. Why do Habib, Mahmud, and the author decide to write the sock newspaper? How does the publication of the newspaper change the author? Are his new traits important for a journalist? How does the government react to the success of the newspaper? Why is it important to the government that dissident voices be silenced?

15. How do the neighbors demonstrate their feelings for Uncle Salim when he dies? Why do you think he earned their admiration? How does the author feel about the loss of his friend? Do you think you would like Uncle Salim for a friend and advisor? Why?

16. How do Mahmud and the author respond to the final arrest of Habib? Why is their action so important in a country where the government restricts the dissemination of the truth? Do you think you would have the courage to do the same? Is this a question that can really be answered?

17. Read the author's postscript. How does he explain the title of his book? Do you think his thoughts are necessary for all oppressed people?

Projects

1. The second half of the twentieth century has been filled with instability and political changes in Syria. Prepare a timeline from 1950 to the present illustrating important events in its political history.

2. Draw a picture of the author's home and its surroundings from the descriptions given in the novel.

3. The madman has written his message in many languages. Make a poster or a *PowerPoint* presentation illustrating a word in each of these languages.

4. Uncle Salim is a great storyteller. Select one of his stories and present it orally to the class.
5. Mahmud is a Muslim and the author is Christian, probably a Catholic of one of the Eastern Rites of this religion. Research these religions and compare and contrast their basic precepts.
6. Kahil Gibran, the Lebanese author and artist, is mentioned in the text. Investigate his life, and prepare a written report of your findings.

Vocabulary

Each of the following quotations chosen from *A Hand Full of Stars* includes one or more vocabulary words in **bold print**.

1. "But I am used to his **griping**."
2. "The street belongs to the children, the beggars, and the **itinerant** peddlers."
3. "Earlier we had been told that imagination resided in **exaggeration** alone, but now Mr. Katib teaches us that **fabulous** tales **transpire** in the simple events of our everyday lives."
4. "he said he would have been a rich man long ago had he not been forced to feed her large and **voracious** family . . ."
5. "who was severely punished for **allegedly** having **depraved** the character of a child."
6. "As I **jubilantly** burst into our courtyard . . ."
7. "But he paid no attention to me, no matter how much I tried to make myself **conspicuous**."
8. "though he himself had no such **sublime** schooling behind him."
9. "I wish my teachers would lie a little so their lessons would be as **fascinating** as Uncle Salim's stories."
10. "After about an hour, they were all sitting at my mother's, **harmoniously** drinking coffee."
11. "Soon we are **enthralled** and stop **interjecting** stupid remarks."
12. "I have **thalessemia**, a **congenital** Mediterranean **anemia**."
13. "When I came home, again my mother **scurried** out of the room."
14. "She let the police know that she would **forfeit** the deposit if Ismat would withdraw his complaint."
15. "but she seems to **savor** her father's frustration."
16. "The street merchants **extol** their wares in a splendid way . . ."
17. "The man who sells fish is the true master of **embellishments**."
18. "I really must be **uniquely** stupid."
19. "We all presented our themes **extemporaneously**."
20. "smiling his repulsively **conciliatory** smile, as he often does after some **obnoxious** act."

About the Author

Born in Syria in 1946, Rafik Schami was forced to immigrate to Germany in 1971. The author of many adult and young adult novels in German, his novels have been translated into many languages, but until recently, never into the Arabic language. A continuing theme throughout his works is that people should understand each other and understand the unity despite the ethnic, social religious, cultural, and gender differences. For many years, he has worked toward reconciliation between Israelis and Palestinians, and often lectures and holds workshops on this topic.

Note: Since there is some implied sexual activity in this novel, it would be wise to read the book before presenting it to young readers.

The Heart of a Chief
Author: Joseph Bruchac
Publication date: 1998

Characters
Chris Nicola
Doda
Celeste
Katie
Belly Button
Gartersnake
Pizza
Mito
Mr. Douglas
Father Benet
Coach Takahashi

Character Traits
Citizenship
Cooperation
Courage
Dependability
Helpfulness
Integrity
Loyalty
Resourcefulness
Respect
Respect for the environment
Self-respect
Trustworthiness

Setting
Present day—Penacook Indian Reservation, New Hampshire

Plot
Chris Nicola, a young Penacook Indian, has always lived and been educated on the reservation, but this year he is to enter the middle school in the neighboring town, Rangerville. With him go his closest friends, Belly Button, Gartersnake, and Pizza, a group of boys so varied in appearance and backgrounds that they call themselves the "Rainbow Coalition." Fearful of the new situation, they enter the school as a group trying not to be noticed. Chris soon finds that school is not as daunting as he has feared. Through his natural intelligence and leadership, he

soon wins the respect of teachers and students alike, and even finds a special friend in Katie, an American Indian, who does not live on the reservation.

There are sharp contrasts on the reservation: the seedy shacks and trailers in which many live and the beautiful island that is a special place to Chris. Changes are pending; there is a talk of building a casino on the island to bring in needed income. When the trees are marked for destruction, Chris and his friends pull up the stakes, temporarily thwarting the construction.

At home, Chris and his sister, Celeste, live with their grandparents for their mother has been killed in an automobile accident and their father is waging a battle against alcoholism—a battle that he has lost many times before. Chris's grandparents are good, caring people, but they are aging and Chris must accept responsibility in caring for them. His grandfather, Doda, is a wise man who has imparted to Chris the history and folklore of the Penacooks as well as explaining that their family has always been one that works for the people.

At school, Mr. Douglas, the English teacher, has divided the class into groups, each to select a controversial topic, research the facts, and present a report to the class. Chris's group chooses "Using Indian Names for Sports' Teams." Their careful research and excellent presentation bring about a change in the policy. As for the casino, Chris and his father present the tribe with an alternative location that will save the island but still provide income for the tribe.

Questions for Discussion

1. Why are the children from the reservation trying not to be noticed when they arrive at school? Why are the other children confident? Is this a common situation in school life? Why do you think it occurs, and what can be done to alleviate the problem?

2. When Chris meets Thumper Wheelock, a sports hero at school, what does he expect? How are Thumper's actions different from what Chris expected? What does it tell you about making assumptions about people?

3. Chris and his three friends call themselves the "Rainbow Coalition." Why? Does their description fit with your picture of children living on a reservation? Do you recognize similarities to children in your community? What does this tell you about people?

4. How does Coach Takahashi help Pizza in his first football game? Why does the result both excite and depress Chris? Can you understand his feelings? Does this insight change your ideas about names for sport teams and ways of cheering for them?

5. Pizza, now Tony, changes after succeeding on the football team. Why do you think he does? What has success given him that he did not possess previously? What has it taken from him?

6. Doda, Chris's grandfather, tells him stories of the old ways of the Penacook nation. What are some of the customs that Chris wishes his people still followed? What saddens him about the way his people live now?

7. Mito, Chris's father, is a complex man. What are the good qualities he possesses? Why do you think he abuses alcohol? How does this affect Chris and his family? What are your feelings toward this man?

8. Chris, Katie, and several other students choose the topic, "Using Indian names for sports teams." What type of controversy does this cause in the school community? Has this topic occurred in any schools in your vicinity? If so, how was it settled; if not, what do you suppose would happen?

9. Coach Takahashi states to Chris that he does not like prejudice. Does he know about it through firsthand knowledge? Do you think he would be totally accepted in your school? What are the reasons for your answer?

10. How do Chris and his family settle the thorny issue of the gambling casino? How do you feel about Mito's letter? Why do you think it impressed the members of the tribe?

11. Would you like Chris as a friend? Name several of his qualities that make you feel this way?

12. What ways of the traditional Penacook native would be admirable qualities to be practiced by our society? What can be done to help the conditions on reservations? What can you do to make a difference?

Projects

1. With a partner, prepare and present a debate on the pros and cons of casino gambling from the Native American point of view.

2. Alcoholism is a serious problem among Native Americans. Investigate the reasons for this and offer a program of solutions for the problem. Be sure to investigate the ongoing programs attacking the problem.

3. Prepare an illustrated oral or *PowerPoint* presentation on the game of lacrosse, providing some historical background but concentrating on explaining the game itself.

4. There are several folklore stories about Gluskabe; select one and present it orally to the class.

5. Prepare a written report on the Penacook Indians.

6. Create a diorama of a Penacook village as it appeared in the 1600s.

7. If possible, visit an Indian Reservation and speak with tribe members. Prepare a newspaper report on your findings.

8. Chris's class chose four topics on which to report. With several other classmates, select one of these topics and prepare a report using the same procedures described in the novel.

9. Celeste's doll is named for two famous women. Select one and research her biography. Prepare a written report on your findings, stressing her contributions.

Vocabulary

Each of the following quotations chosen from *The Heart of a Chief* includes one or more vocabulary words in **bold print**.

1. "The kids at the school take an extra **enrichment** class in Penacook."

2. "Even though her fingers are stiff from **arthritis**, it sure has brought good health to Auntie."

3. "The house is built the way a **wigwam** would have been built back then."

4. "I'll draw the other **diagonal** tonight to make an X."

5. "The other kids are the **confident** ones."
6. "'The big one over there,' he says, his voice sort of **wistful** 'that's Thumper Wheelock.'"
7. "One of them does a **spontaneous** cartwheel for her friend."
8. "which looks like a **maximum** security prison I saw in a movie."
9. "It's **psychosomatic**."
10. "In Rangerville Junior High, that is probably going to be my **maxim**."
11. "He stood me in front of the bathroom mirror with white **scrolled** ferns all around the edge of it."
12. "invisible signals in the air that only a kid's **antennae** can receive."
13. "I'll be late to gym class but detention is better than being **disemboweled**."
14. "Instead there is an **ominous** silence."
15. "He **hefted** another stone and hurled it."
16. "I am getting **hysterical**."
17. "paddles around on the **fiords** being chased by trolls and reindeer."
18. "I sit down and the other three members of the **Coalition** sit with me...."
19. "Like the time I got the word **peripheral**."
20. "**Subanthropoid**."

About the Author

A native New Yorker as well as a Native American, Joseph Bruchac was born in Saratoga and educated at Cornell, Syracuse, and the State University at Albany. A fiction writer, poet, and storyteller, he has published over 100 works depicting the diversity of the Native American culture. His works show the cultural strengths and traditions; the awareness of the land, and the pride of the Native American in America's past and present. He hopes to make the different cultures accepted and understood.

From the Author

"One of my greatest influences as a writer has been my dear friend Chinua Achebe, who is one of modern Africa's greatest novelists. Chinua, who was on my doctoral committee, once told me that his first novel; *Things Fall Apart*, was written as a direct response to a book written by an English author that was about Achebe's own Igbo people. To truly tell his people's stories, good and bad, became Chinua's life work as a writer.

In a small way, I have tried to do the same. Many of my books on American Indian themes are attempts to offer another side of a story that has previously been told to the detriment of American Indians. But, like Chinua, I have tried not to shy away from that which is controversial or even tragic.

The Heart of a Chief, in a sense, is one of those books. People, including other Indians, had been telling me for years that they wished there more books out there for younger readers that presented American Indian life as it is today—not as it was in some past century. In *The Heart of a Chief* I tried to do just that, by telling the stories of a number of Native kids in a fictitious New England reservation that very much reflects life as I have seen it in other northeastern reservation communities. My main character, Chris, has to deal with an alcoholic father, has lost his mother in an accident, and is trying to come to terms with such things as racism (including Indian racism against one of his friends who is part African-American and part Indian) and a proposed gambling casino. His problems are those of many Indian kids today and one reason why teenage suicide in America is highest among Native Americans. By having Chris suffer through these problems and find ways to come to terms with them, I hoped that I might give some of the Native kids who read this book the idea that they, too could find hope. Of course, the book is not just for Indian kids. Some of Chris's problems—like the first day as an underclassman in a new school—are pretty universal. And I hope that this book can both entertain and teach. One of my primary messages in most of what I write—is that we need to find ways to resolve conflict without violence . . .

One last thing, Chris (and most of the other Indian characters in the book) is real. I've had the good luck over the last thirty years to meet Chris many times, to listen to him and watch him grow. The names of those Native kids who became Chris are different, but their faces are like Chris's face as I see it in my heart. Faces that have known pain but never lost hope."

Homeless Bird
Author: Gloria Whelan
Publication date: 2000

Awards
   National Book Award
   YALSA Best Books for Young Adults

Characters
   Koly
   Maa and Bapp, Koly's parents
   Hari Mehta
   Mr. and Mrs. Mehta, Koly's sassur and sass
   Chandra
   Raji
   Maa Kamala
   Mala
   Mrs. Devi
   Mr. Das

Character Traits
   Courage
   Fairness
   Kindness
   Optimism
   Patience
   Perseverance
   Resilience
   Self-control

Setting
   Present day—India

Plot
Thirteen-year-old Koly lives in India, the daughter of a poor scribe. Because her mother believes school is not useful for girls, Koly never learns to read although she yearns to do so. Koly's mother has taught her how to embroider, and for her dowry, Koly embroiders a quilt picturing her family and the important memories of her early life that she wants to take with her. She knows that when a marriage is arranged for her and she leaves home, there will be more food for the rest of her family. Relatives and friends do find a husband for Koly, sixteen-year-old

Hari, whose father, like Koly's, is a Brahmin, the highest Hindu caste. Koly's family has to sell several items including their cow to pay the dowry. Still the bridegroom's family demands jewelry, and Koly's mother gives the earrings she had worn as a bride.

Besides being most interested in the dowry, the Mehtas have not been truthful about Hari's age or his poor health. Furthermore, Mrs. Mehta is demanding and mean. Because of their lying, Koly feels justified in not giving her mother's earrings to Mrs. Mehta and instead hides them in the wall. Koly learns from Chandra, Hari's sister, that her parents want Hari to marry so they can get the dowry that will enable them to travel to the Ganges to cure Hari. When the family reaches the sacred river, Hari is at first energized by going into the water, but he dies soon after.

As a widow, Koly must wear the widow's white sari. She cannot return to her parents. Her in-laws keep her widow's allotment from the government, and her sass, or mother-in-law, constantly screams orders at her. Koly's respite comes from making a quilt, being friends with Chandra, and learning to read with the help of her father-in-law. However, Koly's hope vanishes when she learns that Chandra is marrying with a dowry paid by her widow's pension, and Koly's kind sassur, or father-in-law, dies.

Her sass's cruelty continues with no one to provide a buffer for Koly. When her sass threatens to sell a book of poetry treasured by her husband, Koly turns over her earrings. One day, Sass receives a letter from her brother offering to take her in, so she sells her house and cow for the ticket for both of them to Delhi. Before they reach that city, Sass leaves Koly in Vrindavan, the city of widows. Raji, a rickshaw driver, takes Koly to Maa Kamala, a woman who shelters widows and urges them to think of hopeful futures. In return for his kindness, Koly teaches Raji to read. Mrs. Devi, a benefactor of the widow's house, sees Koly's dowry quilt and introduces Koly to Mr. Das, a sari maker who hires Koly to embroider garments. Koly can confide in Raji, and he tells her of his plans to return to his village, rebuild his family's home, and plant crops. Koly never expects Raji to propose marriage to her, a widow. She agrees to marry him when her new dowry quilt is completed.

Questions for Discussion

1. How are the Mehtas dishonest in arranging a marriage for their son? What circumstances make Koly and her parents unhappy? Why do her parents still go through with the wedding ceremony?

2. Although Koly is angry at the Mehtas, she is sympathetic to their desires for their son. Do you think Koly's feelings are admirable? How would you feel in a similar situation?

3. Even though their doctor advises against taking Hari to the Ganges, his mother still insists that they go. Do you understand her feelings?

4. What is Koly's position after Hari's death? Why are widows treated this way? Why can't Koly return to her family? Do you know of any group that is subject to discrimination like this? What can an individual do to eliminate discrimination?

5. How would you characterize Sass? Why does she treat Koly as she does? Does she ever change? Do you think Koly reacts properly to her treatment by Sass? How would you have reacted?

6. Compare and contrast Koly and Chandra. Is Chandra a good friend to Koly? How does Koly feel when Chandra marries? How would you have felt?

7. How is reading important to Koly? Why has she not been educated? What does Sass think of reading? How does Chandra's opinion of the importance of reading change? How important is reading to you?

8. Why does Koly hide her earrings? Why does she give them to Sass? Do you admire this action? What would you have done?

9. Chandra knows that Koly's widow's pension has been used for her dowry. Why doesn't she tell Koly? Do you admire Chandra for what she says? Do you admire Koly for how she feels? Do you admire Sass's reaction when confronted by Koly?

10. How does Koly see herself changing before she meets Maa Kamala? Does she like her new attitude? What does Kamala offer her? How does it help her to talk with other widows?

11. Why does Maa Kamala object to Koly spending the night with Mala? Is she right about Mala? What do you think of Mala's reason for stealing the wedding veil?

12. What kind of man is Raji? What admirable qualities does he possess?

13. Why does Koly feel sorry for Mala and Sass? Do you think she is right in feeling this way?

14. Koly reads a poem about a homeless bird that always flies to another place. What is the significance of this poem as the title for the book?

Projects

1. Koly works as a sari maker. Draw a sketch of this traditional Indian clothing worn by women and men.

2. Koly makes a quilt for her dowry on which she embroiders pictures of the important people and things in her life. Make a paper quilt including pictures of people and things important to you. You may include pictures cut from magazines, photographs, and drawings.

3. The fathers of Koly and Hari are both Brahmins. Locate information, and write a report on the Indian caste system.

4. What traditions and customs govern the marriages of Koly and Chandra? What customs are followed at Hari's funeral? Write a report comparing and contrasting these wedding and funeral customs with those that are familiar to you.

5. The music of the sitar and tabla is played at Koly's wedding. What kind of instruments are these? Locate pictures of them, and make a model of one.

6. The descriptions of Koly's and Chandra's weddings include examples of Indian food. Compile a cookbook of typical Indian recipes.

7. Locate information on the Hindu religion. Why is the River Ganges important to the religion? Who is Krishna? What are the Vedas? What are the dif-

ferences among the various sects, such as the Jains and Sikhs? Organize your information into a *PowerPoint* presentation.

Vocabulary

Each of the following quotations chosen from *Homeless Bird* includes one or more vocabulary words in **bold print**.

1. "My bapp, like all fathers with a daughter to marry off, had to find a **dowry** for me."
2. "I felt the sharp pokes of elbows in my side and the crush of other people's feet **treading** on my feet."
3. "I thought it **inauspicious** that Hari should be on a train with so many dead people."
4. "That is what my sass was doing to me, worrying and **badgering** me with her never-ending orders and scoldings."
5. "Now that the **monsoon** had come, everything was damp."
6. "If I answered back, I was **impudent**. If I kept silent, I was **sullen**."
7. "Instead of a frightened **gawky** girl and a young and doomed bridegroom, there were a handsome young man and a happy and beautiful bride."
8. "A **pariah** dog would **slink** into the courtyard from time to time in search of a **morsel** of food."
9. "Its dirty yellow fur was **mangy**."

About the Author

Gloria Whelan was born in Detroit, Michigan, and received both her bachelor's and master's degrees in social work from the University of Michigan. She has been a social worker, a supervisor of group services, and an instructor in American literature. She always loved books and began writing as a child. She and her husband live on several hundred acres of land on a small lake in northern Michigan.

From the Author

"I have had hundreds of letters and e mails from young readers of *Homeless Bird*. I am amazed at how easily and deeply the readers enter into and are touched by a story about a country so different from their own. I suspect it is because the emotions in the book: jealousy, love, fear, uncertainty, and joy are common to us all.

I'm sometimes asked, 'How can you write about a widowed girl living in India?' I was asked the same kind of question when I wrote about a Vietnamese family, an African American girl, a Native American boy. I don't see how one can say authors have no right to imagine themselves into the lives of others. Imagining ourselves into the lives of others is not unique to authors. It's something we all do every day. Without our identification with other people, without being able to imagine how others feel, there would be no compassion. That imagining ourselves into the lives of another is what makes life tolerable and makes us all human."

Homesick: My Own Story
Author: Jean Fritz
Publication date: 1982

Awards
Newbery Honor Book Award
American Book Award
Christopher Award
New York Times Book of the Year
Child Study Award
Boston Globe/Horn Book Honor Book

Characters
Jean Guttery
Mr. and Mrs. Guttery
Lin Nai-Nai
Yang Sze-Fu
Ian Forbes

Character Traits
Citizenship
Compassion
Cooperation
Courage
Helpfulness
Kindness
Optimism
Patience
Respect
Respect for the environment
Self-control
Self-respect
Tolerance

Setting
1925–1927—China

Plot
Jean Guttery's father is an official with the YMCA, and Jean has grown up in China. Jean attends a British school and is exposed to the unique culture of China before the Revolution, including coolies, rickshaws, and foot binding, but she longs to go to America, the country of her parents' birth that she herself has

never seen. She corresponds regularly with her grandmother in Pennsylvania and counts the days until she will be there.

Jean is a spirited girl; she refuses to sing "God Save the Queen" in the British school she attends, skips school to walk through the city where she makes friends with the little Chinese boy, and is tempted to teach Lin Nai-Nai incorrect phrases, like greeting an American with the phrase "sewing machine." Jean believes that her mother is most concerned about her being good, a trait that she doesn't believe she naturally possesses, preferring instead to be clever. One of the closest people to Jean is Lin Nai-Nai who is employed by Jean's family, although she is not of the servant class. Lin Nai-Nai walks on stumps since her feet were bound according to ancient custom, but she rebelled against custom by running away from her husband when he took another wife.

As the time nears for the family to leave China, the turmoil within the country grows. The Communists are trying to force the city of Wuchang to surrender by cutting off its food supply. The British school that Jean attended closes, and she is taught by her mother at home. Her father, in his work with the YMCA, is involved with relief efforts. The family is scheduled to leave in July, but has to leave in March when all women and children are evacuated from the city. Although she'd counted the days until leaving, when this happens, Jean has mixed feelings. The family travels by ship and car to their family in Pennsylvania. On her first day of school, she corrects the teacher's pronunciation of Yangtse and fights with girls who call the Chinese "Chinks" and "Chinamen." She also makes a friend, Donald Burch.

Questions for Discussion
1. What does Jean's attitude about singing "God Save the King" tell you about her? How does she deal with the bullying of Ian Forbes? What do you think of her father's solution to the problem?
2. What qualities does Lin Nai-Nai possess? What does she demonstrate by leaving her husband? Why is it so important for her to see her family after the siege of Wuchang is over? How does her father react to her? Is the reaction understandable?
3. Jean is afraid that her mother just wants her to be good, and she doesn't think this trait comes naturally to her. Do you agree? Jean would rather be clever. Do you think she is clever? What traits do you think Jean possesses? Does she usually do the right thing?
4. Why doesn't Jean like her name? What name would she rather have? What kind of name does Jean want for her baby sister? Do you think it is important for a person to like his or her name? Do you like your name?
5. How does Jean feel when she sees the beggars? Why has she been told that one cannot give the beggars money? What do her feelings tell you about Jean?
6. Why is it important for Jean to make friends with the little boy that she meets the day she skips school? Why does he change when they meet again? How does Jean react to this change?

7. Do you think Jean's parents acted appropriately in not telling Jean that her mother is pregnant? Would you have reacted as Jean does? Why doesn't Jean want a sister who will be perfect in every way?

8. Jean cannot wait to go to America, yet after she leaves China, she has mixed feelings. Is this understandable? Have you ever experienced feelings like this? How did you deal with them?

9. What qualities do people like Jean's parents, who move to other countries to help others, possess? What do they gain by their experiences? What do they lose? Do you think that you could work overseas in jobs like this?

10. Would you like to have Jean Guttery for a friend? What qualities does she have that would make her a good friend?

Projects

1. Locate information on the Yangtse River and other major rivers in the world. Make a poster with a drawing of the river and the cities and other geographical features that border it. Include data comparing the Yangtse with other rivers of the world.

2. Select one of the following topics. Locate information on the topic, and write your information into a news or feature story for a newspaper:
   a. foot binding
   b. coolies
   c. Chinese junks
   d. Chinese customs or holidays
   e. The Revolution
   f. Sun Yat-sen
   g. Chiang Kai-shek

3. Jean's mother has a long period of recovery after the death of her baby. Locate services in your community to help parents deal with the death of a child or a sibling. Organize your information into a booklet.

4. Jean has never been to an American school when she enters the eighth grade in Pennsylvania. Prepare a welcome packet of materials for new students who are entering your school for the first time. Include information on school routines, clubs, activities, and rules. Make the information fun, interesting, and attractive to the new students.

5. To ease the adjustment of new students to your school, develop a plan for activities that could help them adjust, like a buddy system and get-togethers. Present your plan to your principal or student government.

6. Jean's father is a relief worker for the YMCA. Locate information on this organization and its work today. Organize your information into a *PowerPoint* presentation.

7. What areas in the world are in need of the kind of relief efforts that were being provided in China when Jean's family lived there? What agencies exist to provide the relief for the people in these countries? How can anyone help with these efforts? Organize a campaign to support the work of one of these organizations, and prepare a flyer to support your effort.

Vocabulary
Each of the following quotations chosen from *Homesick: My Own Story* includes one or more vocabulary words in **bold print**.

1. "I was looking up at a little white cloud **skittering** across the sky when all at once someone tramped down hard on my right foot."
2. "**Snarling** bulldog face."
3. "Part of me wanted to laugh at the thought of Lin Nai-Nai maybe meeting Dr. Carhart, our minister, whose face would surely puff up, the way it always did when he was **flustered**."
4. "and my father would swing his cane in that **jaunty** way that showed how glad he was to be a man."
5. "He was leaning back, **teetering** on the two hind legs of his chair, the way he always did after a meal, the way that drove my mother crazy."
6. "There were demonstrations and marches and **agitators haranguing** about how foreigners ought to be kicked out of China . . ."
7. "Once long ago she had explained to me that she had **disgraced** her family when she had run away from her husband . . ."
8. "I had read about **sieges** like this in my English history book, but in ancient days soldiers had worn armor and ridden horseback and used battering rams against the city walls."
9. "It didn't make a bit of difference that I **intended** to write stories, not time-tables, when I grew up."
10. "Crowds of Chinese were **milling** around but they didn't look like organized riotmakers, just ordinary Chinese who had come out of curiosity to laugh at the foreigners **scuttling** away."
11. "With the steel plates up, the deck was dark and **dismal** and prisonlike."
12. "**Flimsy** things, they looked as if they didn't want to let Shanghai go, but of course as the ship moved farther away, they broke, fell into the water, or simply hung **bedraggled** over the ship's side."

About the Author
Jean Fritz's parents were missionaries in China where she spent much of her childhood. At this time, she began to keep a journal into which she copied the writings of others and communicated her own emotions. She used this journal later when she began to write for children. She graduated from Wheaton College in 1937, has been a children's librarian and teacher, and began her career as a writer of children's picture books in the 1950s. Soon after, she began to write biographies distinguishing herself as a biographer of American historical figures. Mrs. Fritz lives in Dobbs Ferry, New York, and enjoys reading and traveling.

From the Author
"As to why I chose to write *Homesick*—I wanted to create a permanent record of my childhood in China."

The House on Mango Street
Author: Sandra Cisneros
Publication date: 1991

Awards
Before Columbus American Book Award

Characters
Esperanza Cordero
Magdalena Cordero, "Nenny"
Mama
Minerva
Rachel
Lucy
Alicia
Mamacita
Elena
Sally

Character Traits
Compassion
Dependability
Perseverance
Respect
Responsibility
Self-respect

Setting
Modern day—Chicago

Plot
Esperanza Cordero lives in a house on Mango Street. Esperanza and her family have lived on many other streets, but this is the first house owned by the family. Though they no longer have the restrictions of apartment living, but the house is a disappointment—small, dark with no front yard—and all six family members sharing the same bedroom. Esperanza is a young adolescent who is still very much child, though quickly coming-of-age. In short, lyric vignettes, she explores her neighborhood and the people who live there. In each brief episode, she presents her family members and the characters who inhabit her block. In her depiction of each, she shows their impact on her development as the strong, independent person she will be one day. She grows from the youthful person who enjoys dressing up in high heels to the mature young woman who will leave

Mango Street where she does not belong, but who will return for those who cannot leave.

Esperanza is introduced to her new street by Cathy, who offers to be her friend but only until Tuesday when they are moving since the wrong kind of people are moving into the neighborhood. She does not care that Esperanza is new to the block. Esperanza plays on the street with her little sister, Nenny, and her two friends, Rachel and Lucy, and observes the lives of her neighbors. As she matures into young women, the people on Mango Street shape her decisions about herself. Among them are the Vargas's who are so many and so undisciplined that no one, including their mother, cares for their welfare. Also on the block are Alicia, who attends the university and studies all night to better her future prospects of employment, Mamacita, who speaks little English and cries for her pink house in Mexico, Elena, who tells fortunes, and Sally,who marries young even though she is not ready.

Questions for Discussion

1. Esperanza says Nenny is not her friend but her responsibility. Does she take her responsibility seriously? What does Esperanza mean when she thinks of herself as a red balloon with an anchor? Why does she feel a best friend would free her of the anchor?

2. Named for her great-grandmother, Esperanza feels a kinship with her and her youthful wildness. Why does she not want to be like her in later life? How would you behave if you lost everything you wanted? Why do you think she could not change her situation? What does this tell you about the culture in which she lived?

3. Esperanza and Henny do not look alike, but they have similarities; they laugh alike and sometimes even think alike. Do you have anyone in your family who is like you? Why is this a comforting feeling?

4. Louie's cousin stole a Cadillac and came to the neighborhood to give everyone a ride. What do you think was his motivation? When he is arrested, the children wave as he is hauled away. What does this tell you about the expectations of the children and their attitude toward crime?

5. What does Esperanza say about neighborhoods? Do you agree with her? What could be done to allay this fear?

6. Esperanza, Lucy, and Rachel enjoy dressing up in the high heels until they meet a bum man. How does he change the enjoyment? Why do you think Rachel is tempted to take the dollar? Why is she lucky to have a sister like Lucy? When the shoes are thrown away, no one complains. Why do you think this is so?

7. What happens when Esperanza stays in school for lunch? Did the experience meet her expectations? Have you ever been disappointed by an experience you had expected to enjoy? What did you learn from this?

8. In the vignette "Hips," Nenny makes remarks that Rachel and Lucy might ridicule. How does Esperanza show her loyalty to Nenny? Do you feel protective toward members of you family even when you do not agree with

them? Why do you think this is so? What does this tell you about Esperanza?

9. Esperanza's aunt listens to her poems and tells her to keep writing, for it will set her free. What does she mean by this? From what do you think Esperanza must be freed? How do you feel about the environment in which you live? Do you feel the need to escape; if so, how do you plan to do so?

10. How do the four trees on the block inspire Esperanza? Why does she feel an affinity with them?

11. Mamacita longs for her home in Mexico. Why does it break her heart when her baby begins to speak English? How could her husband have helped her overcome her sorrow? How could her neighbors have helped?

12. Minerva is a battered wife. Why do you think she keeps letting her husband return home? Is this common in many marriages where abuse is a factor?

13. With a sigh, Mama says that she could have been somebody. Why did she quit school? How does she feel about her decision? What is her advice to Esperanza? Why do you think she gives this advice to her daughter? What do you think you could do for someone like Mama?

14. Early in this book, Esperanza says that Mexican men do not like their women strong. State examples from the book that illustrate this premise.

Projects

1. With a group of your friends, learn to jump rope in the Double-Dutch fashion. Put on a demonstration for your classmates.

2. Cumbia, salsa, and ranchero are dances mentioned in Marin's story. Draw a floor pattern that shows how your feet would move in doing one of these dances.

3. Geraldo was a "wetback" (an illegal immigrant) to the United States. Study the problem of illegal immigration and the reasons for it. With another student, prepare a debate on the pros and cons of the issue.

4. As a recent immigrant, write a letter home describing the people you have met and the happenings that you have experienced.

Vocabulary

Each of the following quotations chosen from *The House on Mango Street* includes one or more vocabulary words in **bold print**.

1. "Just like that, as if she were a fancy **chandelier**."

2. "Or like **marimbas** only with a funny little plucked sound to it like you were running your fingers across the teeth of a metal comb."

3. That up there, that's **cumulus** and everybody looks up."

4. "And don't forget **nimbus**."

5. "His feet were fat and doughy like thick **tamales**."

6. "I'm no Spartan and hold up my **anemic** wrist to prove it."

7. "when I finally come home at three p.m. you would **appreciate me**."

8. "golden **goblets**, sad-looking women dressed in old-fashioned dresses, and roses that cry."

9. This card, the one with the dark man on a dark horse, this means **jealousy**, and this one sorrow."
10. "Here is a **pillar** of bees, and this is a mattress of **luxury**."
11. "Just another **wetback**."
12. "Ruthie, tall, skinny lady with red lipstick and blue **babushka**, one blue sock and one green sock because she forgot, is the only grown-up we know who likes to play."
13. "but leap and somersault like a n **apostrophe** and a comma."
14. "every once in a while lets out a cry, **hysterical**, high, as if he had torn the only skinny thread that kept her alive, the only road out to that country."

About the Author

Born in Chicago of a Mexican father and a Mexican-American mother, Sandra Cisneros spent much of her youth traveling between the United States and Mexico. Because of these frequent moves, she never felt she belonged in either place, suffered divided cultural loyalties, and felt the shame of grinding poverty. Her writing embodies the emotions of a Latina woman trying to bridge the gap between the Anglo and Hispanic influences. Her writings, both prose and poetry, address the degradation of poverty and the finding of oneself as a woman and an Hispanic.

How I Became an American
Author: Karin Gündisch
Publication date: 2001

Awards
Mildred L. Batchelder Award

Characters
John Bonfert
Maria and Peter, John's parents
Peter, Emil and George, John's brothers
Regina and Eliss, John's sisters
John and Helen Smith and their children, Helen and Janusz
Maria
Rosina

Character Traits
Cooperation
Courage
Dependability
Helpfulness
Loyalty
Optimism
Perseverance
Resilience
Resourcefulness
Responsibility

Setting
Early 1900s—Heimburg, Austria-Hungary, and Youngstown, Ohio

Plot
Johann Bonfert, also called Johnny or John, narrates the story of his family and their emigration to the United States from Austria-Hungary. In their homeland, his father is a weaver, but business is poor, and along with other people from their region, he is encouraged to emigrate to the United States, specifically Youngstown, Ohio, where he can find work in a steel mill. Mr. Bonfert leaves when John is eight years old, and the family is confident that he will work, save money, and send for them, although other men from their region have left and abandoned their wives and children. Next, seventeen-year-old Peter leaves to join their father in Youngstown, and finally the rest of the family begins the journey. It is 1902, and John is ten years old.

The voyage across the ocean is difficult. They are traveling in third class, steerage, crammed with luggage and beds. Passengers stay in these quarters most of the time because it is so cold outside; many are seasick, and Mrs. Bonfert's milk for her nursing baby dries up. Because of fog, the voyage takes eleven days instead of nine.

Soon after they arrive in Youngstown, baby Eliss dies. Father and Peter are working in the steel mill, and Regina and John are going to school. While many immigrants are careless about the English they speak, Mama is concerned that they learn and speak English correctly. John learns to get around in the city from his new friend Helen, the daughter of Mr. and Mrs. Smith who ran the first boardinghouse in which they lived. Soon Peter becomes part of a group demanding better and safer working conditions in the steel mill; he is also incensed that many immigrant children leave school to work for very little money in factories, mills, and slaughterhouses. He decides to leave Ohio and move to California for a better life.

John is doing well in school and even skips a grade. The family works hard; Mama sells eggs, chickens, and milk, Regina apprentices as a housekeeper, and John sells newspapers. Eventually they buy a house and welcome new immigrants who are settling in Youngstown by converting their barn to a boardinghouse. Mama decides to take in Maria and Rosina not only to help with the work, but also because Rosina reminds her of Eliss. In a letter home to relatives who are thinking of emigrating, they note the differences between life in America and in Europe. They have become Americans, working hard, never forgetting the good about their native country, and appreciating the best of what America can offer.

Questions for Discussion

1. Why do the men typically go to America before their families? Why is John teased after his father leaves?

2. When John and his family leave their native country, they are sure that they will never see their friends or family again. How do you think they feel about this? How would you feel in a similar situation?

3. Peter is unhappy with life in Youngstown, and Regina is unhappy because she feels her parents have not taken on American ways. How does each deal with this frustration? Does John do the right thing in not telling his parents about Regina going to the dance hall? Would you have done the same thing? How does the strength of the family unit support Peter and Regina in the end?

4. The Bonferts gather with other German-speaking immigrants at the Society House. Why is it important for them to maintain these connections with people from their homeland? Have you ever moved? Do you try to maintain relationships with friends from your old home?

5. After John leaves to look at cars as his baby brother is sleeping, he returns to find his mother sad and disappointed in him. How does John feel and what does he promise her? What does this incident tell you about John?

6. The Bonfert family Christmas is a blend of old-world and American holidays. How do they combine the different customs?
7. Why does Mama want to take in Maria and Rosina? What does this tell you about her?
8. Throughout the book, John offers comparisons between life in the old country and life in America. What are the differences? Which of these differences would have bothered you, and which could you have ignored?
9. How does John adjust to life in this country? How do members of his family adjust? Why does Mama want her children to learn proper English? Why does Mama not want to give up some of her old ways, like making soap?
10. How do the members of the Bonfert family work together to build a life in this country? What do you admire about them?
11. What kind of boy is John? What admirable qualities does he possess? Would you like to have John for a friend?

Projects
1. Access the website www.ellisisland.com. Select the site map, and then Immigrant Experience, Overseas Passage, or Inspection Process. Gather information on your selected topic, and present your information in the form of a *PowerPoint* presentation.
2. Access the website www.historychannel.com/ellisisland/index2.html. From the menu, select Gateway where you can experience the various tests faced by actual immigrants. Follow the maps. At the end of your virtual experience, write your reflections on this experience in the form of a letter to your best friend who is still in your homeland.
3. A new student has arrived in your school from another country, and you have been asked to help this person acclimate to being an American student in your school. Make a scrapbook of life in your school using whatever artistic techniques with which you are comfortable, for example, drawing, collage, or clip art. Include phrases that your new friend should know, information about classes, rules, and recreational activities.
4. Draw a map of the Bonfert's journey from Austria-Hungary to Youngstown.
5. Locate information on the process of making steel. Organize your information into a report.
6. Locate information either on the conditions in steel mills or child labor at the beginning of the twentieth century. Pretend that you are a citizen living at that time who is interested in eliminating the abuses of these conditions, and write an editorial for your local newspaper outlining the situation and necessary reforms.

Vocabulary
Each of the following quotations chosen from *How I Became an American* includes one or more vocabulary words in **bold print**.

1. "Out of fear of God's punishment, the real **culprit** then came forward, and the plot against my father was **exposed**."
2. "Many folks were hoping for a better life and **prosperity** in Youngstown."
3. "Only a few weeks after the **departure** of the visitor from Bremen, . . ."
4. "And so my mother was very **dismayed** . . ."
5. "Even Sepp was **impressed** that there were such big factories in Youngstown."
6. "At first, he didn't want to believe me, but when Regina **confirmed** it, he left me alone."
7. "Mother didn't **begrudge** her sister-in-law her wealth, but from then on, she took our own **poverty** that much harder."
8. "She dried slices of apple and plum and stitched together **haversacks** for Regina, Emil, me, and herself to carry **provisions** for the trip."
9. "She took an **apprentice** position as a housekeeper with a **prosperous** German family who have been living in America for a long time already."
10. "Besides that, the room was so **crammed** with people that I couldn't make out one from another."
11. "the couple went back into the hall and I was **dismayed** to find that I couldn't get down from the shed, . . ."
12. "and **admonishing** the young people to think about the future."
13. I was only when I looked into Mama's **stern**, **reproachful** face,that I could **compose** myself enough to once again follow the sermon."
14. "They want to know exactly what life in America is like, because they're **contemplating** immigrating."
15. "I enjoy writing letters, but only when you can do so **spontaneously**."

About the Author
Born in Romania, Karin Gündisch emigrated to Germany. Emigrating and getting used to life in a new place are common themes in her novels. Her books have won awards in Germany and Romania.

From the Author
"This book is linked to my biography. It is true that I did not emigrate to America in 1902, but I emigrated from Romania to Germany in 1984. Then I wrote a book with direct reference to my biography: "In the land of chocolate and bananas", in which I narrate what is happening when two children and their parents leave their home and emigrate to a foreign country. I thought with it I would have finished the chapter emigration-immigration for me. But then I discovered by chance a letter from 1902 written by a woman who has emigrated from my native country to Youngstown/Ohio. She was writing to her parents and brothers and sisters back home in Transylvania. After reading this letter I realized that I would write a book about this emigration to America. . . .

Not only me and my family, not only Johnny and his family emigrated. Now, my book has also emigrated to another country and to another language. I'd like that many American pupils and, of course, many German pupils read this book and that they like Johnny. During my writing I got to like him very much."

Journey Home
Author: Yoshiko Ucheda
Publication date: 1978

Awards
IRA Children's Choices
National Council for the Social Studies/Children's Book Council Notable
   Children's Book in the Field of Social Studies

Characters
Yuki Sakane
Papa and Mama Sakane, Yuki's parents
Mrs. Jamieson
Emi Kurihari
Grandmother Kurihari
Mr. Oka
Ken Sakane, Yuki's brother
Stephen and Emma Olssen

Character Traits
Citizenship
Compassion
Cooperation
Courage
Generosity
Helpfulness
Integrity
Kindness
Loyalty
Tolerance

Setting
1944—Topaz Internment Camp and Salt Lake City, Utah
1945—Berkeley, California

Plot
It is the 1940s, and the United States and Japan are engaged in a bitter and bloody war. Feelings run high and the citizens on the West Coast, through hatred and fear of the enemy, have persuaded the government to intern all people of Japanese origin living there. After a year in the Topaz Internment Camp, the Sakane's have been paroled to live in Salt Lake City. They cannot return to their home in Berkeley, California, because no one of Japanese extraction is permit-

ted to live on the West Coast. Ken, Yuki's brother, has enlisted in the army and is serving with the 442nd Regimental Combat Team in Italy.

Though no longer at Topaz, Yuki still has nightmares about the camp, the barracks, and the dust storms and yearns to return to her once happy life in Berkeley. When the exclusion order is finally lifted toward the end of the war, the Sakane's return to Berkeley. But, things have changed; no jobs or houses are available, and the Sakane's and other persons from the camps must live in a hostel behind their church. Joined by Yuki's friend, Emi, and her grandmother as well as Mr. Oka, whom they met in the hostel, the Sakane's start up a grocery business that is almost destroyed by a malicious fire. Their new neighbors, the Olssen's, befriend them and help them rebuild the store.

Ken, seriously wounded in Italy, returns but is not the same, for he is depressed by the loss of his best friend who died saving his life. When Ken begins to build his life again, Yuki, who keeps waiting to really come home to her old life, learns that things change, and home is not necessarily a house but rather a togetherness with family and friends.

Questions for Discussion

1. Why does Yuki have nightmares about Topaz? How do you think you would feel about living in a concentration camp? Why is she confused about being incarcerated by her own country? Why does she wish to return to California?

2. Mrs. Sakane asks, "How can I pack our whole life into boxes and cartons in just ten days?" Look around your home and imagine that you must decide what you might want to keep and what you want to sell or give away. Can you understand Mrs. Sakane's dilemma? How would you feel if you had to get rid of your most prized possessions?

3. Why is Papa in a prisoner of war camp? Do you think the government had valid reasons for this action? What do you think might have been a better solution?

4. Before moving to Topaz, the Sakane's were under a five o'clock curfew. What was the reason for this? What did Ken mean when he said that they might get shot? Can you understand the feelings of the citizens toward their Japanese neighbors?

5. When Yuki arrives in Salt Lake City after the internment camp, her landlady, Mrs. Henley, questions her about why the government had sent them to a concentration camp. How did her questions make Yuki feel about Mrs. Henley? How can you explain why Mrs. Henley would offer the Sakane's an apartment, and bring them a casserole, but still would not believe in their good faith?

6. Why do you think Yuki refused to learn to speak Japanese? Do you think this is a common occurrence among children of immigrants? Do you think it is a wise decision?

7. Why does Yuki feel that saying good-bye is leaving behind a small piece of herself? Why does Mama say this is a good thing? Do you agree with her?

8. In Berkeley, Yuki finds that much has changed. Why does she feel that Emi, not Mimi, is now her best friend? What do you think caused the space between them?

9. Mr. Oka does not like white folks. What has caused his bitterness? How would you feel if you had suffered the abuses that Mr. Oka had? Why did he finally decide to stop nurturing his hatred?

10. Returning to Berkeley was not easy, for they are surrounded by the hatred and distrust caused by the war. What type of person would set fire to the grocery? How did people react to the destruction of the store? What does this tell you about human nature?

11. The Olssen's had lost a son at the battle of Iwo Jima in the Pacific. How do they feel about the Japanese? What does this tell you about them? Were the Sakane's lucky to have them as neighbors?

12. What finally makes Ken forgive himself for being alive when his friend was dead? Have you ever heard of reverse psychology? Is this what Mr. Oka used, and how successful was it?

13. What does Yuki finally learn about home? What have you learned about the Sakane's and their friends? Do you think you would like them as friends?

Projects

1. In World War II, the United States was fighting Japan, Germany, and Italy. Research how each of these immigrant groups was treated by the government. Write an essay describing your findings and the conclusions that you have drawn concerning the differences.

2. Obtain a copy of the movie, "Go for Broke." Show it to your class, and lead a discussion of the issues involved for the Japanese-American soldiers depicted in the film.

3. Yuki must live up to the noble tradition of her Samurai grandfathers. Research the history and code of the Samurai Warriors, and present your findings in a *PowerPoint* presentation.

4. Pretend you are Mrs. Sakane, and create the first poem that she wrote in a notebook and not on a scrap of paper. Mrs. Sakane's writes in the thirty-one- syllable style the Japanese call "tank." See if you can write the poem in this style.

5. Charles Robinson illustrated *Journey Home* with beautiful pen and ink drawings. Illustrate a scene from the novel in the medium of your choice.

6. Create a timeline highlighting the important dates in Japanese immigration and naturalization. Briefly state your opinion of the fairness of the government.

Vocabulary

Each of the following quotations chosen from *Journey Home* includes one or more vocabulary words in **bold print**.

1. "stifling her and wrapping her in a **smothering cocoon** of sand so fine it was like dust."

2. "Her damp fists were **clenched** tight."

3. "when Papa had been threatened by a small group of **agitators**."
4. "She was **famished**."
5. "Some things needed to be **savored** in private without **curious** eyes watching."
6. "with their Japanese talk and **genial** bows and eventually he smelly pickles they brought to picnics."
7. "He's been **evacuated** to a hospital, but he's all right."
8. "Here poor Ken was lying in some hospital with **shrapnel** in his leg."
9. "'I'm sure I can find a **sponsor** to **vouch** for me.'"
10. "A cold shiver of nervous excitement **surged** through her."
11. "'You mustn't make a **nuisance** of yourself.'"
12. "Mama was **peering** out the car window trying to see how the garden looked."
13. "Yet it seemed **shabbier** and somehow battered."
14. "'They're all **scoundrels**.'"
15. "Yuki **blurted** before she realized how unfriendly that sounded."
16. "She didn't quite understand the **brusque** old man, but she was beginning to like him."
17. "It **shrouded** the living as well as the dead, covering everything in a **hazy** gray mist."
18. "She was **rummaging** in another carton and pulled out one of Ken's old records."
19. "where Papa and Grandma Kurihara were **frantically** trying to put out the **smoldering** fire."
20. "Why then was he still **nurturing** his hate?"

About the Author
Born in Alameda, California, in 1921, Yoshiko Ucheda became a teacher before becoming a full-time writer. Her teaching career included teaching elementary students while confined in a relocation camp in Utah. Her writings for children deal with the Japanese-American experience and the feeling of isolation from mainstream America. Her books tell of the Japanese customs and traditions and offer a great insight into that portion of American society. In 1992, Ms. Ucheda died in California where she had lived most of her life.

Kit's Wilderness
Author: David Almond
Publication date: 1999

Awards
Michael L. Printz Award
Smarties Silver Award
Arts Council Award for Outstanding Literature for Young People
YALSA Best Books for Young Adults

Characters
Kit Watson
John Askew
Allie Keenan
Grandpa
Mr. and Mrs. Watson
Mr. and Mrs. Askew

Character Traits
Compassion
Dependability
Helpfulness
Kindness
Resilience
Respect
Responsibility
Self-control
Self-respect

Setting
Present day—Stonygate, England

Plot
Kit and his family move to Stonygate to be with his grandfather after his grand-mother's death. Stonygate is a coal-mining town with coal mines, shafts, and holes still beneath the surface, and Grandpa tells Kit of his days as a worker in the mines. Kit knew that like his family before him he would be a coal miner, and he both dreaded and looked forward to his work. Grandpa tells Kit of the children lost in the mine and never properly buried, like Silky, a gentle bright spirit who occasionally appears to him. He shows Kit the monument of the mine disaster in 1821 when over 100 workers were lost; among the names written on

the monument are the names of two thirteen-year-olds, Christopher Watson and John Askew.

Soon after his arrival in Stonygate, Kit meets the current John Askew, a student in his school who with his dark and brooding ways intimidates Kit, especially with the pronouncement that they are alike. John is part of a poor, unfortunate family, who have worked for generations in the mines. His father is the town drunk. Both boys are talented—John as an artist and Kit as a writer. Although he is afraid, Kit is also drawn to John, and goes with him into a cave to play the game of Death in which a spinning knife stops on the "victim," who is asked questions like "Do you abandon life?" When the knife lands on Kit, he is struck unconscious and sees the images of the lost children.

After the game is discovered, John is expelled from school and disappears from town. His mother cares for her small baby, all the while not knowing the fate of her son. Kit composes a lengthy story about Lak, who in prehistoric times, saves his baby sister from a bear and goes in search of his family. John eventually returns and calls for Kit to meet him in one of the abandoned draft mines. John tells Kit about life with his father and his wish to kill him. The two boys become blood brothers, and Kit encourages John to illustrate his story.

In the meantime, Grandpa's health deteriorates, and he shares more of his memories. He sees repeated visions of Silky and the pit children, and wonders what is a dream and what is real. John helps to care for his sister, very much like Lak in Kit's story. John returns to school and illuminates Kit's words with his drawings. Grandpa dies, and Kit brings his precious possessions into his own room. He sees around him a world filled with those who have lived there before, and feels the presence of his grandparents.

Questions for Discussion

1. What kind of boy is Kit? How does he relate to others? Would you like to have Kit for a friend? Why?

2. What has influenced John to become the person that he is? What does Grandpa mean when he says that John never had a chance to be a child? Do you agree with him? Does John overcome the difficulties of his life?

3. What does Grandpa tell Kit about the Askew family? Does he give an explanation for the behavior of Kit's father? Do you think his explanation is an excuse for Mr. Askew's behavior? Are there scenes in the novel when Mr. Askew acts differently than his usual self? Do you think his change at the end is a permanent one? Why?

4. Why does John seek out a relationship with Kit? Why is Kit both frightened by and drawn to John? How is each boy affected by their friendship? Have you been affected differently by various friendships you have had?

5. What is Kit's relationship with his grandfather? How is his attention important to Grandpa as his health fails? Have you ever been in a similar situation with an ailing loved one? Have you been able to offer the kind of comfort that Kit was able to offer his grandfather?

6. Why don't all people see the pit children? What do John, Kit, and Grandpa have in common that enables them to see children like Silky?

7. How is the story of Lak important to the entire novel? Why do you think the author included the entire story instead of just telling us a little?
8. How does the author use light and dark in the novel? Consider such elements as Silky, the mines, the darkness of death, and Allie in *The Snow Queen*.
9. How is the setting important in this novel? Could the story have been told in any other locale?
10. What does Grandpa mean when he tells Kit that they would go on forever along with those who had come before and those yet to come? Do you think this is one theme of the novel? Are there other themes?

Projects

1. Locate information on coal mining. Find out how coal is mined, and where it is still mined today. What measures are taken to insure the safety of miners? Organize your information into a news story for your local paper.
2. As a talented artist, John Askew illustrates Kit's story of Lak. From Kit's words, illustrate the significant scenes from the story in the medium of your choice.
3. It is important to Grandpa that he pass on his memories to Kit. Talk with an elderly person, a member of your family, a neighbor, or a friend. Before your conversation, write questions that will encourage discussion. If your subject is willing, videotape your discussion and later present the person with the tape. As an alternative, write your subject a letter, telling the person what memories most impressed you.
4. Read a version of the folk tale *The Snow Queen*, such as the one written by Hans Christian Anderson. Rewrite the tale as a play, and perform it before your class.
5. Project Kit and John ten years into the future. What are they doing as young men in their twenties? If you believe they are still in Stonygate, write another chapter to the book that updates their lives. If they are living at a distance from one another, write a series of letters between the two. Be sure that your projections are in keeping with the original novel and the characters created by David Almond.

Vocabulary

Each of the following quotations chosen from *Kit's Wilderness* includes one or more vocabulary words in **bold print**.

1. "Candles burned in **niches** in the walls."
2. "Lampposts and telegraph poles were twisted and **skewed**."
3. "There was Bobby Carr, the others, then Allie standing silent on the **fringes**."
4. "He leaned toward me; his heavy body **loomed** in the candlelight."
5. "I was certain she would **scoff** at me."
6. "the clouds began to break and weak beams of sunlight shone on to the **sodden** wilderness."
7. "But I stood there **sullen** and silent."

8. "Frost **relented** in the mornings, took hold again each afternoon."
9. "The world out there was **distorted** and confused by a thousand beads of water, by sudden trickles of water."
10. "He **lurched** out of the dark, the dog beside him blacker than the night."
11. "It was great to **trudge** with Allie through it on our way to school, to hear her giggles **muffled** by the dead still snow-padded air."
12. "I thought of Askew, of the fear and **revulsion** he caused around him."
13. "She'd been **enticed**, cast under a spell."
14. "At other times he stared past us through empty eyes into the **immense** absence that surrounded him."
15. "The moon shed its light onto the wilderness as we walked to school. It stunned the light from stars. It made snow **luminous**."

About the Author
David Almond grew up in northern England and, as a child, wrote stories and compiled them into books, dreaming that his books would be in a library some day. He received a degree with honors from the University of East Anglia, and taught school at the primary and adult levels as well as in the area of special education. He eventually stopped working full time, moved to a commune, and put his energy into writing. Early in his career, he wrote for adults; his first novel for young adults, *Skellig*, was published in 1998. He lives in England with his wife and daughter.

From the Author
"[The book is] very linked to the scenery of my childhood and the stories and history of the place where I grew up. I'm also asked about the origin of the story that Kit writes. That story just bounced into life. I thought, oh gosh, where's this come from, and I wondered, can I manage this? I remember taking a deep breath and saying, yes, believe in it. In my mind, it was Kit who was writing that story, and when it came time for it to be put to paper, I could relax because it was Kit who was the writer. I know that sounds daft, but that's the way it felt. I think when characters come alive they begin to do the work for you."

The Maestro
Author: Tim Wynne Jones
Publication date: 1995

Awards
> *Boston Globe/Horn Book* Award
> Governor General's Award for Children's Literature in Canada
> Canadian Library Assn. Young Adult Best Book of the Year
> Master Christie Award shortlist
> NYPL Books for the Teen Age

Characters
> Burl Crow
> Cal and Dolores Crow, Burl's parents
> Nathaniel Orlando Gow, "Maestro," "Nog"
> Natalie and David Agnew
> Bea Clifford
> Reggie Corngold
> Japheth Starlight

Character Traits
> Compassion
> Courage
> Resilience
> Resourcefulness
> Trustworthiness

Setting
> Modern day—Northern Ontario, Canada

Plot
Running away from his abusive father, Cal, and drug-weakened mother, Dolores, fourteen-year-old Burl Crow follows the path of a piano he saw flying through the sky suspended from a helicopter. He finds the remote cabin of the renowned and eccentric pianist and conductor, Nathaniel Orlando Gow, whom Burl calls Maestro but also has the nickname Nog. Gow is himself escaping the pressures of his busy world to create his bid for immortality— a dramatic oratorio for orchestra and chorus. One day after Burl arrives, Gow returns to Toronto, leaving Burl and his oratorio in the cabin.

Learning of Gow's death, Burl returns to civilization with Bea Clifford, the bush pilot who flies in supplies. Burl claims to be Gow's love child, and Bea convinces Burl to go to Toronto in an attempt to inherit the cabin. He tries out his believability on Reggie Corngold, a close friend of Gow's. When he tells her of the oratorio, she impresses him with its importance. Though it is late fall in the North Country, Burl is determined to return to the cabin to obtain the manuscript for Reggie. To do this, he must return to the home he fears to gather some equipment he will need for the endeavor. His mother is gone and her replacement, Tanya, tells Cal of his visit. Hiding from Cal while waiting for the train back to the cabin, he encounters his former teacher, Natalie Agnew, who offers him a home with her and her husband.

Arriving at Mile 29, the train's stop for the cabin, he finds that Cal has followed him and is his drunken, abusive self, eventually burning down the cabin and forcing Burl to choose between saving Cal or the oratorio. On the return ride, Japheth, the prospector who owns the land, makes him see that the true beauty and importance of the Ghost Lake has not been destroyed by the fire and will be there for Burl in the future.

Questions for Discussion

1. What types of abuse does Cal inflict upon Burl? Which form do you think causes greater damage toward a person's self-esteem? Why do you feel this is so?

2. Why is Burl such a good secret-keeper? Why doesn't he tell his teacher about the piano? Why did Burl leave Mrs. Agnew's book in school? What must it be like to always live in fear?

3. How does Burl's anger exhibit itself? Have you ever found yourself angry and not know where the angry should be directed? How do you handle this situation?

4. What is Burl's first impression of Nog? Would the Nog's actions puzzle you as well? Why does Burl wish to stay at the Nog's camp? What must it be like to have no place to go? How does Burl convince Nog that he should stay? What qualities does he exhibit in this interchange with Nog?

5. How does Nog earn the title "Maestro"? How is Burl affected by the lesson? What inspires you to strive for perfection?

6. What do you think Nog means when he calls winter the perfect cure?

7. How does the appearance of the bear affect Nog? Why does the fact that Nog takes drugs affect Burl? What do you think the discussion between Nog and Burl about drugs tells you about each? What do you think the difference is between being "sick" and being "sick and tired"? Why does Burl get rid of Nog's pills? Can you understand his reasons? Do you think he had a right to do so? What do Burl's actions during his time alone at Ghost Lake tell you about him?

8. What is Burl's first reaction to hearing of Nog's death? Why do you think he tells Bea that he is Nog's son? What motive does Bea have in convincing Burl to go to Toronto? Do you find her reason admirable? Why did Burl think that vermin were in his skull? Is this a good description of a guilty conscience?

9. Burl feels he is a nobody. What has caused him to feel this way? How does he show that he does not really believe this of himself? Do you think you would have the courage to do what Burl has done and what he plans to do?

10. When Burl reaches Toronto, he sees his first black person? Does this tell you something about the region that is Burl's home? What other firsts does Burl encounter in Toronto?

11. Why did Burl approach Reggie Corngold before going to the Maestro's attorneys? Was his reason very admirable? How does Reggie's attitude encourage him in his quest for the "Maestro's" immortality?

12. When hiding from Cal, Burl again encounters his teacher, Natalie Agnew, and her husband, David. What does their repartee with each other and with Burl tell you about their marriage and about them as individuals? Would you like Mrs. Agnew for a teacher?

13. When Cal follows Burl to the cabin, he immediately begins to put Natalie and David down. Why do you think he does this? Do you know other people who do this? How do you react to the situation?

14. In his drunkenness, Cal sets the cabin on fire and injures his leg at the same time. Burl has to make the decision whether to save the oratorio or his father. Do you think it was a hard decision for him to make? What would your decision have been? Does Cal show any gratitude for his son saving his life? Do you think he is capable of such emotions as humility and gratitude?

15. What changes does Burl's conversation with Japheth, the prospector who owns the land where the cabin stood, create in Burl's opinion of himself and of the destruction at Ghost Lake?

16. Burl has not had an easy life with an abusive drunken father and ineffectual drunk addict mother. Do you think his story would help others in poor situations to rise above the situation and become strong, useful human beings? Why do you feel as you do?

Projects

1. The character, Nathaniel Orlando Gow, is modeled after the Canadian musician, Glenn Gould. Research his accomplishments, and write an illustrated magazine article about him.

2. Select a tale from *The Red Fairy Book*, and tell it to the class.

3. The Trans Canada is a most important highway in Canada; trace its entire route noting places of historic, cultural, and recreational significance along the way.

4. Read "The Book of Revelations" in the *Bible*; explain its importance to the Christian religions.

5. Prepare a scientific study on the pesky blackfly that plagues Burl while he is in the woods.

6. Tim Wynne Jones uses his intimate knowledge of the plant and wildlife of Ontario to create the atmosphere for Burl's story. Write a creative story that incorporates a description of the plants and wildlife in your community.

7. Toronto, where Burl goes to see the lawyers, is a large and beautiful city in Canada. Northern Ontario is a vast area inviting the adventurous. Select one of these locations, and create a travel brochure or a television segment that would encourage people from your area to travel there.

Vocabulary
Each of the following quotations chosen from *The Maestro* includes one or more vocabulary words in **bold print**.
1. "and Cal was on him as quick as a bear on a **spawning** sucker."
2. "a **silhouette** coming straight for them."
3. "He ran along the rails a way, breathing in hot **creosote**, putting a thousand railway ties between him and his father."
4. "Deep **gouges** in the weathered slabs indicated a bear's work."
5. "He took a **tentative** blow."
6. "He came to a place where the still stream widened out into a **sphagnum** bog."
7. "Gravity was tugging him down at its own **relentless** speed."
8. "he said in an **imperious** voice."
9. "'You don't appreciate my **masquerade**,' said the man without turning back."
10. "his attention freed from his host's **penetrating** gaze, Burl noticed a letter lying open."
11. "I'll make a note to myself to **eradicate** from my vocabulary."
12. "Standing, he played a rapid **arpeggio** at the high end."
13. "He mumbled on like this in **sporadic** bursts."
14. "He laughed a little **hysterically**, coughed, and nodded."
15. "A boy-of-the-woods like you must think me a complete **nincompoop** living here like this."
16. "'Tonight's **episode** convinces me that I must go back to **civilization**.'"
17. "But he only stared at the fish, and then with eyes frosted over, he **scrutinized** Burl."
18. "He watched the train drawing to a **clamorous** stop."
19. "He felt like someone **evacuated** from a place under siege, a village in the path of a forest fire."
20. "Burl, on the other hand, was **writhing** inside."

About the Author
Born in Britain, but raised in Ottawa, Canada, Tim Wynne Jones is an award-winning author for adult and young adult fiction as well as children's picture books. A graduate of the University of Waterloo, Mr. Jones is a visual artist, though he does not illustrate his highly popular children's picture books. Themes that appear in his novels and are very prominent in *The Maestro* are the relationships between children and adults, the need to conquer fear, and the struggle for survival.

From the Author
"The Maestro came about in a rather peculiar way. In March of 1992, a producer from The Canadian Broadcasting Corporation (CBC) phoned me about writing a radio play to celebrate the life of the great Canadian pianist, Glenn Gould. That fall, the CBC was going to be airing a variety of tributes to Gould; it was the

tenth anniversary of his death. The producer, Bill Lane, was an old acquaintance. I used to write a lot of radio plays for him, and I would be pleased and honored to give it a try.

When I was a teenager, Gould was often in the news, and he was a really curious character, brilliant and very eccentric. I wasn't a pianist, but it was hard not to be intrigued by him. So, yes. I said sure. Then Bill said he needed an outline or at least a good, solid idea by the following week. Yikes!

Writers get deadlines all the time but seldom such short ones. Still, I gave it a try. I spent the whole weekend reading articles and books about Gould, listening to his music, trying to come up with an angle that interested me. He was a real person, and yet I was being asked to write a "story" not a documentary, so I needed an incident or event to start from.

It turned out that this world-famous pianist had a lot of trouble with fame, and sometimes he would just run away. He would hop in his great big, black limo and drive off into the wilds of Northern Ontario and "hide out." Hmmm, interesting. Apparently, he would stay in little motels along the Trans Canada Highway, places where no one would know him. I started thinking, wouldn't it be cool if he actually had a secret cabin up there, in the woods somewhere, on a beautiful lake. Someplace not even his closest friends knew about.

Writing is all about playing the "What if?" game. If Gould did have a secret cabin on a northern lake, he would have to have a piano. That's when I got the idea of a grand piano being air-lifted by helicopter. It was such a beautiful image, a piano flying over the boreal forests. But that was all I had when Bill phoned on Monday.

'Great image,' he said, 'It'll look great on radio.' We had a good laugh about that. Clearly, I needed a lot more of an idea, and there just wasn't time. So, we abandoned the radio play. But the image wouldn't go away.

About three months later, I woke up very early one morning, about 2 a.m., with that piano burning in my mind's eye. There it was flying over the landscape, but the big difference was that now I had someone who could see it. A boy. A boy named Burl. I'm not sure where that name came from, but it seemed a good, solid name. A name I could begin to build a person around. (It doesn't always happen that way. Sometimes you go through a ton of names before arriving at just the right name.) Not only was Burl seeing this weird thing, this flying piano, he had a reason to want to see it. He was in a bad way. He was in the middle of a terrible moment and then—poof!—there's a piano flying overhead, and it kind of saves his life.

You can't have a story until you have a character you love, a character you're ready to spend every day with for a year or two. I can never start a story without an image and a scene that reveals to me this character. And that character better have something going wrong in his or her life—terribly wrong. A writer needs a needy character, someone full of motivation. And there he was, Burl Crow, three months after this tiny spark of an idea came to mind.

Burl Crow would go looking for that piano. It would have been cool if Burl had just taken wing and followed it, but I'm not a fantasy writer. So he took off over land. And who would he meet when he found the secret cabin? Glenn

Gould, of course. I ended up fictionalizing the character after the first draft, for legal reasons, but also to loosen him up. I wanted to invent this character, using Gould as a model. Nathaniel Orlando Gow, I called him. A person who would seem exotic and scary and completely other-worldly to boy who had grown up in harsh surroundings, both emotionally and physically. I couldn't wait to write the scene where these two very different creatures finally met each other. I didn't know what would happen. Not exactly, I never do. I write to find out. That's what makes writing fun for me."

Miracle's Boys
Author: Jacqueline Woodson
Publication date: 2000

Awards
Coretta Scott King Award
YALSA Best Books for Young Adults

Characters
Lafayette
Ty'ree
Charlie
Aaron
Milagro (Miracle)

Character Traits
Dependability
Loyalty
Perseverance
Resilience
Responsibility
Trustworthiness

Setting
Present day—New York City

Plot
Thirteen-year-old Lafayette tells his story of life with his brothers, Ty'ree and Charlie, Miracle's boys, after the death of their widowed mother from diabetes. Their father had died many years earlier from hypothermia incurred after he jumped into the water to save a drowning woman and her dog.

Ty'ree has been accepted at MIT but gave up college to care for his brothers. Charlie has recently been released from Rahway correctional facility after robbing a store. Lafayette calls him Newcharlie because he has changed from a caring and sensitive brother to an ill-tempered and difficult one. The Charlie who wanted to adopt stray animals and prayed to St. Francis for their protection is the Newcharlie who burned all but two of the pictures of their mother and calls Lafayette "Milagro killer" because he was the one who was with their mother when she died.

Ty'ree explains to Lafayette that they each carry these burdens of regret, like the monkeys that addicts are said to carry on their backs. Lafayette blames himself for freezing up and not acting quickly enough to save her. When she died, Charlie was already in the correctional facility, and he regrets that the last time she saw him he was being taken away in handcuffs. Ty'ree admits that he was with his father when he ran into the water, and, in fact, told their father to save the woman and her dog. As Ty'ree says, Charlie has the biggest burden of all because he wasn't with either parent when they died and was isolated from their family.

Both Lafayette and Ty'ree go to the police station after Charlie is picked up for breaking parole and riding in a stolen car. Charlie insists that he didn't do anything wrong. He went to a party, not realizing it was a gang initiation. When he refused to fight, someone offered to take him home and punched him a few times to make him tougher.

In one of the pictures of his mother that remains, Lafayette is handing her something. He has a vision of her and remembers that in the picture, he is handing her a leaf and promising that he won't fight with Charlie anymore. He begins to talk to his brother and admits that their mother was not dead when he found her, and that she opened her eyes and tried to speak before she died. Charlie reveals that he robbed the store for the money that would take the four of them back to their mother's home in Puerto Rico.

Finally, the three brothers are able to talk about their mother and share their memories. Lafayette, feels "good and safe and free."

Questions for Discussion
1. Ty'ree put aside his plans for attending MIT to take care of his family. What admirable character traits and values does this show?
2. In what ways has Charlie changed after his return from the correctional facility? How does Lafayette react to these changes?
3. Why does Charlie burn the pictures of his mother? How does Lafayette feel about this? What explanation does Ty'ree give for what Charlie has done? What does this tell you about Ty'ree and Charlie?
4. Ty'ree says that he chooses his arguments with Charlie. Why does he decide to deal with Charlie in this way? Have you ever used this strategy in dealing with a difficult person?
5. What feeling does Charlie have when he realizes that Aaron had brought him to a gang initiation? What is the appeal of gang membership? Why does he resist? What does this tell you about the strength of his character?
6. What is the meaning of the quote from one of Mama's favorite writers Toni Morrison, "The function of freedom is to free someone else"?
7. Ty'ree says that they all have burdens that they are carrying around. What are their burdens? Do you think they begin to overcome these by the end of the novel? How?
8. How have the brothers changed throughout the book? Are the changes for the better or worse? Do they make up a strong family unit? Why?

Projects
1. Mama dies of diabetes. Locate information on this illness from sources like the website of the American Diabetes Association, www.diabetes.org. What

are the signs of diabetes? What steps can a person use to promote a healthy lifestyle? Organize your information into a *PowerPoint* presentation or a booklet.

2. Lafayette and his brothers have a difficult time dealing with the death of their mother. What resources exist in your community to assist people, especially children, when a loved one dies? Create a flyer that lists these resources.

3. Imagine what the lives of Lafayette, Charlie, and Ty'ree are like ten years after the end of the novel. Write an afterword to the book telling us what has happened to the brothers. Are they still living together? Has Ty'ree gone on to college? Has Charlie permanently turned his life around? What is Lafayette doing at the age of twenty-three? Be sure that your afterword is a logical extension of the material in the original novel.

4. Mama was not interested in letting Lafayette be part of the Fresh Air Fund because it was specifically for poor children. Locate information on the history, purpose, and activities of the Fresh Air Fund from the source of your choice; for example, you may use the website of the Fresh Air Fund, www.freshair.org. Using this information, create a poster to encourage families to host children. Contact a social service agency in your community to see if your poster can be used to encourage participation in the Fund.

Vocabulary

Each of the following quotations chosen from *Miracle's Boys* includes one or more vocabulary words in **bold print**.

1. "Or the time our big brother, Ty'ree, stopped him from **snatching** this little kid's Halloween bag."
2. "Aaron didn't take the bag, but he kept **glaring** over his shoulder as me and Ty'ree and the kid walked away."
3. "Not all Chinese people know karate, he said. That's a **stereotype**."
4. "The dog and the lady lived, but my daddy died of **hypothermia**."
5. "Little outside never hurt nobody, Ty'ree said, **mimicking** me."
6. "Newcharlie turned away from me, went over to the corner, and **crouched** down against the wall."
7. "He stayed that way, **glaring** at his hands."
8. "the fish wiggled and wiggled, their rainbow scales **flickering** in the sun."
9. "I **shrugged** and stared down at my plate."
10. "I stood at the token booth with my hands in my pockets trying not to notice the people standing in line behind Ty'ree getting **impatient**."
11. "Ty'ree **clenched** his hands."
12. "Only it wasn't a party, it was—it was an initiation."
13. "Smitty and PJ were sitting on my **stoop** rolling a basketball back and forth between them."
14. "But there were only black **smudges** of paper left—and ashes everywhere."
15. "It was like the pictures were **chiseled** into my brain."
16. "Newcharlie **winced**, and I wondered if it was because of his hurt eye or what I was saying."

About the Author
Jacqueline Woodson was born in Columbus, Ohio, lived in New York City and South Carolina as an adolescent, and now makes her home in Brooklyn. She has a B.A. degree in English and has taught in the Goddard College Writing Program in Vermont, at the MacDowell Colony in New Hampshire, and at the Fine Arts Work Center in Provincetown, Massachusetts. She has also worked with runaway children as a drama therapist. The winner of several writing awards, she writes about the forgotten in society and strives to show the value of the individual differences in all people.

The Night Journey
Author: Kathryn Lasky
Publication date: 1981

Awards
ALA Notable Book
Jewish Welfare Board Book Council National Jewish Book Award
Association of Jewish Libraries Sidney Taylor Book Award

Characters
Rachel Lewis
Nana Sashie, Rachel's great-grandmother
Nana Rose, Rachel's grandmother
Ed and Leah Lewis, Rachel's parents
Ida and Joe, Sashie's parents
Ghisa, Sashie's aunt
Zayde Sol, Sashie's grandfather
Wolf Levinson
Reuven Bloom

Character Traits
Citizenship
Compassion
Cooperation
Courage
Helpfulness
Optimism
Perseverance
Resilience
Resourcefulness
Respect
Responsibility
Trustworthiness

Setting
Present day—Minnesota
1900—Russia

Plot
Thirteen-year-old Rachel is part of an extended and loving family, comprised of her parents, grandmother, and great-grandmother, Nana Sashie. Rachel is supposed to talk to Nana Sashie each day but is told to avoid topics that would

make the elderly lady upset, especially topics about the past. Nana Sashie, however, tells Rachel that her past is what she wants to talk about because she is fearful that she will forget it. Now Rachel's visits with her great-grandmother are no longer boring; she is obsessed with finding out about Nana Sashie's childhood.

Nana Sashie grew up in Russia. Her Jewish family experienced many kinds of persecution at the hands of the authorities. Jews could not own land; their villages were burned. Rebecca is shocked to learn that her great-great-great grandparents were murdered. As a nine year old, in 1900, Sashie thought up the escape plan that enabled her family to flee Russia and the dehumanizing treatment to which they were subjected. She suggested that they leave as Purim players.

The family all collaborated to work out the problems of the escape. Aunt Ghisa suggested they should put on their costumes when they are close to the border; Mama suggested that the costumes be reversible so they didn't have to be carried separately, and that they bake the gold to be paid to the sentries into cookies. Papa thought of the person who could help them with a horse and wagon. This person was the haunted and terrified-looking Wolf Levinson, whose own village was destroyed by the Tsar's troops and who lived in the furnace room of the factory in which Papa worked. Wolf agreed to help them, but the family had to travel under coops as Wolf transported chickens. Their journey was fraught with danger including encounters with the Tsar's army. They come upon a town that has been totally destroyed by the army. After Wolf left them, the man Sashie eventually would marry, Reuven Bloom, brought them a new wagon for the rest of their journey. Near the end, the family had to reverse their clothing to the dark side and pretend they were going to a funeral, with Zayde Sol as the corpse.

Nana Sashie dies soon after telling her story to Rachel. Five years after her death, Rachel opens a letter from Nana Sashie that explains why Wolf was such a haunted man; he had left his family. A year later, Rachel is ready to tell her great-grandmother's story.

Questions for Discussion

1. Describe Rachel's family. How do the members of her family support each other? Are these qualities similar to those shown by Nana Sashie's family? What family values are demonstrated by both families?

2. What special qualities does Nana Sashie have? In what ways does she surprise Rachel and you? What kind of child was she? What qualities did she demonstrate as a child?

3. How does Rachel feel about spending time with her great-grandmother? Have you ever spent time with an elderly person? What has been special about this time for you? Why do the other adults want Rachel to avoid certain topics with Nana Sashie? Why is Rachel so interested in Nana Sashie's childhood?

4. What positive character traits does Rachel have? What kind of friend is she? Why does she stop working on the play? How does she treat her great-grandmother?

5. Describe the plan the family develops for escaping from Russia. How do they cooperate to put the plan together?

6. Why does Joe ask Wolf Levinson for help? What is there about Wolf that frightens people? Why was Wolf upset by the dead squirrel? What did Nana Sashie tell Rachel about Wolf in her letter?

7. What difficulties does Sashie's family have to endure on their journey? What qualities do they demonstrate? What emotions do the various members of the family experience? Can you think of any group today that faces obstacles such as this in seeking a better life? What gives them the courage to continue in their quest?

8. The family's Purim costumes are reversible. Sashie wonders which side, the player or the mourner, is real. What does she mean by this?

9. What is a samovar? How is this object an important link between Rachel's family and Nana Sashie's family? Why is the samovar important to Nana Sashie?

10. Rachel's father is concerned about his daughter's values when she comments on the copyrighting of McDonald's arches. Explain his concern. What does he want Rachel to value?

11. How do you think Nana Sashie feels after she has told her story to Rachel? Why was it important to her that the story be told?

12. Why do you think Rachel wants to tell her great-grandmother's story? Why did she have to wait to do this?

Projects

1. Locate information on the mental, emotional, and physical conditions of the elderly. Organize your information into a *PowerPoint* presentation.

2. Interview an elderly family member or friend about his or her early life. Record your interview, and write a summary of your conversation. Give both the tape and the summary to the person whom you interviewed.

3. Contact the volunteer services director at a local nursing home to see if an "Adopt-a-Grandparent" program is available or could be started. Then, organize a group of students who would like to visit the elderly in a nursing home on a regular basis. It might be helpful to work with a service organization in your school or community to get this project under way.

4. Rachel's father describes Tsar Nicholas II as a weak leader. Find information on the Tsar and his rule, and write a news story about an aspect of his life that is particularly interesting to you.

5. Locate information about the Jewish holiday of Purim. What does it commemorate? Make a poster showing the important details, the costumes, and the food.

6. Members of Nana Sashie's family can only take one thing, no bigger than a grown chicken, on their journey. If you had to make the same choice from your possessions, what would you select and why? A concrete poem is writ-

ten by arranging the words in a particular shape so that the arrangement of the words adds meaning to the poem. Create a concrete poem, writing the words in the shape of your selected object; include in the poem a physical description of the object and its importance to you.

Vocabulary

Each of the following quotations chosen from *The Night Journey* includes one or more vocabulary words in **bold print**.

1. "**Incredulous**, Rache stared into the calm eye of the woolly storm."
2. "But between Rache and Nana Sashie's story was an **interminable** number of errands and unforeseen events."
3. "the high rounded cheekbones becoming even more **prominent** as their mouths broke into the exclamation that was her name."
4. "Zayde Sol's, the grandfather's, plan was that they should do it after he died, which he was sure would be **imminently**."
5. "straining and sweating and twisting his body like a **contortionist** in order to look at the dishwasher's plumbing."
6. "Again Nana Sashie's almost **translucent** eyes seemed to turn brown in a **flickering** of dim reflections from **unimaginable** distances."
7. "Ghisa's eyebrows **collided** to form a dark knot over the bridge of her nose and her spectacles slid down a bit."
8. "Joe's positive approach was **contagious**."
9. "For a family that had never owned a pushcart or a bicycle—or anything with wheels—a horse and wagon seemed like a **preposterous** leap in the economic and social order of things."
10. "Occasionally he **ventured** upstairs . . ."
11. "Within seconds there was a deafening roar of fiery **combustion** that seemed to shake the whole building."
12. "It was such an uncharacteristic gesture for an old lady, but that's what Rachel loved—the **transformations**, the odd **juxtapositions**, the slidings back and forth between two realities . . ."
13. "She had become so **mesmerized** by the transformation . . ."
14. "gold braid and bright tassels to **embellish** the costume side of the reversible outfits she was making."
15. "She dared not step on the wide old floor boards and unleash their **cacophony** of squeaks and groans."
16. "She sensed there would be no **digressions**, no **petulant meanderings**."

About the Author

Kathryn Lasky was born in Indianapolis, Indiana, and received a Bachelor's degree from the University of Michigan and a Master's degree from Wheelock College. She always enjoyed making up stories and writing, but didn't decide to pursue writing as a career until she began to share her stories with her family. She writes a variety of works, from children's picture books to adult books, from informational books to young adult novels. Kathryn Lasky lives in Cambridge, Massachusetts, with her husband and children.

Nory Ryan's Song
Author: Patricia Reilly Giff
Publication date: 2000

Awards

Association for Library Service to Children Notable Children's Book

YALSA Best Books for Young Adults

Characters

Nory Ryan

Granda, her grandfather

Maggie, her sister

Celia, her sister

Patch, her brother

Anna Donnelly

Sean Red Mallon

Francey Mallon

Devlin, the rent collector

Lord Cunningham

Character Traits

Compassion

Courage

Fairness

Helpfulness

Kindness

Perseverance

Resilience

Respect

Responsibility

Setting

1845—Ireland

Plot

Nory lives with her father, a fisherman, her grandfather, sisters, and brother on Maidin Bay. Her father goes to sea to fish and leaves his children with their grandfather. Everyone around them is poor and subsists by farming, mostly potatoes, and fishing. Their situation is compounded by the cruel treatment of the Irish by the English, in the person of Lord Cunningham. When they cannot pay their rent, he runs them off the land and levels their houses so that his sheep can graze. When Nory sees a family she knows driven out of their house, she runs to

Anna Donnelly to borrow a coin that she has seen in the thatch of Anna's roof. Nory fears Anna because Anna is believed to harbor evil creatures and to possess magical healing powers. Anna lets her borrow the coin in return for Nory's help in gathering herbs. At this point, Francey and Maggie are so disturbed by this last eviction that they decide it is time to sail to America. Before she leaves, Maggie tells Nory that she is the heart of their family with her songs.

An overpowering, sickening smell is the first hint that the family's potato crop is going bad. Then they see the leaves wilting and the stems rotting; there is a slimy mess where the potatoes should be. They will all surely starve, and will certainly have no eyes to plant for the next year's crop. Anna is kind to them, giving them milk from her cow. She teaches Nory cures for illnesses using herbs and natural medicine. She even saves the last milk from her cow before the rent collector takes the animal. Nory promises her that she will never leave her. In turn, Anna remembers a small girl, whose mother she could not save, singing and dancing over the land; the child was Nory. Anna has always loved Nory for her spirit and has decided to pass on her healing magic to Nory.

When Devlin, the rent collector, comes and demands the rent and their animals, Granda decides to go to Galway to find their father. Celia accompanies him while Nory stays behind with Patch. When Sean Red and his mother leave for America, they offer his deceased grandmother's ticket to Nory, but she gives it instead to Patch. Nory stays with Anna when the tax collector comes to her to be healed. Surprisingly, a stranger comes along in search of Nory to give her two tickets for America from her father. At first, Nory does not want to leave Anna, but the old lady insists, telling Nory that she is bringing with her the cures that Anna has taught her.

Questions for Discussion

1. How do you describe the treatment of Nory, her family, and her neighbors by Lord Cunningham and Devlin? Do situations like this exist in the world today?
2. What is the relationship between Nory and Celia at the beginning of the novel? How does their relationship improve? Why?
3. Before she leaves, Maggie tells Nory that she is the "'heart of this family'" and "'Celia is loyal and true'." Do you agree with her? By their actions, do Nory and Celia prove her assessment correct?
4. Why is Nory afraid of Anna? Why does she overcome her fear to ask Anna for the coin? What does this tell you about Nory?
5. How would you characterize Anna? What admirable qualities does she possess? What does Nory learn about her as the novel progresses? How do Nory's feelings about Anna change from the fear she had originally? What does Nory's experience with Anna show about judging people?
6. Before Nory can open the package from Maggie, it is stolen. What do you think is in the package? If you were Nory, what would you want in the box?
7. Nory, Celia, Patch, and Sean Red observe a frightening scene at the bakery. Why does this happen? Do scenes like this happen today?

8. Describe the friendship between Nory and Sean Red. How do they count on each other? What qualities do you look for in a friend? Would you like either of them for a friend?
9. What do you think of Nory's plan to feed her family by retrieving eggs from the nests of the cliff birds? What does this tell you about Nory?
10. Why does Nory give up the ticket that the Mallons offer her in favor of Patch? What does this tell you about Nory?
11. What vow does Nory make to Anna? Why does she do this? What does this tell you about Nory? How does Anna convince Nory to leave at the end of the novel? What does this tell you about Anna?
12. What effect has Nory's life had on her character? Do you think that Nory has become stronger because of her difficulties? Do you know anyone personally whose character has been strengthened by adversity?

Projects

1. In July 2002, a memorial to Irish famine victims opened in New York City. Find information on its exact location and design of the memorial. What is the significance of the cottage brought from Ireland, the flowers, and the stones that are included at the site. Present your information in the form of a travel brochure encouraging people to visit the memorial.
2. Anna lives in a house with a thatch roof. How is a thatch roof made? In what climates is it most popular? Draw a poster including a drawing of a house with a thatch roof and information about the construction.
3. Anna teaches Nory about healing herbs. Locate information about the cultivation, appearance, and uses of these plants. Organize your information into either a booklet or a *PowerPoint* presentation.
4. Nory and her family were among the thousands of Irish who emigrated to the United States. Write a news story for a New York City newspaper about the Ryan children. Interview Nory, Celia, Maggie, and Patch. How have they adjusted to life in the United States? What are they doing?
5. Nory and her family would have entered the United States through Ellis Island. If your own ancestors came through Ellis Island, go to the Ellis Island website, www.ellisisland.org, and try to find information about your family. Include this information with family pictures in a scrapbook.

Vocabulary

Each of the following quotations chosen from *Nory Ryan's Song* includes one or more vocabulary words in **bold print**.

1. "Every creature who walked by would be **gaping** at it."
2. "Cat would be sobbing, her tiny face **blotched**,"
3. "picturing Cunningham's face, red and **mottled** from too much mutton."
4. "And Patch was **burrowed** under the straw of his bed,"
5. "ragged bits of mist still **hovered** over the fields, . . ."
6. "We went on down the path with Patch pulling on my hand, **veering** this way and that to pick up stones for his collection."
7. "It **shimmered** in the sunlight, . . ."

8. "Da on a ship, sails **billowing**."
9. "She was off in an instant, ears back, **loping** across the field."
10. "the milk **sloshing** over the edge of the pail."
11. "A **splotch** of mud."
12. "The rain was so much colder now and the damp **seeped** through our clothes."
13. "The lines and **furrows** in her face had to do with worry."
14. "I hardly felt the rain as it **pelted** down on me,"
15. "I kept moving with him, trying to find a space to **wedge** him in."

About the Author

Patricia Reilly Giff was born in Brooklyn and was educated at Marymount College, St. John's University, and Hofstra University. She has worked as a teacher and reading consultant. She says, "Six of my eight great-grandparents lived through the famine." They never talked about the famine, but the author made many trips to Ireland to learn about their experiences. She lives now in Weston, Connecticut.

From the Author

"At last, I ran my hands over the rough walls of my great-grandmother's house, the house that was there during the famine, and I walked up the road and tied a piece of my jacket sleeve to the tree over Patrick's Well. I tucked a manuscript page between the rocks and made my wish. 'Let me tell it the way it must have been. I want my children and grandchildren to know. I want everyone to know.' "

The Other Side of Truth
Author: Beverly Naidoo
Publication date: 2000

Awards

Carnegie Award for Children's Literature
ALA Best Books for Young Adults
Smartie's Silver Medal
National Council for the Social Studies/Children's Book Council Notable
    Children's Book in the Field of Social Studies
Jane Addams Book Award
Arts Council Writer's Award for work-in-progress

Characters

Sade Solaja
Femi Solaja
Folarin Solaja
Uncle Dele
Mrs. Appiah
Mr. Nathan
Aunt Gracie
Uncle Roy
Miriam

Character Traits

Courage
Kindness
Integrity
Patience
Resourcefulness

Setting

1995–1996—Nigeria and London

Plot

Folarin Solaja is a journalist who has received death threats in response to his articles condemning the regime of the dictatorial general who rules Nigeria. One morning as Sade and Femi, his children, prepare for school, their mother is murdered. Fearing that this is only the first attempt to still Solaja's protests, the children are smuggled out of the country to their Uncle Dele, a professor at the London College of Art. The plan is for their father to follow as soon as false papers can be obtained. Upon arriving in London, they are deserted by the woman who has illegally brought them into the country and are unable to locate their uncle. Soon Sade and Femi are on the streets with no resources and no money, for they have been robbed of what little they had. They come to the notice of the authorities when accused of thievery by a shopkeeper. Fearful of causing harm to their father and of being deported back to Nigeria, they give false names and information to the social workers.

Due to the misinformation, no trace of their parents can be found, and they are placed in a foster home under the care of Aunt Gracie and Uncle Roy. The strain of the murder of their mother, fear for their father's safety, and the strangeness of their new surroundings cause Sade to have nightmares and Femi to withdraw into himself. Enrolled in Presentation High, Sade is introduced to Mariam, a refugee from Somalia, who will help her become familiar with the school routines. Mariam is little help when Sade is intimidated by two of the school's bullies. Forced by threats of violence against Femi, Sade steals a lighter from Mariam's uncle's store. Sade is filled with remorse, but is afraid to reveal the truth to anyone.

Fearful for the safety of his children when he cannot contact his brother, Mr. Solaja enters the country with false papers and does not immediately ask for political asylum so he can go in search of is children. Caught, he is placed in prison where Mrs. Appiah, the social worker, chances upon him. The children are permitted to see their father, but the authorities doubt his story and there is danger that he will be sent back to Nigeria. Desperate, Sade and Femi tell their story to a television newscaster, who after checking for its veracity, broadcasts their story, bringing Uncle Dele out of hiding and raising public consciousness of their plight. Mr. Solaja is released from prison and reunited with his children.

Questions for Discussion

1. Still in shock from the murder of their mother, Sade and Femi are smuggled out of the country by a complete stranger. What do you think were their thoughts and feelings during this time?

2. What must it be like to be alone, cold, and hungry in a strange place? Why do Sade and Femi not go to the authorities for help? What experience have they had with the police? Can you imagine some of the terror that the two children must feel? How would you feel if you no place to go for help?

3. When the police turn Sade and Femi over to the social worker, why do they give false names and information? Do they have powerful reasons for not telling the truth? What did Mama say about the truth? Do you know what the proverb means? Why is Sade so conflicted about telling the truth?

4. As the older child, Sade takes the responsibility for telling their story. How does Femi cope with their situation? Does his remoteness make Sade's life even more difficult? Does having someone with whom you can speak about your problems make them easier to bear?

5. Why does school become a source of panic for Sade? What reason do you think causes Marcia and Donna to behave as they do? What could you have done to make things easier for Sade? Why do you think Mariam does not

help? Do you agree with Papa that the bullies are cowards? If so, what is the best way to handle them?

6. When you hear Mariam's story, does it make you realize the plight of many children in the world? Does this knowledge make you appreciate your own situation? Do you think you would be able to shoulder adult responsibilities as Mariam's brother does?

7. Why is Mr. Solaja detained when entering England? Do you think government regulations are unfair to the refugees of the world? Why must governments have some rules about people entering the country? What do you think can be done to make these regulations more responsive to the needs of refugees?

8. What do Sade and Femi do to help their father? Do you agree that public opinion is a strong force is shaping policy? Have you seen any examples of this in your community or nation?

9. Throughout this novel, Sade has conflicting thoughts about telling the truth. Who is her main influence in this regard? What are some of the colorful thoughts about telling the truth or lying that Sade remembers? What else does she remember that makes her fear the truth? What does the title *The Other Side of Truth* mean to you?

Projects

1. Draw a political map of Africa as it appears today, placing the date of origin within each country's boundaries.

2. Several items of clothing are mentioned in the text and described in the glossary. Locate actual pictures of the items, and create a poster illustrating them; or if you have access to the actual garments, model them for the class.

3. Nigeria is a member of the British Commonwealth of Nations. Report on the history, membership, and significance of this group.

4. Research the United States' involvement with Somalia, Mariam's homeland, and prepare a television presentation or magazine article about it. Be sure to include illustrations in either project.

5. Sade was a typical twelve year old living in Lagos, Nigeria. Find out what her everyday life was like. As Sade, write a journal describing one day in her life. Describe the home in which she lives, the school she attends, the courses she studies, the games she plays, and the food she eats.

6. Refugees live in many of the world's countries. Locate agencies in your community that deal with the problems facing refugees. Write to them inquiring what you can do to help refugees in your area.

7. Religion plays an important role in the lives of the Nigerian people. Investigate the geographic, educational, and social differences of the various religious groups. With other members of your class, prepare a panel discussion of your findings.

8. Ms. Naidoo paints many brilliant pictures with words. Review the text, and make a list of those that most impressed you. Try to make some pictures with your own words.

Vocabulary

Each of the following quotations chosen from *The Other Side of Truth* includes one or more vocabulary words in **bold print**.

1. "She races to the **verandah** pushing past Femi in the doorway."
2. "as she covered Mama's face with the corner of the **embroidered** bedspread."
3. "She ran to her room, feeling **impelled** to strip away the uniform."
4. "Papa seated behind the desk in a full-length, ink-black **agbada**."
5. "Femi **scowled** and shrugged his shoulders."
6. "Femi **flinched** as Mama Buki placed her hands on his shoulders."
7. "The doctors have to do a **post-mortem**."
8. "Each movement carried different **vibrations**."
9. "Already Femi was **squirming** . . ."
10. "her **furrowed** skin crumpling."
11. "like a **grim** sports **commentator**."
12. "Uncle Tunde turned away, almost **brusquely** . . ."
13. "His eyebrows and forehead **puckered** with **suspicion**.
14. "before he flung it onto the **conveyor** belt."
15. "loudly enough for the **kiosk** lady to hear although she pretended not to."
16. "but began to **grouse** about having to drag her baggage all around London."
17. "Femi's voice **quavered**."
18. "He cursed **hooligans** and he cursed the police for taking so long."
19. "Once again the car became a **capsule** traveling to some unknown destination."
20. "'It sounds as if we shall have to apply for **asylum** for you,' Iyawo-Jenny said finally."

About the Author

Raised in white South Africa, Beverly Naidoo was unaware of the problem of apartheid until attending the university. While there, she became active in the fight against racism, spending eight weeks in solitary confinement for her work. She continued her education in England and became a teacher. It was then that she realized the dearth of educational materials concerning apartheid and wrote *Journey to Jo'burg* and *Censoring Reality*; both were banned in South Africa. The hanging of the author, Ken Saro-wiwa, for writing of the crimes of the military government in Nigeria inspired the writing of *The Other Side of Truth*.

Parrot in the Oven: Mi Vida
Author: Victor Martinez
Publication date: 1996

Awards
> National Book Award
> Pura Belpre Author Award
> Américas Award for Children's and Young Adult Literature
> NYPL Books for the Teen Age

Characters
> Manuel Hernandez
> Manuel's parents
> Nardo, his brother
> Magla, his sister
> Garcia brothers, Bobby, Stinky, and Little Tommy
> Lencho
> Albert
> Mr. Giddens

Character Traits
> Cooperation
> Dependability
> Helpfulness
> Perseverance
> Resilience
> Respect
> Self-control
> Self-respect
> Trustworthiness

Setting
> Present day—United States

Plot

Manuel tells of his life as a Mexican American in an unspecified city. His father calls him *Perico*, or parrot, because like the bird in Mexican legend that complains about the heat while sitting in an oven, Manny trusts others too much and "would go right into the oven trusting people all the way—brains or no brains."

Manny's father has lost his job and spends his days in a pool hall drinking and complaining about his life. After he chases his wife with a rifle in one of his drunken rages, he is arrested, and she is happy for that. However, she welcomes him home when he is released. Manny's sister Magla is meeting a boyfriend in secret, and her mother warns her not to make the same mistakes that she herself made. Magla does not heed her mother's advice and gets pregnant, but loses the baby. When she starts to run a high fever, her father, never having been told what is going on, puts her in a tub. They are amazed that he has taken action. His lazy brother Nardo also starts to drink, and Manny, fascinated by his father's gun, is petrified that he has hurt his little sister when the gun goes off in his hands. Manny thinks about his siblings and his mother, who continually cleans, and his father, who cannot stop fighting himself.

Unlike most of the boys they hang out with, Manny and his friend, Albert Sosa, both do well in school, and Manny is surprised when the bully, Lencho Dominguez, recruits Albert for his boxing team. Lencho is a member of the Berets, which believes that whites and Mexicans are enemies. Lencho can be a bully, but he also encourages ethnic pride among the Mexicans and Chicanos, calling them special people. However, all the fighters, including Albert and Lencho lose, and Lencho is kicked out of the Berets.

Manny is initiated into the Callaway Projects gang and begins to lie to his mother who trusts and believes him. When Eddie, a member of the gang, steals a woman's purse, Manny experiences an epiphany and realizes then who he really is. At home again, he knows he is where he should be.

Questions for Discussion

1. How does Manuel describe his attitude toward work? Does this differ from his brother's attitude? How do the brothers' work habits compare with that of the wetbacks? How would you describe your attitude toward work?

2. What kind of man is Manuel's father? Why does he become angry when Manny's teacher gives him $20? Why does he drink? How does his drinking affect his family?

3. How would you describe Manny's mother? How does she deal with the turmoil in her family? Were you surprised at her reaction to her husband's arrest or to his release from jail? What does she mean when she tells Magla not to make the same mistakes she made?

4. How do the Garcia brothers treat Manny? Should he have dealt with them differently? How would you have reacted to these bullies?

5. Lencho is also a bully, yet he is able inspire other Mexican Americans. How does he do this? How does he convince Albert to join his boxing team? Why is Lencho kicked out of the Berets?

6. What attitude about school do Albert and Manny share? If you were a teacher, how would you encourage other students to share this attitude?

7. How are Manny's mother and Magla treated when they go to the hospital? Why doesn't his mother want to go back? Why does she hit Manny when he insists that they should? Are you surprised when Manny's father takes over Magla's treatment?

8. How would you describe Manny? His dad calls him a parrot because he trusts too much. Do you agree with his father? What are Manny's strengths

and weaknesses? How does he react to his family situation? Is he strengthened or weakened by his environment?

9. Why does Mr. Giddens want Manny to go to his daughter's party? Why do
Nardo and Magla think Manny is foolish for going? How is Manny treated
at the party? If you were a guest at the party, how would you have behaved
toward him?

10. Why does Manny join the gang? Does being a member change him for the
better or for the worse? What makes him realize what he should do and who
he really is?

Projects

1. Go to the website for the U.S. Border Patrol, cbp.customs.gov, and click on
Border Patrol. Find information on its history, mission, responsibility, and
methods of operation. Organize your information into either a news story or
a *PowerPoint* presentation.

2. Grandpa had grafted saplings of plum, almond, and peach tree onto a cherry
tree. Try an experiment similar to this with plants that are available to you.

3. Manny accidentally shoots his father's gun and is afraid that he has killed
or injured his sister. Using online databases or magazine indexes, locate articles on gun control, and write an editorial for your local newspaper that
expresses your position on the issue.

4. Manuel's family is dramatically affected by his father's alcoholism. Alateen
is an organization for young people in situations similar to Manny's. Go to
its website, al-anon.org/alateen.html, and find out how young people can
benefit from membership. Take the website's twenty-question test for
Manny to help him decide if he could benefit from membership. Then write
Manny a letter explaining what you have found.

Vocabulary

Each of the following quotations chosen from *Parrot in the Oven: mi vida* includes one or more vocabulary words in **bold print**.

1. "I could tell how **searing** it was by the dragged-out way my mom's roses
drooped every morning after I watered them."

2. "He'd yell and **stomp** around a little space of anger he'd cut in our living
room, . . ."

3. "The leaves were **sparse** and **shriveled**, dying for air, and they had a coat of
white **pesticide** dust and **exhaust** fumes so thick you could **smear** your
hands on the leaves and rub fingerprints with them."

4. "This **lured** workers from Mexico needing quick cash for rent or emergency
food, . . ."

5. "There was fast talking in Spanish and **frenzied commotion** as suddenly
forty or so people all at once jumped up and started running."

6. "If I grew a bit too **raucous**, he's put a **vise** grip on my shoulder and whis-
per hot breath inside my ear."

7. "Suddenly a dog crashed out of some side bushes, grunting and **hunkering**
low, **froth** blowing from his mouth."

8. "grumbling and **haranguing** until he **gnawed** her patience down to **shreds**."
9. "It was the way he said it, too **nonchalant**, too nervously **offhand**, too guilty, actually, that made Mom suspicious right away."
10. "pointing a **menacing** finger at us."
11. "Steam rose from the hoods in thin ghostly clouds, and **blanched** by the sun, the windshields shone like morning frost."
12. "I climbed over the hood of my uncle's truck and walked over to the cherry tree, **clambering** up on a branch."
13. "they stood over by the exit doors **intimidating** anyone who happened to walk into their space."
14. "The fight was lopsided from the beginning, . . ."
15. "and **rumpled** like she'd crushed it in her hands before putting it on."
16. "Mondo **squelched** that with another **prolonged** Naaah."

About the Author

Victor Martinez was born in Fresno, California, the fourth of twelve children. He attended California State University at Fresno and Stanford University. His jobs have included teaching, driving a truck, firefighting, and working as a field laborer. Mr. Martinez credits his background with giving him the material for his writing, which includes poetry, short fiction, and essays. This is his first novel.

Playing Beatie Bow
Author: Ruth Park
Publication date: 1980

Awards
> CBCA Book of the Year Award
> *Parents'* Choice Award for Literature
> *Boston Globe/Horn Book* Award
> International Board on Books for Young People Honour Award
> COOL Award (Canberra's Own Outstanding List)

Characters
> Abigail Kirk formerly Lynette Kirk
> Beatrice Bow, "Beatie"
> Alice Tallisker, "Granny"
> Dorcas Tallisker, "Dovey"
> Judah Bow
> Gilbert Bow, "Gibbie"
> Samuel Bow
> Natalie Crowne
> Robert Bow

Character Traits
> Compassion
> Courage
> Generosity
> Kindness
> Loyalty
> Patience
> Resilience

Setting
> Modern day and 1873—Sydney, Australia

Plot
Lynnette Kirk changed when her father left her mother for a younger women; she became a loner who did not fit in with her peers. Four years later, Lynnette now Abigail, has rejected even her name because it is too reminiscent of the father she adored but now hates. An unhappy and confused fourteen year old, she rebels against her mother when she learns that her father now wishes to come back, and her mother is ready to accept him. Abigail cannot understand either either of them or the meaning of love.

While watching children play the game called Beatie Bow, Abigail spies a raggedy girl and follows her through the streets of Sydney to a section known as The Rock. However, suddenly it is not the Sydney she knows but the same streets at an earlier time, 1873. All that remains the same is the little girl who is the real Beatie Bow of the game.

Samuel, Beatie's father, suffers spells of violence caused by an injury sustained during the Crimean War. In one of his rages, he injures Abigail who is is taken in by Beatie's family: wise and kind Granny Tallisker, Beatie's grandmother, gentle Dovey Tallisker, her cousin, and strong and loving Judah and whiney, sickly Gibbie Bow, her brothers. As she heals from her injuries, she learns that the family has "the gift," the ability to see the future, to heal, and other special powers. "The gift" that comes from the Tallisker side of the family can be handed down by the men in the family; it is only possessed by the women. As Granny ages, her powers, once strong, are weakening, and no one else in the family has her abilities. Abigail also learns that the family believes her to be the "Stranger" who comes to the family every time "the gift" weakens. They believe she is there to perform some feat, which will allow "the gift" to continue in future family members. For this reason they keep from her the piece of clothing she needs to return to her own time. In the months Abigail spends with the Bows, she matures into a young person who falls in love but learns from Granny that true love is unselfish. In an act of bravery, Abby rushes into the burning Bow home and rescues both Dovey and Gibbie, fulfilling Granny's prophesy and helping to carry on "the gift." While in the Sydney of 1873, Abigail learns the goods and evils of the people of the period. She sees the generosity and work ethic of the people, but she also sees the poverty, the unsatisfactory hygienic conditions, the incurable illnesses, and the working conditions for all, especially the children.

Returning to her own time, Abigail is able to accept her father's return and moves with her parents to Norway. Four years later, returning to Sydney, she learns the truth about her role as the "Stranger."

Questions for Discussion

1. Why do you think Abigail changed her name from Lynnette? What are her feelings toward her father? Abigail changed her name after he left., Why do you think she did so? Do you know anyone like Abigail? How could you make friends with her?

2. What frightens Abigail about moving to Norway? Why do you think she feels so vulnerable?

3. When Abigail touches Beatie, she is transported back in time to the Sydney of 1873. How does she react to waking up in the Bow's house? How would you feel in this situation? What would you do faced with what Abigail overheard about who Granny thinks she is?

4. What does Dovey do when Abigail asks for her clothes? Is this something Dovey is comfortable doing? What does this tell you about Dovey?

5. What is Beatie's great desire? Why is this difficult for her to achieve? Would it be as difficult if she were a boy? What does this tell you about the status of girls and women during the Victorian Era?

6. Why does Abigail wish to return to her own time? How does Beatie change toward her when Abigail speaks of her reason? Why do you think the change occurs?

7. How does Abigail feel about Gibbie? What does she find unacceptable in his behavior? Would you like to have Gibbie for a relative? How do Dovey and Beatie feel about Gibbie? What good character traits do they exhibit? Are they ones who you would find hard to emulate? Why?

8. Abigail asks Dovey about how they clean themselves and their clothes. Do her answers offer a picture of the people and the period? Do you think you could live in this period? What would you like about the life and what would you most miss?

9. What are some of the ills of the Victorian Era mentioned by Beatie to Abigail? Have these ills been rectified in modern times? Give examples that substantiate your answer.

10. What did Beatie want to know about Abigail's time? What can she accept easily, and what does she find hard to believe? What is the difference between the things she can believe and those she cannot? Can you give a reason for this?

11. When Abigail is kidnapped, Granny uses "the gift" to find her so that she can be rescued by Judah and his friends. How do you feel about the validity of extrasensory perception? What is it about Abigail that amazes Judah's friend? Why do you think she is different from girls of this period?

12. What does Abigail begin to understand about herself when she realizes her love for Judah? How can her wishes and actions be both tender and callous?

13. What is Beatie's attitude toward Abigail when she learns of her love for Judah? Is her loyalty to the gentle Dovey an admirable quality? Do you feel the same toward members of your family? How do you express these feelings?

14. What ambivalent feelings does Beatie's news cause in Abigail? What does Granny advise Abigail about the nature of true love? How does Abigail demonstrate her acceptance of Granny's wisdom?

15. How does Abigail's stay in Victorian Sydney affect her feeling about love and her parents? Tell why you think she is a better person.

Projects

1. Draw a picture showing the Sydney Opera House and the Sydney Harbor Bridge.

2. New South Wales and Sydney had an interesting origin. Write a play about the people who founded the colony.

3. In *Playing Beatie Bow*, the country of Australia does not exist; Sydney is in the colony of New South Wales, a part of the British Empire. Create a timeline depicting the important events of the federation and the development of Australia as an independent country.

4. Select one of the projects about the Victorian Era suggested next:
    - Create a catalog illustrating articles of women's clothing.
    - Create a catalog illustrating articles of men's clothing.
    - On a world map, identify the extent of the British Empire.
    - Research child labor during the period, and prepare a persuasive essay to eradicate the problem.
    - Compare and contrast the roles of rich and poor women.
    - Select an occupation of the period, and describe the working conditions involved.

Vocabulary

Each of the following quotations chosen from *Playing Beatie Bow* includes one or more vocabulary words in **bold print**.
1. "It must have been the **anaesthetic**."
2. "and when asked why she either looked **enigmatic** as though she knew twenty times more about boys than any one else, or said she'd never met one who was half-way as interesting as her maths textbook."
3. "So she **cultivated** an expressionless face."
4. "Most times people took her for twelve, which was **humiliating**."
5. "Justine was so **jubilant**."
6. "Abigail thought **callously**."
7. Kathy looked **rueful** and **fidgety**, for she hated to be on the outs with anyone."
8. "She **riffled** through the fox-marked pages to the wildflowers."
9. "Something lay between them, an **ineradicable** memory of rejection of love...."
10. "The child whipped around in what seemed **consternation**."
11. "At the thought of this her sensation of **vulnerability** grew so strong she almost cried.
12. "when **tormented** beyond **endurance** by the **demonic** Vincent."
13. "Out of the doorway bounded a **grotesquely** tall figure in a long white apron, **brandishing** what she thought was a rusty **scimitar** above his head."
14. "I'll bet I had one of Granny's **possets** in the cocoa or something."
15. "The **trundlebed** had been slept in but was unoccupied."
16. "Beatie **dawdled** in and gave Abby a **sullen** look."
17. "he announced in an important and yet **tremulous** voice."
18. "Gibbie peered out of his huddle of shawls like a small **wizened** monk."
19. "Typical Victorian **morbidity** about the sick and the dead . . ."
20. "clung to the **lintel** of the door and looked eagerly and **urgently** about her."

About the Author

Born in New Zealand, Ruth Park spent her early years in the wilds of Australia where her father's work took them. She credits these years with developing the introspection necessary for a writer. The majority of her adult years were spent in Australia, where she met and married Niland. Together they wrote short stories, radio plays, westerns, and romances among other forms of literature. They even authored a light-hearted autobiography, *The Drums Go Bang!* Ms. Park has written extensively for children and adults, and has the sensitivity to combine fantasy, adventure, history, and coming-of-age in one novel, which she did so admirably in *Playing Beatie Bow*.

The Real Plato Jones
Author: Nina Bawden
Publication date: 1989

Characters

Plato Jones
Constantine Llewellyn Jones, Plato's Welsh grandfather
Nikos Petropoulos, Plato's Greek grandfather
Maria, Plato's mother
Aliki, Plato's sister
Tasso Psomodakis
Aunt Elena
Jane Tucker

Character Traits

Courage
Integrity
Kindness
Loyalty
Tolerance
Trustworthiness

Setting

Modern day—Greece, London, and Wales

Plot

Plato Jones is a short, skinny, near-sighted, asthmatic boy who lives in London; but his father, who has divorced his mother, is Welsh, and his mother, who is bereft by the loss, is Greek. Aliki, Plato's younger sister, lives in New York with Plato's father who has remarried. There is definite conflict in Plato's life, for although he lives in London, he is not English, when he is in Wales, he feels very Greek, and when in Greece, he feels very Welsh. His Welsh grandmother belittles Plato's Greek heritage at every opportunity and his mother says, "The Greeks were building great cities and temples . . . while the Welsh were still grunting away at one another like illiterate monkeys." Plato knows that his Welsh grandfather was a hero during World War II living in the mountains with the Greek guerillas who were fighting the Germans. Learning that Constantine Llewllyn Jones's (CLJ) presence and activities have been betrayed to the Germans, a young girl, Elena, Plato's mother's aunt rushes to his rescue.

When Plato and his mother and sister travel to Greece for his Greek grandfather's funeral, he is mystified by the hostile attitude of the townspeople. His Aunt Elena relates the history of his grandfathers, CLJ and Nikos Petropoulos, telling Plato that it was his grandfather who told the Germans where to find the guerillas and CLJ. The men of the town have never forgiven the act, though the women are grateful since he did it to save the old men and the children from being killed by the Germans. Returning to London, Plato is further conflicted with what he considers his heroic and cowardly heritage.

A later visit to Greece clarifies his feelings, and he accepts the truth that both grandfathers were heroes in their own way.

Questions for Discussion

1. Describe and explain the prejudice exhibited by Plato's grandmother and mother. How does Plato feel about their attitudes and his mixed heritage? Have you experienced similar attitudes in people you know? What do you think is the best way to eliminate such attitudes?
2. What happens to Plato's family following the divorce? How does the divorce affect each member of the family? Why do you think each reacts as he or she does? Do you have experience with split families? What are your feelings about the problems of divorce?
3. Describe the scene in the Athens airport. How do the actions of the people and Plato's reactions to them illustrate some of the differences in the personalities of the Greeks and the Welsh? Do you think the opposing traits are difficult for Plato to assimilate? What would you advise to help him?
4. Meeting his younger sister at the airport, Plato is suddenly aware that she is taller than he. How does this affect his self-esteem? Are his feelings common for a boy approaching adolescence? Do you think sharing his feelings with another person might help him understand his inadequacies? Why?
5. How does Plato's mother answer him when he asks about her about the hostilities at his grandfather's funerals? Does her idea that "children wouldn't understand and therefore should not be told" reflect the attitudes of many adults? Do you think this causes some of the tensions between parents and children? How do think this can be rectified?
6. How does Plato feel about the developing relationship between Tasso and his mother? Why is his reaction different from Aliki's? What does this tell you about the children and about their relationship with their mother?
7. How does Plato find out the secret about Nikos? Why is it Elena who tells him instead of his mother? Does her story explain his Welsh grandmother's attitude toward the Greeks? Why does she choose to hate because of the evil done to her husband rather than love because of the kindness shown him? How does the truth conflict Plato's feelings about his heritage?
8. What does Plato's friend, Jane, advise him to do about the mystery of Nikos's betrayal? Is her advice a good idea? Does CLJ's words clarify the picture for Plato? Does his attitude demonstrate a trait of the Welsh people? Are Uncle Emlyn's insights more helpful than CLJs? Do they paint a different picture for you to view Nikos's actions?
9. How does Plato's mother change after her involvement with Tasso? What does this tell you about her?

10. How does Plato's mother overcome the attitude of the townspeople? What does this tell you about the Greek people? How does Plato finally begin to understand his conflicting heritages? Would his knowledge be an attribute for all people?

Projects
1. The Petropoulos's are of the Greek Orthodox religion. Research the basic tenets of the religion, and report your findings in essay form.
2. The burial customs of the Greeks are described in the novel. Find out why these customs originated, and compare them to those in your community.
3. Olive trees are an important factor in the economy of Molo. Go to a super-market and locate the many products derived from the trees. Select one product and find a Greek recipe containing it.
4. Find out facts about the Greek Resistance during World War II. Imagine you are a guerilla, and tell of your adventures in a journal.
5. Several classic cars are mentioned in the novel. Design a poster with pictures of them.
6. Draw a picture of the town of Iria as described in the novel.
7. Compare and contrast the customs and lifestyles of the Welsh and the country people of Greece.
8. Gypsies have a colorful and interesting history. Research their origin and their customs; prepare an illustrated magazine article with your findings.

Vocabulary
Each of the following quotations chosen from *The Real Plato Jones* includes one or more vocabulary words in **bold print**.
1. "stabbing with a specially **venomous** look...."
2. "That was a pretty discommunious affair, I can tell you. Or as some people might say, **discombobulating**."
3. "for someone of even my **minuscule** mental capabilities . . ."
4. "A bit **reproachful** but still a smile."
5. "Not even some way behind in the **queue**."
6. "So he gave up trying to **ingratiate** himself and put on a tape."
7. "I had a distinctly **squalid** experience with braces on my teeth."
8. "The silence, and the absolute stillness that went along with it, was suddenly **menacing**."
9. "It was a dreary and **desolate** place."
10. "This seemed a **ghoulish** thought to me, but Aliki was pink with excitement."
11. "not **gloating** over some stranger's old bones."
12. "I had woken up to find myself **slithering** about on the floor of the car . . ."
13. "and chattering away to him in **staccato** Greek."
14. "But it had a **dire** effect on Aliki."
15. "when I thought most **preoccupations** were fairly foolish if not downright **despicable** . . ."
16. "a **masochistic** passion for vertical living."

17. "**camouflaged** by scrub and trees."
18. "No more startling flashes of **illumination**."
19. "Or maybe they simply get more **hypocritical**."
20. "CLJ had just parked his **antediluvian** Morris Minor between a Rolls Royce and a Bentley."

About the Author

A lifetime native of London, Nina Bawden writes for both the adults and children, having written ten novels for adults before her first for children's book, *The Secret Passage*. Many of her books for children draw on her childhood experiences, including her evacuation from London during the blitz of World War II. Her novels focus on the interplay between adults and children, seeing this as an area that has not been properly handled in children's literature.

The Return
Author: Sonia Levitin
Publication date: 1987

Awards
   National Jewish Book Award in Children's Literature
   PEN Los Angeles Award for Young Adult Fiction
   Association of Jewish Libraries Sidney Taylor Book Award
   Catholic Children's Book Prize (Germany)
   Austrian Youth Prize
   Dorothy Canfield Fisher Award nomination
   Parent's Choice Honor Book citation
   ALA Best Book for Young Adults

Characters
   Desta
   Almaz
   Joas
   Uncle Tekle
   Aunt Kibret
   Dan
   Melake
   Weizero Channa
   Hagos

Character Traits
   Compassion
   Cooperation
   Courage
   Generosity
   Integrity
   Perseverance
   Self-respect

Setting
   1984—Ethiopia, Sudan, and Israel

Plot
The year is 1984; drought and famine plague the eastern part of Africa, but in the mountains where the black Ethiopian Jews live, there is food. What does not exist is freedom; these people are subject to persecution and discrimination by their fellow countrymen. They are called Falasha, a term meaning Stranger.

Missionaries and members of the government come among them to force them
to accept the cross. Many do; others are martyred, and the race is dying. Young
boys are kidnapped and forced into the armies of the opposing groups.

Desta is a young girl, who with her brother, Joas, and sister, Almaz, lives with
her aunt and uncle in a small village high in the mountains. Like others girls in
her tribe, she is betrothed at an early age and educated only in the skills needed
for married life. Desta is not sure that this is what she wants for her life, feeling
the need to learn by going to school. She is very envious of her brother who has
been allowed to go to school.

Visitors from America come to the village with news of Israel and inspire
Joas. He prevails upon Desta that they and their little sister join the others who
are walking to the Sudan for the mercy airlifts to Israel. Forced to leave unex-
pectedly when a band of rebels arrives looking for recruits, they miss the group.
Searching for the main body of their group, Joas is killed by bandits. Desta and
Almaz must continue the journey alone. Reviled by people along the way, they
are kept from starvation by a Muslim family. They finally rejoin their group,
which now only includes Dan, Desta's betrothed, Melake, and Weizero Channa;
the others have been captured and imprisoned.

At the border, Dan sacrifices his freedom so the others may cross into the Sudan. They reach the refugee camp where food availability and sanitary conditions are horrendous. Even there, they must hide their true identities for fear of
persecution. Finally, they are airlifted to Israel where they are schooled and
eventually reunited with Dan.

Questions for Discussion

1. Desta lives in a country where the animals roam free but she and her people
   are not. What do you think it would be to live like that? How would you
   cope with such a situation?
2. Why do you think many of the Ethiopian people revile Desta and her people? In what ways do they show their dislike and distrust?
3. Why is Joas more anxious than Desta to escape to Israel? What are Desta's
   concerns about making the trek to the Sudan? Can you understand her feelings? How would you react if asked to leave your home and everyone and
   everything you know and love? What convinces her that they must make
   the trip? What does this tell you about Desta?
4. What does Joas's behavior on the trip tell you about him? What qualities
   does he display that you would like to emulate?
5. What is Desta's first reaction to Joas's murder? Can you understand her anger and desire for revenge? After burying Joas, what does Desta realize
   about the change in her life? How does she handle her new role as an adult?
   What strengths does she show in caring for Almaz and continuing their
   journey?
6. How do Desta and the Muslim family help each other? Why do you think
   Desta feels she had never had a better meal than the one shared with the
   Muslim family?

7. Desta's group has hired a guide to lead them to the Sudan. What type of a person is he? Why must they deal through him, even though he is not honest in his handling of their affairs? How would you feel faced with this dilemma? How does Desta show her new strength in her dealings with the guide? What can you learn from her?

8. Dan and Desta speak of Joas. What are some of their memories of him? Do you think you would like him for a friend? Why?

9. What are some of the hardships endured by the group during their journey? What do you think gave them the strength to endure? Do you have something or someone in your life that would help you face adversity?

10. At the border, Dan sacrifices his freedom so the others can escape. As you think of Dan's leadership of the group, what admirable qualities does he exhibit?

11. When asked if they are Falashas, Melake answers that they are Ethiopians. Why do you think he answers in this manner? What happens when he is discovered to be a Jew? Have you ever experienced this discrimination because of your race or religion? If so, how did you handle it?

12. The Ethiopian Jews are known by the term Falasha, but they call themselves Beta Yisrael. Why is one term acceptable to them while the other is not?

Projects

1. Operation Moses was followed by Operation Joshua and Solomon. As an Ethiopian Jew who was rescued in one of these operations, write a factual essay describing your adventure, including what happened upon your arrival in Israel.

2. There are several explanations concerning the origin of Judaism in Ethiopia. Select the one that most appeals to you, and describe it in detail.

3. Walk around your home looking at all the items that you take for granted. Make a list of things that would be completely new to Desta. Describe their uses in a manner that Desta would understand, or make a video demonstrating the use of the items you selected.

4. Ethiopia has a long and distinguished history. Haile Selassie, the Dergue, the Glorious Revolution, and the People's Unified Liberation Party are all mentioned in this novel. Research and report on one of these topics, or select one of your own choosing that deals with the country's history.

5. Do a follow-up on the Ethiopian Jews in Israel. Prepare a television presentation or a magazine article on their present status.

Vocabulary

Each of the following quotations chosen from *The Return* includes one or more vocabulary words in **bold print**.

1. "Now the government has locked up our **synagogues** and schools."

2. "My pretty aunt frowned, then puffed out her long skirt of white **homespun**."

3. "You could hear the **wheeze** of the **bellows** and hear the clink of my uncle's hammer."

4. "Dust clouded our vision, but from the size of the **spiral** we could see it was several donkeys."
5. "The guide began to **swagger**."
6. "Words flew, rattling from the woman, onto Petros, who **translated**."
7. "'They are **ignorant**,' said the guide with **contempt**."
8. "I gazed at him, **envious**."
9. "He has a **visa**."
10. "They have their **quota** to bring to the army."
11. "Almaz took up the **gourd** and began to **churn**."
12. "Aunt Kibret's face changed; it seemed to **wither**, and she turned away."
13. "he and his wife had watched our **humiliation**."
14. "Would I have to return the **betrothal** pendant to Dan?"
15. "With his long legs he has an **ambling gait**, even uphill."
16. "in some waters there are **parasites** that can squirm in under the skin."
17. "'I won't,' she said, **subdued**."
18. "**distracted** now beyond courtesy."

About the Author

In 1938, at the age of three, Sonia Levitin and her family fled from the horrors of Nazi Germany and eventually, with the help of compassionate Jews and non-Jews alike, settled in the United States. Educated at Berkeley, Ms. Levitin became a teacher and a writer. The importance of her Jewish heritage has been an important theme in her novels, with her first novel being the story of her family's escape from Germany. Diversity is an also important theme in her writings and is descriptive of her literary endeavors, for she has written in many genres.

From the Author

"One morning the *L.A. Times* featured an article that changed my life! It told of a secret rescue mission, Operation Moses, in which some 8,000 persecuted and destitute Ethiopian Jews had been airlifted to Israel and freedom. The article went on to explain the history of these black Jews, their descent from the Queen of Sheba and the Jewish King Solomon, their triumphant ascendancy into a great nation, their eventual decline and fear of extinction.

I was fascinated by their story. My own people, the core of European Jewry (including my own grandparents and dozens of other relatives) had been murdered by that same kind of hatred that these Ethiopians endured. But my black co-religionists had been saved! It was exactly the kind of story that I love to tell —a story of personal courage and the goodness of strangers, leading to survival and freedom. The story had its parallel in my own life, as my family did escape the Holocaust because of the courage of my parents and the kindness of strangers. So, you see things come around again. I embarked on a year of research, met wonderful, interesting people who have remained my dear friends, and presently I am involved in creating a musical of this story, called *Children of Sheba*. Researching the book also took me to Israel, where I discovered my own religious roots, resulting in some profound changes in my personal life."

Rodzina
Author: Karen Cushman
Publication date: 2003

Awards
> Parents' Choice Award—Historical Fiction
> *Booklist* Editors' Choice Award
> Western Writers of America Spur Award

Characters
> Rodzina Brodsky
> Mr. Szprot
> Miss Doctor, Catriana Anabel Wellington
> Lacey, Mickey Dooley, Joe, Sammy, Gertie, and other orphans on the train
> The Clench family
> Mr. and Mrs. Tuttle

Character Traits
> Compassion
> Cooperation
> Courage
> Dependability
> Helpfulness
> Kindness
> Optimism
> Patience
> Perseverance
> Resilience
> Resourcefulness
> Responsibility

Setting
> 1881—American West

Plot

Twelve-year-old Rodzina is left alone after her parents and brothers die. After she fends for herself for a time on the streets of Chicago, she is taken to the Little Wanderers' Refuge and subsequently put on an Orphan Train with other children bound for the West, where hopefully there would be people willing to adopt them. Rodzina and many of the other children believe, however, that they are going west to be sold as slaves. On the train to supervise the children are Mr. Szprot and Miss Doctor.

At various stops along the way, for example, Omaha, Grand Island, the Wyoming Territory, and Ogden, the children are taken one by one. In Cheyenne, Rodzina is taken by Mr. Clench. When she arrives at the family's underground house, she is horrified at her new surroundings with dirt everywhere, at the food they eat, including snake, and at the way the children of the family neglect their ill mother. They talk about their mother dying and their father taking a new wife, and Rodzina soon realizes that she is the intended wife. When the sickly Mrs. Clench rises from her sickbed to protest her husband's advances toward Rodzina and the possibility that he will ruin Rodzina's life as he has ruined hers, he consents to let Rodzina return to the orphan train in Cheyenne.

Mr. Szprot and Miss Doctor seem cold and unfeeling. However, Rodzina eventually learns that they do care for the children. Mr. Szprot hits a man who strikes one of the children. Rodzina believes Miss Doctor has left Gertie in Omaha because she whined and dirtied Miss Doctor's suit. However, she learns that the doctor diagnosed the child as having rheumatic fever and arranged for her to be taken to a hospital in Omaha. Miss Doctor also tells Rodzina about her estrangement from her mother because she wanted to be a doctor and the discrimination she has endured in this pursuit because of her gender. When she is the last orphan left without an adoptive family, Miss Doctor makes plans to enroll Rodzina in the Boys' and Girls' Training School near San Francisco. Rodzina sees this as the path to a desolate life and, seeing a posted advertisement for mail-order brides, she sneaks onto a train bound for Virginia City. When she arrives there, she realizes that she is just a child and must go to the school and grow up. She returns to Reno to find Miss Doctor frantically looking for her. On their way to California, they decide that they will live together: Miss Doctor has a job in Berkeley, and Rodzina can go to the high school there.

Questions for Discussion

1. What do you learn about Rodzina's family from what she says about her them? What difficulties did her family face? What values has she received early in life that help her when she is alone?
2. What kind of emotions do you think Rodzina experiences when she is left alone in Chicago? What dangers does she face? How does she feel about going west on the Orphan Train? Describe Rodzina's feelings when, one by one, the others are adopted and she is not.
3. What do you admire about Rodzina? Would you like her for a friend? Why or why not?
4. Which of the children on the Orphan Train do you like the best? Why? How do the various children deal with their plight? Did you suspect that Joe and Sammy are not brothers?
5. What are Rodzina's hopes for an adoptive family? Do you think her hopes are realistic?
6. What is Rodzina's reaction to the meetings when people had a chance to select an orphan? Why can't she beg people to take her? Do you think Lacey does the right thing by telling people she is slow? What do you think of the reactions of Rodzina and Miss Doctor when a woman calls her a half-wit.

7. What do you think about the way the Clench children treat their mother? What do you learn about Rodzina by the way she treats Mrs. Clench? Did you suspect that Mr. Clench intended to marry Rodzina after his wife died? Why does Mrs. Clench stand up to her husband on Rodzina's behalf?
8. Do you think Rodzina is correct in her initial assessment of Miss Doctor? Are you surprised by what Miss Doctor eventually tells Rodzina about herself? Have you ever changed your opinion of someone after learning more details about the person? What does this tell you about judging others?
9. Why does Rodzina decide to leave Miss Doctor and go to Virginia City? Why does she decide to return to Reno and go on to the school in San Francisco?
10. What do you think life will be like for Miss Doctor and Rodzina living together? From what you have learned about them, how do you think they will get along?

Projects

1. Use the Internet to locate information on the history of the Orphan Trains and children who rode the trains. Organize your information either into a *PowerPoint* presentation with downloaded pictures or a news story.
2. Use the Internet to find the routes taken by various Orphan Trains. Draw a map of the United States at the time of the trains, and indicate the routes on your map.
3. Rodzina misses the Polish food that she had eaten. Make a cookbook of traditional Polish recipes; cook or bake one of the items to share.
4. Rodzina is stunned when she is taken to the underground house. Find out about the typical houses in the American West in the late 1800s, and sketch each one.
5. Rodzina is surprised that, according to the terms of a treaty, Indians cannot ride inside the trains. Locate information on the treaties between the United States and Native Americans in the late 1800s. Write an editorial for your paper about the fairness of these treaties to Native Americans.
6. Miss Doctor faced many forms of discrimination in her pursuit of a medical degree. The first woman to receive a medical degree in the United States was Elizabeth Blackwell. Find out about the difficulties faced by Dr. Blackwell, and, in an essay, compare and contrast her obstacles with those of the fictional Miss Doctor.
7. Write an afterword to the novel taking the story of Rodzina and Miss Doctor ten years into the future.

Vocabulary

Each of the following quotations chosen from *Rodzina* includes one or more vocabulary words in **bold print**.

1. "A lady, standing straight and tall in a black suit and stiff white shirtwaist, put her hands up to her mouth and shouted, but I could not hear much over the **din**."
2. "its smokestacks **belching** sparks. . . ."

3. "Her black robe **billowed** like the sails of a ship."
4. "The **intruder** next to me interrupted with a gentle tap on my arm."
5. "As we passed the lady doctor's seat, the train started with a **lurch**."
6. "The gamblers shouted and squealed, their **ruckus** accompanying the squealing, jangling, and tooting of the train. . . ."
7. "I **slouched** behind the others so no one could see me."
8. "I watched the other orphans **peering intently** into strange faces, trying to decide who might be good to them and who wouldn't."
9. "She didn't want to eat, kept shaking her head and turning away, so I **distracted** her mind by telling her about the orphan train and Miss Doctor."
10. "He **stalked** outside and never came back all that night."
11. "The whole way back to Cheyenne I sat stiff, my suitcase on my lap, ready to jump down and run if Mr. Clench seemed **liable** to grab me again."
12. "feeding the fire was something for me to do besides **fret**."
13. "The **ascent** was so steep, we were pinned back in our seats."
14. "Or be **stranded** in the mountains with nothing to eat but bear paws, elk nostrils, and snow."
15. "Miss Doctor turned around, but the woman was waving to a **portly** gentleman in a straw hat."

About the Author

Born in Chicago, Illinois, Karen Cushman received a B.A. degree in English and Greek from Stanford University, an M.A. degree in human behavior from United States International University, and an M. A. degree in museum studies from John F. Kennedy University. After a teaching museology, she began to write historical fiction. Her first book, *Catherine, Called Birdy*, was a Newbery Honor Book, and her second, *The Midwife's Apprentice*, won the Newbery Medal. After she decided to name the heroine of this book after her great-grandmother, she learned that Rodzina is actually the Polish word for family; but she kept the name since this is the story of a search for a family. Mrs. Cushman lives on Vashon Island in Puget Sound; her interests are gardening, reading, and the music of the Middle Ages.

Sadako and the Thousand Paper Cranes
Author: Eleanor Coerr
Publication date: 1977

Awards
West Australian Book Award
OMAR Award

Characters
Sadako Sasaki
The Sasaki family
Chizuko, Sadako's best friend
Kenji

Character Traits
Courage
Kindness

Setting
1954–1955—Hiroshima, Japan

Plot
Nine years after the World War II atomic bombing of Hiroshima, the Sasaki family is living a loving, satisfying family life. Sadako, one of the four children, is a happy, healthy eleven year old who loves to run. Chosen as a member of the relay team for the big race on Field Day, she runs with all her strength. Finishing the race, she feels strange and dizzy for the first time in her life. The joy of winning quickly overcomes the dizziness. Each day, Sadako runs in the hopes of making the junior high team in the next year and often experiences more dizzy spells, but tells no one. When one day a bad spell happens in school, her father is notified and takes her to the hospital. The tests show that Sadako has leukemia due to her exposure to the bomb's radiation.

Hospitalized, Sadako is visited by her best friend, Chizuko, who reminds her of the old story of the crane, and the belief that if a sick person makes a thousand cranes, the gods will make her well. With this, she gives Sadako her first crane and the tools to make the rest. Bolstered by this hope, Sadako begins to make her cranes. but the disease progresses and Sadako loses her fight, dying on October 10, 1945. She has completed 644 cranes. Her classmates made the remaining 356 cranes so that she was buried with the thousand paper cranes.

Questions for Discussion

1. What type of person is Sadako? On what qualities do you base your opinion? Is she a person you would like for a friend? Why?
2. Describe the Sasaki's morning ritual. What does this tell you about the family? How does this compare to how your family starts the day?
3. How does Mr. Sasaki describe Sadako? What are his feelings concerning her? Are these feelings felt by many parents about their children? What are some qualities that cause parents to be proud? Do you often display these qualities?
4. On August 6, the Sasaki family attends the memorial at Peace Park. What is the purpose of this memorial? How do the Sasaki's venerate the day?
5. How does Sadako react when she enters the Red Cross Hospital? How does she feel when she learns that she has leukemia, the atom bomb sickness? How would you feel if diagnosed with a fatal disease?
6. How do her parents and siblings react? Do you think their love will be a source of comfort?
7. What does Chizuko say to her friend when she visits her in the hospital? Is she pleased that she has found a way for Sadako to get well? What is her solution? How does this change Sadako's attitude toward her illness? Do you think being optimistic is helpful when facing serious problems? Why?
8. Sadako meets Kenji in the hospital. Why does she think that he cannot have leukemia from the bomb? What is the truth about the effects of radiation?
9. Sadako thinks of Kenji's bravery facing his illness without the support of family. What do you think this must have been like for him? How do you think you would react in similar circumstances? How does Sadako react to Kenji's death? What does the nurse do to change her thinking? Is this a wise move?
10. How does Mrs. Sasaki try to fend off Sadako's weakness? Do we often use food or other favorite things to brighten a bad situation? What else did Mrs. Sasaki do? Why was the kimono so important to Sadako?
11. When Sadako succumbs to her illness, what do her classmates do? What does this tell you about how her classmates feel about Sadako? How do you feel about Sadako and her family?

Projects

1. Using the Internet or more traditional sources, research one of the following topics:

    The United States and Japan in World War II
    The historical development of the atomic bomb
    Harry Truman and his decision to drop the bomb
    Peace Day in Japan
    Enola Gay and Little Boy
    Leukemia, causes and treatments
    Origami
    Family life in Japan
    Hiroshima, then and now

Select one of the following methods to report your findings, or create your own method.

Written report
Television interview
One-act play
Diary
Newspaper report from both perspectives
Timeline

2. Read other books about the results of the atomic bombings of Hiroshima, and lead a class discussion about the serious effects on the people of Japan.
3. Create a mobile of paper cranes or other origami figures that you have learned to construct.
4. Identify some of the similes used in the book. Explain their meaning or illustrate them using your favorite medium: charcoal, pencil, water color, etc.
5. Make a list of the Japanese dishes mentioned in the book, investigate how they are made, and create one dish for the class.

Vocabulary

Each of the following quotations chosen from *Sadako and the Thousand PaperCranes* includes one or more vocabulary words in **bold print**.

"She **fidgeted** and **wriggled** her bare toes while Mr. Sasaki spoke."

1. "And he prayed that his family would be protected from the atom bomb disease called **leukemia**."
2. "It had filled the air with **radiation**—a kind of poison—that stayed inside people for a long time."
3. "Sadako plopped down with a thud on the **tatami** mat."
4. "She tried to **convince** herself that it meant nothing that the dizziness would go away."
5. "Mrs. Sasaki looked beautiful in her best flowered silk **kimono**."
6. "She smiled **mysteriously** as she held something behind her back."
7. "Sadako was **puzzled**."
8. "It must be a good **omen**."
9. "her eyes **twinkling** with **mischief**."
10. "Sometimes the **throbbing** headaches stopped her from reading and writing."
11. "The nurse was **flustered**."
12. "Soon everything in the room smelled **musty**."
13. "Sadako was pale and **listless**."
14. "her father said **gruffly**."
15. "As soon as she **concentrated** on something else, death crept back into her mind."

About the Author

Eleanor Coerr, who was born in Kamsack, Saskatchewan, in 1922, first visited Japan as a journalist for the *Ottawa Journal*. Lacking knowledge of the language, her job as an interviewer was not successful. Undaunted, she lived with a Japanese family for a year and remained in Japan for three years, writing newspaper articles and a book for children. Later returning to Japan, Ms. Coerr became inspired by the rebuilt Hiroshima and the statue of Sadako in Peace Park. Her story *Sadako and the Thousand Paper Cranes*, published in 1977, is the result. Her journeys to other parts of the world have garnered information for other children's books: Japan—*Circus Day in Japan*, Thailand—*Mystery of the Golden Cat*, Taiwan—*Twenty-Five Dragons*.

Samir and Yonatan
Author: Daniella Carmi
Publication date: 2000

Awards
Mildred L. Batchelder Award
UNESCO Prize for Children's Literature in the Service of Tolerance, Honorable Mention
Middle East Outreach Council Book Award
ALA Notable Children's Book
Notable Book for a Global Society

Characters
Samir
Yonatan
Andan
Samir's parents and Grandpa
Tzahi, Razia, Ludmilla, and other patients in Samir's room
Vardina and Felix, nurses

Character Traits
Courage
Kindness
Perseverance
Resilience
Tolerance

Setting
Present day—Israel

Plot
Samir, a Palestinian boy, tells his own story of his life in the war-torn Middle East. After he severely injures his knee falling off a bike, his parents secure a permit for him to have an operation at a Jewish hospital. At the hospital, he is placed in a ward with four other patients. Besides two girls, Razia and Ludmilla, there are two boys Tzahi and Yonatan. Tzahi is wild, loud, and boisterous. Yonatan is quiet and introspective, spending much of his days reading about the stars and planets.

Samir is alone in the hospital waiting for the operation that will help his knee. His parents cannot come to see him because the borders have been sealed off. He thinks about his family and friends. Since his brother Fadi was killed by the Israelis, his father has stopped communicating, and Samir misses him very much. He thinks of his friend Andan who, in his boldness, resembles Tzahi. From the first day when he made fun of Samir's name, Tzahi has not been friendly to Samir. In fact, one night Tzahi appears at the side of Samir's bed and, with a voice that frightens Samir, tells him that his brother is a soldier. Samir wonders if Tzahi's brother is responsible for his own brother's death. When Tzahi's brother comes to visit, Samir sees that he is carrying a cardboard box with a name on it from a town near his own. Samir cannot stop thinking of the possible connection between the brothers. He says, "This thought is turning in my belly like a snake. It's freezing me alive."

Yonatan, on the other hand, frequently talks to Samir at night as he stands on a chair observing the night sky. They talk about the planets, stars, and their families. The first time he talks to Samir during the day, he tells Samir that they will go to Mars as soon as Samir's operation is over. The operation is a success, and after Samir returns to their room, Yonatan appears at his bedside with a wheelchair and takes Samir to a room with a computer. On the computer are a green boy and a blue boy, exactly alike except for their color. On the computer, the boys travel to Mars together, landing where the Viking spaceships landed, on Utopia. They make improvements so the planet can be habitable, and Yonatan says that when they are discouraged with their world as it is, they can always return here. Samir feels closer to Yonatan than he has ever felt to another person. He feels that his life has changed. He has peace with his brother's death when he realizes that his brother was simply too discouraged to fight for his life. He and Yonatan have created a new world, better than the old one. On the day he is going home, Tzahi reaches out to Samir who realizes with wonder that he, a Palestinian from the West Bank, is laughing with a Jewish boy.

Questions for Discussion

1. Samir's grandfather says that in war everyone thinks he is right. Do you agree with him? Do historic events support this view? Based upon personal conflicts that you have observed in which you have been involved, do you believe this statement is correct? How should conflict be resolved if this is true?
2. What are some of the difficulties of his everyday life that Samir thinks about? How has his life been affected by war? Do you think these events have made Samir a stronger or weaker person?
3. How does Samir feel when he's admitted to the hospital? Do you admire his behavior? Do you understand his fears?
4. Compare and contrast Tzahi and Yonatan. What qualities do they have that make them good or poor hospital roommates?
5. Why does Tzahi treat Samir the way he does from the beginning? What makes him change? Why is the change in Tzahi important to Samir?
6. Samir thinks a lot about his friend Adnan. Describe their friendship. Would you like to have Adnan for a friend? Why?
7. Carefully read the dream Samir has when he's under an anesthetic. How does this dream mirror the events of Samir's life?

8. The nurse Vardina is very upset when a flowerpot from the mother of a former patient is broken. Yonatan says they are all to blame. Who is responsible? What do you think of Yonatan for making this statement? What does this tell you about him?
9. Why does Samir say that he would like to be like Yonatan? What does Yonatan have that Samir would like to have?
10. What does Yonatan understand about people that many others do not understand? How is this message important for all people?
11. Samir thinks he might be completely different after his hospital stay. How have his life and his attitudes changed? What caused this change?
12. How is the trip to Mars that Samir and Yonatan take important to the message of this book? Why is it significant that they landed on Utopia?

Projects

1. Imagine that Samir and Yonatan correspond with each other regularly after their hospital stay. Write a series of letters between the two in which they talk about their daily lives. Have them discuss a project in which they are both involved to build bridges between their people.
2. The Middle East is constantly in the news; major events happen there daily. Use either one of the following websites: www.middleeastdaily.com or news.yahoo.com, and track the events in the Middle East over a two-week period. Compile the information into a timeline.
3. Gather information on one of the following topics and organize the data into an article for your school newspaper: Palestinians living on the West Bank, the creation of Israel, or the significance of the city of Jerusalem to all parties in the Middle East conflict.
4. Using a current atlas, draw a map of the Middle East.
5. Samir's father is consumed with grief over the death of his son. Find out what services exist in your community to help parents and others deal with the death of loved ones. Create a flyer including the names of the organizations and the methods of contacting them.
6. Yonatan tells Samir that every living creature is composed of the same materials uniquely combined; in other words, we are all alike inside. Create a poster that illustrates this theme using different nationalities, ages, and social classes.
7. Yonatan gazes up at the sky each night. Look up in the sky on five different nights, and with the aid of a reference book on astronomy, identify what you see. Draw diagrams of the night sky for each evening including labels of stars and constellations.

Vocabulary

Each of the following quotations chosen from *Samir and Yonatan* includes one or more vocabulary words in **bold print**.

1. "Since morning I've been waiting for a **curfew**."
2. "but I'm **woozy** from the examinations and the X rays, . . ."

3. "I stare at her **pudgy** arms."
4. "There's a **bulge** under his blanket beside his legs."
5. "There's an iron **contraption** on his other hand, so he can't move it."
6. "I'm so hungry my ears are **twitching**."
7. "But the nurse grabs me and pulls me up and hands me the crutches, and I **hobble** through the room after her."
8. "Now it's standing in the empty lot full of bullet holes—ever since the day when somebody thought it was the car of a **collaborator**, and finished it off."
9. "with Mom telling him that the cigarettes are making him **shrivel** up."
10. "I can see she wants to, only somebody **forbade** her to touch food."
11. "And so many kinds of animals have **evolved** here on earth, so many species and types."
12. "You're allowed to do whatever you like here. You are **pampered**. You're **indulged**."
13. "I manage to fatten up the rabbit's legs, but they're still crooked and not at all **nimble**."
14. "Or maybe it's just because I kept repeating those sentences as **obstinately** as a mule."
15. "they're so **absorbed** in this world that they can't feel the other one."

About the Author

Daniella Carmi was born in Tel Aviv and attended Hebrew University, majoring in philosophy and communication. She now lives in Jerusalem with her family and writes books, plays, and television scripts.

From the Author

"The main reason for this work was the wish to describe episodes in the life of a young kid living in the occupied territories, (West Bank). It was meant to be for Israeli children, who live sometimes not more far than half an hour by car, from those territories, and who know so little about these kids, who are the same age, very little about their life, their problems, their dreams, being so near and nevertheless so far, due to a perpetual war going on and administered by adults from both sides. . . .

The children themselves, who call me sometimes when they choose to write a book report about Samir and Yonatan, respond better than I could imagine, taking the story as it is, not aware of the many prejudices attached to it, and fulfilling the hope that I always maintain, in the good and pure common sense of these young citizens of the world, everywhere."

Scorpions
Author: Walter Dean Myers
Publication date: 1988

Awards
Newbery Honor Book

Characters
Jamal Hicks
Tito
Mama
Sassy
Randy
Mack
Dwayne
Blood
Angel
Indian

Character Traits
Cooperation
Courage
Dependability
Helpfulness
Loyalty

Setting
Modern day—New York City

Plot
Jamal Hicks is a victim caught in the web of violence and degradation so often caused by poverty and lack of education. He has a father who is sometimes there, a brother in prison for murder, and a mother who works long hours in order to provide for James and his sister, Sassy. For Jamal, every facet of life is a struggle. In school, he is tormented by the bully, Dwayne, and abased by the principal, Mr. Davidson, who has no understanding of the problems faced by Jamal. At home, he is constantly worried about his mother and her struggle to get the money for Randy's appeal. Worst of all is the Scorpions, a street gang formerly led by his brother. Though Jamal is only twelve years old, his brother wants him to take over leadership of the gang. The members, led by Indian and Angel, oppose him, but Mack, a crazy doped-up friend of his brother, pressures him to do so, even supplying him with a gun.

The only bright spot in Jamal's daily routine is his friend, Tito, who shares long walks and dreams of the future with him. The gun becomes a source of consternation between the two because Tito wants him to get rid of it, but Jamal, knowing that it is bad, enjoys the power that the gun gives him. He uses it to intimidate Dwayne, and then asks Tito to hide it for him. When Jamal meets with Indian and Angel to turn over the leadership to Indian, Tito shoots Angel and Indian in order to save Jamal from being knifed. Seriously affected by this act, Tito returns to Puerto Rico, leaving Jamal saddened by his departure but still wondering about the power of the gun.

Questions for Discussion

1. What do you think about Jamal and Sassy, at twelve and eight, being responsible for making their own meals and a being left alone until late at night? Have you ever gone to bed hungry? Do you realize that many children in the your country go to bed hungry every night? What can you do to help these children?

2. Randy, Jamal's brother, is in jail for murder. What does his mother feel about this situation? What is she trying to do to help him? What would you do if you were in her place? Can you understand her feelings?

3. Describe the relationship between Jamal and Sassy. Would you say they have a normal relationship for brother and sister? Relate some of their interactions that support your opinion.

4. How do you think Mr. Davidson's attitude toward Jamal affects his behavior in school? What are some changes in his actions and approach that you would suggest to Mr. Davidson?

5. How do Jamal's teachers treat him? Do you think they do anything to raise his self-esteem and create opportunities for success? How are you affected when those around you treat you negatively? Do you think this occurs in many schools?

6. Randy's friend, Mack, gives Jamal a gun. What is Jamal's feeling concerning the gun? How does his friend, Tito, feel about the gun? What do you think Jamal should have done with the gun?

7. Dwayne makes Jamal feel small inside. What do you think this means? How do you think it affects Jamal's feelings about himself and his relationship with others? Why does Jamal bring the gun into the room with Dwayne? Does it produce the effect he wanted?

8. What kind of a man is Jevon Hicks, Jamal's father? What does he do or say that leads you to this opinion? How does Jamal feel after his father leaves? Would you like to have him for your father?

9. What is your reaction to the school authorities giving Jamal medication? Do you think the proper procedures had been followed before prescribing a medication? How do you think it should be determined if Jamal is in need of this medication?

10. At one point, Jamal states that he wishes Randy would never get out of prison. Why does he feel this? If Randy was your brother, what would you want to happen?

11. Throughout the story, in what ways does Tito demonstrate his loyalty and affection for Jamal? How do these actions affect his life and his relationship with his grandmother and with Jamal? How does Jamal feel about his friend's problems? Why is he unable to help him?
12. Though Jamal has many negative forces working against his growing into a responsible adult, what do you see as positive forces? How can these become the leading factor in his choices?

Projects

1. Using a map of the Manhattan borough of New York City or websites such as www.mapquest.com or www.mapblast.com, chart the walks taken by Jamal and Tito. Compare the mileage covered with what you what you walk each day.
2. Do a study of the effect of gangs on the crime rate in New York City or your own community. Create a poster or a *PowerPoint* presentation to illustrate your findings.
3. Make a sketch of your best friend as Jamal did of his.
4. Research the cultural, historical, or ethnic significance of the Harlem section of New York. Present your findings in an illustrated magazine article.
5. The relationship of poverty to crime has been a source of many conflicting opinions. Study sources available on this topic; then write a persuasive essay supporting your opinion.
6. An interesting website from Calgary, Canada, is www.justiceforyouth.com. Investigate this website, and find out how you can participate in its goals. See if you can develop a local chapter in your community.
7. Locate sources that deal with the problem of schools in low-income areas in your country or state. Present a list of recommendations to improve the status garnered from your search.

Vocabulary

Each of the following quotations chosen from *Scorpions* includes one or more vocabulary words in **bold print**.

1. "He still talking like he ain't got no sense, as far as I'm **concerned**."
2. "He talking about how is gonna **appeal** his case."
3. "Sassy, her eyes still closed, said in a **singsong** voice."
4. "her voice full of **triumph**."
5. "Mama asked, **ignoring** his remark about the tea."
6. "Mack was just foolish, maybe even **addle headed**."
7. "Jamal **shrugged**."
8. "At least try to talk as if you're **civilized**."
9. "**Abuela** said I have to take more **responsibility**."
10. "Jamal saw their **reflections** in the windows."
11. "Mama had said that she had gone to a different **bodega** on the avenue to buy some **plantains** . . ."
12. "Most of the time they sat around and played **dominoes**."

About the Author
Though born in the South, Walter Dean Myers spent most of his childhood years in Harlem being raised by foster parents. Knowing he could not afford college, he quit high school to join the army. Many years later, he received his bachelor's degree from Empire State College. His writings are varied: picture books, fantasy, mystery, adventure, historical fiction, and nonfiction. In his statement, "'Young people need ideals which identify them, and their lives, as central . . . guideposts which tell them what they can be, should be, and indeed are,'" Myers states the purpose of *Building Character through Literature*.

Shabanu, Daughter of the Wind
Author: Suzanne Fisher Staples
Publication date: 1989

Awards

Newbery Honor Book
ALA Best Book for Young Adults
New York Times Book of the Year
Horn Book Fanfare
IRA Young Adults' Choice
IRA Readers' Choice
International Board on Books for Young People Honor List

Characters

Shabanu
Phulan
Shabanu's parents and other members of the family
Sharma and Fatima
Hamir and Murad, promised in marriage to Phulan and Shabanu
Nazir Mohammad
Rahim

Character Traits

Cooperation
Courage
Dependability
Generosity
Kindness
Respect
Respect for the environment

Setting

Modern day—Cholistan Desert, Pakistan

Plot

Semi-nomadic families live in the Cholistan Desert, roaming from area to area in search of water and fodder for their animals. Shabanu is a twelve-year-old daughter of one such family. Still considered a child, she is allowed freedom to tend the camels and even travel to the Sibi Fair with her father in order to sell the camels they have raised. It is there that Shabanu suffers her first disappointment, for Dadi, Shabanu's father, is offered such an extravagant price that he is forced to sell Guluband, her prized camel. Dadi needs the money to provide an elegant wedding and dowry for Phulan, Shabanu's sister, who is to be married this year, and for Shabanu who has been promised for the following year.

Soon after returning from the fair, the toba, a freshwater pond, which is their only water source, dries up. They must travel to their next source, Chanann Pir, a desert shrine, where the women pray and talk of preparations for Phulan's wedding. A fierce sandstorm destroys the toba, forcing the family to travel to Derawar and then to Mehrabpur, home of Phulan's betrothed, Hamir. Hamir and his brother, Murad, are farmers on land owned by Nazir Mohammed, an evil man. One day, Nazir who is out with a hunting party, spots Phulan and desires her. Foiled by Shabanu, he is very angry. The family must flee while Dadi goes to warn Hamir and Murad. Hot-tempered Hamir is killed by Nazir, but the rest of Shabanu's party are protected by the Desert Rangers. Rahim, Nazir's older and more powerful brother, who is shamed by his brother's behavior, offers comfort and resources to the families. He spies Shabanu and wishes her to become his fourth wife. A decision is made: Phulan is to marry Murad, Shabanu's betrothed, and Shabanu is to marry Rahim when she becomes a women. She must decide whether to abide by her father's wishes or to rebel and bring disgrace to the family.

Questions for Discussion

1. Phulan and Shabanu are both promised in marriage to Hamir and Murad while they are still children. How do Phulan and Shabanu feel about this state of affairs? How do their ideas differ? How would you feel if you were Phulan and Shabanu or Hamir and Murad?

2. Shabanu is willful. How does her father correct her when she does not obey him? What does her mother say to her about obedience? What does this tell you about the role of men and women in this society? How does Shabanu feel about this situation? What are your ideas as you read of Shabanu's quandary?

3. Why does Dadi sell Guluband? Do you think he was correct with his decision? How does Shabanu feel after the sale? Have you ever lost something that you prized highly? Did you feel as Shabanu that something had left a hole in your heart? How does Dadi try to make up for the loss of Guluband? What does this tell you about him?

4. When Shabanu's family prepares to travel, the women are dressed in silk and the animals are festooned with silver medallions and silk tassels. Does this fit your image of a nomadic people? What were your expectations? What does this tell you about your knowledge of the world's many cultures?

5. Grandfather tells stories of his past glories. What happens when he tells the stories? Does this remind you of any older people that you know? Is he treated by his family the same way as the older people you know? If there is a difference, what is the difference and how do you feel about it?

6. As the women of the family gather at Channan Pir to pray, they are joined by Sharma and Fatima. Why does Shabanu admire and envy them? Do you think their life is unusual in an Islamic society? Why?

7. What does Phulan do to encourage Nazir's hunting party? Why do you think she does this? How does she react when she realizes the trouble? How does Shabanu react? Which of the girls would you rather have with you in an emergency?

8. How does Hamir react when told of the incident by Dadi? Does he make a wise decision or one fueled by emotion? Have you ever let emotions mar your better judgment? What would be a smart thing to do before taking action?

9. At Hamir's death, both families travel to Yazman to negotiate a settlement between Nazir and Murad's family. What incident occurs at Yazman that changes the course of everyone's life? What do Rahim's actions tell you about the man? How are Phulan's and Shabanu's futures decided? How do your betrothal customs differ from those in Pakistan? What are some positive and negative results of both customs?

10. Sharma and Dadi are two very strong influences in Shabanu's life. Do you think that they both love her? Why do you think their actions are so different? Is Dadi a cruel man, or do his actions reflect his cultural and religious beliefs?

11. What does Sharma give Shabanu that will help her face the future? Is this a lesson to be learned by all, or do you see times when the advice is not helpful? What would be your advice to Shabanu?

Projects

1. The Cholistan Desert offers many attractions for tourists. Design a travel brochure that will educate and entice tourists to travel there. There are several websites that will help you in this endeavor, or contact the Pakistan Embassy in Washington D.C.

2. Pakistan is a fairly young country. Research its origin, and detail how this effects its relations with the neighboring country, India. Report your findings in a televised news segment.

3. Ms. Staples is very descriptive of the foods and clothing of the nomads. Prepare a meal that Shabanu and her family would enjoy, or design a poster depicting the clothing of both men and women.

4. Camels are a vital part of Shabanu's existence. Prepare a written report on the animal, which includes its physical characteristics, its life cycle, its habitat, its biome, its geographical distribution, and its benefits to man. Be sure that you research the type of camel described in *Shabanu*.

5. For many, the knowledge of the Islamic religion and its worshipers is based on terrorist activities rather than the actual tenets of the religion. Using a reliable source, find the basic truths of Islam. Compare them to a religion with which you are familiar. A reliable source might include a person in your community who practices the Islamic religion or an authoritative website such as www.jamaat.org/islam.

6. An important period in the Islamic year is Ramadan. Find out about this period, and then attempt to practice its restrictions for a day. An interesting

website on the Internet for this and other holidays is www.holidays.net. For Ramadan, add /ramadan.
7. If you are a weather buff, research the monsoons of Southeast Asia. Prepare a weather map showing the climatic conditions during a monsoon.

Vocabulary
Each of the following quotations chosen from *Shabanu* includes one or more vocabulary words in **bold print**.
1. "and his black hair is **disheveled** under his turban."
2. "Phulan hasn't gone since her **betrothal** to Hamir."
3. "Dadi will give us each ten camels for our **dowries**."
4. "Dadi earns extra money by taking Guluband to dance at fairs in the **irrigated** areas."
5. "says Dadi, his smile **dazzling** under his thick black moustache."
6. "and Guluband lowers his head to **quench** his thirst."
7. "I think she has been bitten by a **krait** . . ."
8. "All the while he nuzzles me, looking for a teat to **suckle**."
9. "Kalu is ready with a **deft feint**."
10. "nudging their babies into the center of the **gamboling** herd."
11. "**languid** and important with her new status."
12. "Dadi and grandfather have clipped the fur on the camels' flanks into **whorls** and **chevrons**."
13. "Two young males carry new babies in **panniers** on their backs..."
14. "The camels are **hobbled** . . ."
15. "The day passes in a long **monotonous** shuffle."
16. "singing and clapping, and the **camaraderie** of women."
17. "Women whirl like **dervishes**."
18. "Sharma's voice rises and falls in **trills** and **cadences** . . ."
19. "At first I only hear the faint hiss of softly **articulated** air."
20. "The camels move in **syncopation**."

About the Author
Born in Pennsylvania and now living in Tennessee, Suzanne Fisher Staples lived for many years in Asia as a marketing director for a large company and then as a correspondent for UPI. Returning to the United States, she worked the foreign news desk for *The Washington Post* before taking up writing for young adults as a full-time career. She lectures on the status of women in the Islamic Republic of Pakistan; an expertise apparent in her writings.

The Sign of the Beaver
Author: Elizabeth George Speare
Publication date: 1983

Awards

Newbery Honor Book
Scott O'Dell Award for Historical Fiction
Christopher Medal
Children's Study Book Award
ALA Best Books for Young Adults
Teachers' Choice—National Council of Teachers of English
Child Study Association of America's Children's Book of the Year
Americas Award for Children's and Young Adult Literature
New York Times Book of the Year

Characters

Matt Hallowell
Ben
Saknis
Attean
Matt's father, mother, and sister

Character Traits

Courage
Respect for the environment
Resourcefulness
Tolerance

Setting

Mid 18th century—Maine Territory

Plot

The Sign of the Beaver is the story of a new beginning and an inevitable ending. For thirteen-year-old Matt and his father, building the cabin and laying claim to the land is the start of a life in the developing territory of Maine. For Saknis and Attean, the coming of the settlers marks the ending of their way of life and the passing of a culture.

In the spring of 1769, Matt is left alone in the new cabin he and his father built while his father returns to Massachusetts for the rest of the family. Armed with his father's rifle and a supply of food provisions, Matt confidently embarks on the chores and adventures that will keep him occupied for the seven weeks until his family's arrival. Robbed of his rifle by a renegade named Ben, Matt is devastated for he has lost his source of protection and food gathering. However, the creek is stocked with fish, and he soon learns to compensate and to become careless. Returning from a morning's fishing, he finds the cabin door off its hinges and his food supplies gone. A bear had entered the cabin and devoured or ruined everything. After subsisting on fish for days, Matt decides to gather honey from a tree beehive. The result is disastrous, for Matt is severely stung by the angry bees and loses one of his boots in his struggle to escape the swarm. Strong arms lift him from the creek, remove the stingers from his body, carry him to his cabin, and give him bitter medicine to counteract the poison.

With this beginning, Matt meets an old Indian, Saknis, and his grandson, Attean. The old man brings food him and a pair of moccasins to replace his lost boot, and fashions a crutch for Matt who has injured his ankle in his dash from the bees. Remembering his manners, Matt tries to thank Saknis for his kindness with the only thing he has, his copy of *Robinson Crusoe*. Matt is embarrassed by the gift realizing that Saknis cannot read, but Saknis is inspired by the gift to make a treaty with Matt. In return for food, Matt will teach Attean to read so that he will understand the treaties the Indians have with the white man.

The truce between the two boys is tenuous until Matt starts reading parts of the Defoe novel as the reading lesson. Attean is intrigued by the story but angered that Friday should become a slave to Crusoe. Matt wonders why he has never before seen anything wrong with this premise. After finishing the novel, Matt begins with Bible stories. Attean tells a similar story from the Indian folklore.

As the summer progresses, Matt realizes that it is Attean, and not he, who is the teacher. Attean teaches Matt to trap with snares, create and hunt with a bow, and find his way in the forest—the skills that Matt needs to survive in the wilderness. The summer draws to a close but not before Matt has earned the respect of other members of Attean's family. However, he has not ever earned Attean's respect which is the one he desperately wants. Winter is fast approaching, Attean has passed his test for manhood and Matt's family has not arrived. Saknis offers to take Matt with them on the Great Hunt from which they will not return. Though he is afraid of spending the winter alone, Matt refuses, saying he must wait for his family. By this singular act of bravery he acquires Attean's respect.

Questions for Discussion

1. How did Matt feel when left alone in the cabin in Maine? How would you feel in the same situation? Who would be better able to handle the situation, you or Matt? Why?

2. Why is Matt wary when he is confronted by Ben? What in Matt's upbringing makes him offer Ben a meal and a night's lodging? How's he rewarded? What does this tell you about Ben's character? What does Matt ask himself?

3. How is Matt saved when he is stung by a swarm of bees? Why do you think the old Indian showed him such kindness?

4. Matt wishes to pay Saknis for his many kindnesses and presents him with his only possession of value. What is it and why does Matt soon realize it is an inappropriate gift? What does Saknis ask Matt to do instead? What is his

reason for this request? What is Attean's reaction? Can you empathize with his resentment?

5. Matt chooses to use *Robinson Crusoe* as his reading text. How does Attean feel about the relationship between Crusoe and Friday? Does his opinion help to change Matt's opinion of the novel? Why do you think Matt was willing to accept the slavery premise while Attean strongly believed that Friday would never be subject to Crusoe?

6. Though Matt is not very successful in teaching Attean to read, he has become the student. What are some of the things that Attean teaches Matt? Are these skills paramount to his survival in the Maine wilderness? Why does he feel Defoe had the wrong point of view when writing *Robinson Crusoe*? Would Defoe's reading audience have accepted the novel if Friday had been the leader and teacher instead of Crusoe?

7. Though Matt and Attean share experiences and some understanding, what is missing from their relationship? What does Matt want from Attean? Why do you think he does not respect Matt? How do you feel about someone who does not possess the skills that you do?

8. Matt is finally invited to the Indian village for the celebration of the killing of the bear. Why does Attean have him sleep alone? Does Matt begin to have some understanding of the bitterness displayed by Attean and his grandmother? What is his response to Attean's story of the demise of his mother and father? How would you answer Attean's question about why the white man makes cabins on Indian hunting grounds?

9. The morning after the feast, Matt sees the Indian village clearly. What does the condition of the village tell you about the Indians' fortune at this time? Why is their way of life in peril? How would you feel and react if your way of life was no longer possible?

10. How does Matt finally gain Attean's respect? Why do you think this is so? How do the two boys show that they genuinely care for the other? Why are their gifts so meaningful? Does this give you second thoughts about the gifts you give to others?

11. Why does Matt decide that he could never really be a part of the Indian tribe? Do you agree with his reasons? How did his new knowledge improve him as a person? Do you think knowledge is the beginning of acceptance among cultures? How could you improve your knowledge and understanding of other cultures? How could you help others toward acceptance of other races, religions, and cultures?

12. Reflect on the insights of Indian life shown in the book. What are some admirable qualities that you could incorporate into your life?

Projects

1. Draw or make a diorama of the Indian village as Matt describes it.
2. Write Matt and Attean's story from Attean's point of view.
3. Research the history of the Penobscot Indians. Prepare a report, which includes their origin in America, and life after the influx of white settlers in Maine.

4. Bees were brought to America by the English colonists. Discover five other flora and/or fauna that are not indigenous to America and trace their introduction and subsequent absorption into the American environment. Note whether they have been harmful or beneficial to the existing flora and fauna.

5. Blueberries are very prolific in Maine. Locate and prepare a recipe, which might have been used by the colonists.

6. Besides the Bible story of the flood, find another story from the Bible and an Indian myth that are similar. Prepare an oral presentation illustrating the differences and likenesses.

7. In this novel, Attean goes to find his "Manitou," a rite of passage into manhood. Many Indian tribes in the United States have similar rites of passage. Select three tribes from various parts of the country, and compare and contrast their customs.

8. Construct a model of the cabin built by Matt and his father.

Vocabulary

Each of the following quotations chosen from *The Sign of the Beaver* includes one or more vocabulary words in **bold print**.

1. "haul the logs and **square** and **notch** them."
2. "It **coiled** around Matt."
3. "and a sturdy **puncheon** table with two stools."
4. "'I'll take your **blunderbuss** with me,' his father had said."
5. "**Ruefully** he **trudged** back to the cabin."
6. "It was a good life, with only a few small **annoyances** buzzing like mosquitoes inside his head."
7. "His father had been assured by the **proprietors** that his new settlement would be safe."
8. "he was accompanied by the **chirruping** of birds, the chattering of squirrels, and the **whine** and **twang** of thousands of bothersome insects."
9. "Easy to pick up their **lingo**."
10. "It was hard to be **deprived** of the hunting."
11. "he was naked except for a **breechcloth** held up by a string around the waist."
12. "Then, **astonishingly**, the rare white smile appeared."
13. "The boy **glowered** at his grandfather, but he did not dare to speak again."
14. "He flung it **disdainfully** on the table."
15. "Attean had no need to be **finicky**, Matt thought."
16. "The real trouble was that Attean was **contemptuous** . . ."

About the Author

Born and educated in Massachusetts, Elizabeth George Speare became a high school English teacher. She loved this profession, for it enabled her to share her favorite literature with her students. From a very early age, she wrote stories, but after her marriage and the birth of her two children, her life revolved around family activities, leaving no time for writing. As her children grew older, Ms.

Speare resumed her writing, becoming one of America's best historical fiction writers for children. *The Witch of Blackbird Pond* and *The Bronze Bow* are winners of the Newbery Medal, and in 1989, she was awarded the Laura Ingalls Wilder Award for distinguished and enduring contributions to children's literature. Though she died in 1994, her novels are considered classics and are still read by America's children.

The Sign of the Beaver has been criticized for presenting a stereotypical picture of the American Indian, its demeaning use of Pidgin English, and some historical inaccuracies, but the true bond and growth of understanding between the two boys earns its inclusion in this book.

Sing down the Moon
Author: Scott O'Dell
Publication date: 1970

Awards
Newbery Honor Book
Booklist Contemporary Classics for Young Adults
Children's Literature Association Phoenix Award Honor Book

Characters
Bright Morning
Bright Morning's mother
Bright Morning's father
Bright Morning's sister Lapana
Running Bird
White Deer
Tall Boy
Rosita
Nehana

Character Traits
Citizenship
Compassion
Cooperation
Courage
Helpfulness
Integrity
Kindness
Optimism
Perseverance
Resilience
Resourcefulness
Respect
Respect for the environment
Responsibility
Self-respect

Setting
1863–1865—American West

Plot

Fifteen-year-old Bright Morning is a Navaho girl living in the Canyon de Chelly. She is happy that her mother is giving her the responsibility to take her herd of sheep to the mesa to graze, even though the previous year, Bright Morning had left the sheep at the mesa during a storm. From a ledge over the canyon, she and her friends, Running Bird and White Deer, see soldiers from Fort Defiance going to their village. The soldiers threaten to burn the village and murder everyone if the warriors are on a raid. The Navahos respond that they will defend themselves against their Ute and Spanish enemies. In fact, the warriors are on a raid against the Utes, the enemies of the Navahos.

When Bright Morning and Running Bird go back to the mesa to graze their sheep, they are captured by Spanish slavers who, for many years, have stolen Navaho girls and sold them to people in the town to be servants. In town, the girls are taken to separate houses, and in the house in which Bright Morning is living, there is already another Navaho girl, Rosita, who accepts her life and seems happy. On the other hand, Bright Morning sees a girl from the Nez Percé who is anything but happy. When they meet at the market, Nehana tells Bright Morning not to trust Rosita. Bright Morning learns that Nehana had tried to run away, but was caught and beaten.

Using the plan that Nehana develops, she, Bright Morning, and Running Bird escape. Tall Boy finds them and is shot in a skirmish with the Spaniards. The Navahos make it back home, but before long, the Long Knives, or soldiers from the fort, order all of them to leave the Canyon de Chelly. The soldiers destroy the village and all the crops; the Navaho are led into captivity by the Long Knives. Food is in such short supply that the Navahos begin to eat their pets; many, especially the old and weak, become ill and die. Settled in Bosque Redondo, the Navahos are given fields to plant, but both the women and men are idle most of the time, and the men especially are dispirited. During this time, Tall Boy and Bright Morning are married. He is taken prisoner after a fight with an Apache, and after he escapes, Bright Morning and her mother chide him into going back to their canyon. After six days, they find a safe place to build a lean-to where they stay through the summer and into the next spring; their son is born there. In the spring, they continue to the canyon. There they find one of her ewes and a baby lamb. They are home.

Questions for Discussion

1. Describe the friendship between Bright Morning, Running Bird, and White Deer. How is their relationship similar to that of you and your friends? Does this surprise you?

2. What kind of relationship does Bright Morning have with her mother? What do you think of the way her mother deals with her when she leaves the sheep on the mesa? How does this make Bright Morning feel? Is this an effective way to discipline? How does Bright Morning assert herself with her mother when they disagree about Tall Boy?

3. How does Bright Morning deal with being stolen and put into slavery? Compare and contrast the ways Rosita and Nehana handle their captivity as

servants. How can Rosita be calm and happy? What qualities does Nehana display? Which girl would you rather have for a friend? Why?

4. What strengths and positive character traits does Bright Morning possess? Do you think her name suits her? Do you think she is unusual for a fifteen year old? Would you like her for a friend?

5. Why doesn't Bright Morning's mother like Tall Boy? When does she change her attitude? What kind of boy is he? In what ways is he a good warrior? How does he handle his disability? Do you think he is treated fairly and kindly by the other warriors? Why does he fight with the Apache? What traits does he display by his escape from the fort?

6. What do you learn about Bright Morning by the way she takes care of the little girl?

7. What effect did their captivity have on the Navaho spirit? Do you think this is understandable?

8. What drives Bright Morning to want to go home? Why doesn't Tall Boy share her desire? How does Bright Morning prepare for the trip home? Why does Tall Boy change his mind?

9. Why are Bright Morning's sheep so important to her? Why is she so sure they are alive? Why is it important that they find not only a ewe, but also a young lamb? What is the significance of Bright Morning's breaking the toy spear that her husband made for her son?

10. The Navahos and other Native American nations were persecuted by the government that has since compensated them for their losses. Can you think of any other groups that have been persecuted in the past? Are there any groups being treated unfairly today? Why is it important for us to learn about these painful times in our history?

Projects

1. Locate information on the role of women in the Navaho culture. Compare and contrast the information that you find with the references to the life of the women in this novel. Write your findings into a comparison/contrast essay.

2. Find information on the Long Walk of the Navaho into captivity. Organize your information into a *PowerPoint* presentation.

3. Draw a map that includes the settlement of the Navaho in the Canyon de Chelly, the Long Walk, and Bright Morning's journey home.

4. Bright Morning assembles many items that will help on her journey home. Assemble a backpack of survival items that you would need if you were in the wild for an extended period of time.

5. Many years after the Long Walk of the Navahos, code talkers from this tribe made significant contributions to the U.S. effort in World War II. Consult a website, such as www.history.navy.mil/index.html/, select "Wars and Conflicts of the U.S. Navy, World War II 1941–1945, and Code Talkers, World War II." Find information like who devised the idea of using the Navaho language, why that language was chosen, how the language was used as a code, and the number of code talkers that served in the military. Write

this information into an introduction for a code talkers dictionary. Then select at least twenty-five terms from the code talkers dictionary and include
them in the dictionary you are creating.

6. Construct a model of a Navaho village.

Vocabulary

Each of the following quotations chosen from *Sing down the Moon* includes one
or more vocabulary words in **bold print**.

1. "Nor say that I had learned in the days between the two springs that a herder
   of sheep does not leave the flock to **fend** for itself, whether from fear of
   storms or wild animals or for any reason."
2. "They were **goading** me to speak, but still I kept silent."
3. "My mother did not like him, but I did not mind his **haughty** ways."
4. "She was standing on a ledge that **jutted** out over the canyon."
5. " 'A **surly** miss,' the woman said in Spanish. 'Can't you bring me one with
   a better **disposition**?' "
6. "The talked like the Anglos who come to our canyon and **haggle** over the
   price of wool."
7. "Many horses were **tethered** in the cottonwood grove, some **hobbled**, some
   tied to the trees."
8. "At last he looked away and began to **stagger** toward the far end of the
   church, as people made way for him."
9. "The sound of hoofs was **muffled** in the tall grass."
10. "He was pale and **gaunt** faced and kept his eyes closed, even when I spoke
    to him."
11. "This was to make me **industrious** and obedient, my mother said."
12. "I went a little faster and came to the river and **floundered** around, pretend-
    ing to slip on the grass bank."
13. "I tried to make him smile but he would not forgive me for running fast,
    even though he had **taunted** me."
14. "The river flowed slower now and many old people began to **falter**."

About the Author

Scott O'Dell was born Odell Gabriel Scott in 1898 in Los Angeles, California.
He attended Occidental College, the University of Wisconsin, Stanford University, and the University of Rome. He worked as a cameraman and technical director in the movies, was a farmer, and also served in the U.S. Air Force and the
U.S. Army. He began writing full time in 1934 and wrote his first children's
book, *Island of the Blue Dolphins*, when he was in his sixties; this book has received countless awards, including the Newbery Medal, and a designation as
one of the Eleven Best Children's Books of the Past 200 Years by the Children's
Literature Association. He wrote more than twenty additional children's books,
and received many awards for these until his death from prostate cancer in 1989.

A Single Shard
Author: Linda Sue Park
Publication date: 2001

Awards
> Newbery Medal

Characters
> Tree-ear
> Crane-man
> Min
> Ajima
> Kang
> Emissary Kim

Character Traits
> Compassion
> Courage
> Generosity
> Integrity
> Perseverance

Setting
> Mid-to-late 12th century— Ch'ulp'o, a small village on the west coast of Korea

Plot

Though there are not many homeless persons in 12th century Korea, Tree-ear is one. When orphaned at the age of two, he is brought from Songdo to live with his uncle in Ch'ulp'o, but the messenger can neither locate the uncle nor leave him in the Buddhist temple, for the fever that killed his parents is raging there as well. He leaves Tree-ear with Crane-man who, because of a shriveled calf and foot, is unable to work. For ten years, the two live under the bridge with Crane-man teaching Tree-ear the ways of surviving and living in an ethical manner.

When Tree-ear is twelve, he becomes intrigued by the work of Min, the master potter among all the potters of this seaside town. When he breaks one of Min's ceramic boxes, he offers to work off the cost. The cost covered, Tree-ear asks if he may continue to work in hopes that he will someday be taught to throw a pot on the wheel. As Tree-ear works with Min, suffering his cruelties, Ajima, Min's wife, shows nothing but kindness, always sending Tree-ear home with a full bucket of food for his and Crane-man's supper. Perhaps, she is thinking of the son she and Min have lost.

One day, returning home to the bridge, Tree-ear learns the design secret of Kang, another potter. Counseled by Crane-man, Tree-ear knows that he cannot disclose the secret to Min until it becomes public. The opportunity arises when Emissary Kim arrives in the village to bestow a royal commission on the finest potter. Now that Kang's inlaid vases are on display, Tree-ear can disclose the secret to Min. Min's first attempt is a failure, for while the inlaid art is beautiful, the glaze is muddied, causing Min to destroy all the pieces before the emissary can see them. Though he realizes that Min's work is far superior to Kang's, the emissary cannot ignore the value of the new technique and so awards the commission to Kang. Before he leaves the village, he visits Min, advising him that he will reconsider his decision if a piece in the inlay style is brought to him in Songdo. Since Min is too frail to make the trip, Tree-ear volunteers to go in his place. Crane-man constructs a jiggeh that will carry the vases safely to Songdo. Just before he is to undertake the journey, Tree-ear asks Min if he would one day teach him to make a pot. Min's answer is that he will never teach Tree-ear because he is not his son, and the potter's craft is handed down from father to son. Though crushed by Min's decision, he begins the journey to Songdo, wondering why he is doing the task for such an ungrateful man.

As Tree-ear embarks on his journey, he gives Crane-man a small ceramic monkey he has molded with his hands. Crane-man's advice to Tree-ear is that his greatest danger is from people, but it is also people to whom he must turn if in need of aid. After days on the road, Tree-ear is accosted by robbers who, realizing that they cannot sell the vases, throw them over a cliff, smashing them both. Tree-ear is bereft thinking that he must return to Min with the story of his failure. Instead he chooses a large shard that shows part of the inlaid peony and the beauty of the glaze, and continues his journey to the emissary. Realizing the artistry of the shard, the emissary grants a royal commission to Min.

Arriving in Ch'ulp'o, Tree-ear learns that Crane-man has been killed in an accident. Min has the little monkey that Crane-ear was clutching when he died. Realizing the craftsmanship of the piece, Min offers to teach Tree-ear to throw a pot and build a wheel of his own. Tree-ear moves into the home of Min and Ajima, becoming their adopted son.

Questions for Discussion

1. How do Tree-ear and Crane-man get their names? Why are they appropriate? Do they reflect their true characters or their physical appearances?
2. What do you think Crane-man means in his statement, "Scholars read the great words of the world. But you and I must learn to read the world itself." Why is this wisdom so important to them?
3. Why do you think Tree-ear, an orphan, often asks the story of how he came to live under the bridge? As he grows older, he no longer feels the need. Why is that? Do you think you would be happy living in Tree-ear's circumstances?
4. Why did Min feel the need to keep is creations secret? Do you think his attitude is healthy to his art? Do you feel this way about any of your accomplishments?

5. How did Tree-ear feel about having real work to do? Why do you think this was a source of pride? Have you experienced this feeling of satisfaction from one of your endeavors? Explain.

6. Min is never satisfied with Tree-ear's work. Would you like to work for such an employer? Why do you think Min treats Tree-ear in such an unkind manner? Why do you think Tree-ear accepts the treatment? How would you react to such treatment?

7. Why is the lunch prepared by Ajima so special to Tree-ear? After eating the lunch, why does Tree-ear feel guilt? How would you feel in a similar situation?

8. Why does Crane-man feel it is a waste of time to feel sorrow for things that cannot be changed? Do you agree with him? What would be a healthy attitude to such things?

9. How does Ajima show her kindness to Tree-ear? In what ways does he try to repay her? Why does he feel frustration about his efforts? In what ways have you tried to thank someone for kindnesses shown? If you have not, what could you do in the future?

10. Why do you think Tree-ear is so surprised that Min had been a father? What qualities do you think Min lacks that a parent should possess? How do you see yourself developing these qualities?

11. What does Tree-ear do with the jacket and pantaloons given him by Ajima? How does he get Crane-man to accept the gift?

12. How does Tree-ear learn of Kang's pottery secret? What advice does Crane-man give to Tree-ear concerning this knowledge? Do you think this is an ethical approach to the secret? Why?

13. Given a second chance by the royal emissary, Min destroys his work. Why? Do you agree with him? How do you react when one of your endeavors does not meet your expectations? What might be a different approach that Min might have tried?

14. What do you think Crane-man means by his "One day, one village" philosophy? How can you apply this to your life?

15. Why does Tree-ear offer to carry Min's vases to Songdo? How does he phrase his offer? How does this phrasing differ from what you might say in the same situation? How does this reflect a difference in cultures?

16. Why does Min refuse to teach Tree-ear to throw a pot? How does Tree-ear react to this decision? What would you do if faced with this rejection?

17. When Crane-man describes the father-and-son tradition in pottery making, he offers Tree-ear a riddle. What does it mean to you? Have you ever experienced this occurrence? What are some other proverbs that express the same meaning?

18. What does Crane-man mean when he advises that people will be Tree-ear's greatest danger, but he must turn to people when in need? Relate how both come true on his journey. What does this tell you about people?

19. Why was Tree-ear so surprised and impressed by Min touching his shoulder just before his departure? Why do you think Min did it?

20. List at least five ways that Crane-man showed his love for Tree-ear. List at least five ways that Tree-ear showed his love for Crane-man. List at least five things you can do to show someone your love.

Projects

1. Crane-man tells Tree-ear that Korea has suffered many invasions from the powers that surround it. Write a magazine article complete with illustrations about one of these invasions. Include the facts of the invasion and its effect on Korea.
2. Locate a potter's wheel in your school or community Learn to throw a pot and to glaze and fire it.
3. Buddhism is an important religion in many Asian countries. Using a map of Asia, trace its spread from its origin in India. On the map, include the date it arrived in each country and the percentage of the population that currently practices the religion.
4. Research Buddhism: its origin, its important beliefs, including the path, the commandments, and the perfections. Choose a method of reporting your findings, either print or electronic, that best illustrates your findings. Be sure to include your research sources.
5. Using print and electronic sources, locate examples of Korean celadonware. Create a poster or a *PowerPoint* presentation to show the pieces, and give a brief description of each.
6. Start a pen pal dialogue with a Korean child in order to learn more about the similarities and differences of your lives. Either conventional mail or e-mail may be used. Share your correspondence with others in your class or family.

Vocabulary

Each of the following quotations chosen from *A Single Shard* includes one or more vocabulary words in **bold print**.

1. "The man had paused in the road and **hoisted** the wooden **jiggeh** higher on his back, shifting the **cumbersome** weight."
2. "but the two friends cracked them open and worried away every scrap of **marrow** from the inside."
3. "He tilted his head, listening, and grinned when the **droning** syllables of the song-chant reached his ears."
4. "The master was singing, which meant it was a '**throwing**' day."
5. "behind a **paulownia** tree whose low branches kept him hidden from view."
6. "In recent years the pottery from the village **kilns** among those wealthy enough to buy . . ."
7. "and **insistently**, but still without a word, began feeding Tree-ear as if he were a baby."
8. "**Wincing**, he eased the bandage away."
9. "A period of **diligent** chopping and loading, and then a break, was better than several hours of **frenzied** chopping."

10. "the cabbage core he found would add to Crane-man's **culinary** efforts for dinner."
11. "Tree-ear **rehearsed** his words one last time as he neared Min's house."
12. "'I beg the honorable potter to pardon my **insolence**,' he said."
13. "'What are you saying, you **impudent** boy?'"
14. "and water mixed in to form a thick **viscous** mud."
15. "but sometimes with **derision** just below the thin line of banter in their voices."
16. "His frustration at the **meagerness** of his thanks was like the small but constant whine of a gnat in his thoughts."
17. "Despite the joke, Tree-ear shook his head **ruefully** over Crane-man's wasted work."
18. "a thousand **noxious** shoots that threatened the cucumber plants so precious to Min's wife."
19. "all but abandoning their work in favor of long, **lugubrious** visits to the wine shop."
20. "Instead of giving gruff, **terse** commands, he **harangued**."

About the Author
Born in Illinois in 1960, the daughter of Korean immigrants, Linda Sue Park has been reading and writing stories and poems since early childhood. Graduating from Stanford University with a degree in English, she has continued writing as well as teaching English as a second language. Married to an Irish journalist, Ben Dobbin, she now has two children and lives in upstate New York.

The birth of her children awakened the desire to explore her ethnic heritage. The result is several books for young people that richly detail life in Korea. Prior to *A Single Shard*, Ms. Park wrote *The Seesaw Girl* and *The Kite Fighters*. In each of the works, her characters are interesting and believable.

From the Author
"There are several strands that go into the making of any book. One of the most important to me in writing *A Single Shard* was the value of working hard at something you love. I think people who are passionate about their work—whether job or avocation—are very fortunate, and I wanted Tree-ear's story to reflect that."

A Step from Heaven
Author: An Na
Publication date: 2001

Awards
Michael L. Printze Award
IRA Children's Book Award for Young Adult Fiction
ALA Notable Children's Book
ALA Best Book for Young Adults
Horn Book Fanfare List
National Book Award Finalist
New York Times Book Review Notable Book

Characters
Young Ju
Uhmma
Apa
Joon
Halmoni

Character Traits
Compassion
Courage
Integrity
Perseverance
Respect

Setting
Present Day—Korea, United States

Plot
In a series of vignettes, *A Step from Heaven* follows Young Ju Park from age four in a small Korean fishing village to her college entrance in America. With hopes for a better life, the Park family immigrates to America where all good things can be accomplished. From what she has heard, Young is convinced that America is heaven, the idea further enhanced by the airplane trip to the United States. Soon she learns the truth from her Uncle Tim who tells her it is a step from heaven.

Soon the grand illusions are dispelled; the Parks move into a rented run down house with the belief that the move is just temporary. To make ends meet, Young's mother, Uhmma, and father, Apa, work two and three jobs leaving little time to develop friendships or learn American ways. With little or no English,

Young Ju enters kindergarten and begins the Americanization process. Her parents are fearful that she is losing her sense of Korea and place obstacles in her path. Ashamed of their poverty and of her parents' differences from American parents, Young becomes accomplished at lying to both her parents and her friends, leaving her living in a lonely and isolated world. When her brother, Joon, is born, she resents his importance in the family and tells her class that he has died, resulting in much unearned sympathy and more lies.

Moving to America has not changed or cured her father's drinking problem. The failures, the strangeness, and the alienation have instead exacerbated the problem. Through the years in America, he becomes an abusive husband and father. His excesses cause him to lose gardening jobs and to be arrested for drunk driving. His abuse culminates in Young calling 911 when he is angered by her attitude and beats both she and her mother. Her mother refuses to press charges and is angry with Young for her actions, believing she has shamed the family.

No longer able to cope with America's strangeness and his failures, Apa returns to Korea while Uhmma, Young, and Joon remain in America. They begin to prosper, Young is in college on a scholarship, Joon is attending school again, and all three move into their own home.

Questions for Discussion

1. How does Young Ju first learn about moving to America? Why do you think Ju Mi pushes her away and changes her attitude about America? Can you understand how she feels? Have you ever felt anger and jealousy for some unexplainable reason?

2. What does Uhmma tell Young Ju about America? Why does she think it is heaven? How does she find out it is not?

3. What are some of the unusual things that Young Ju finds in her aunt's home? Can you understand why they are a mystery to her? Have you ever been in surroundings that were completely alien to you? How did you feel? Did you become accustomed to the newness?

4. Compare your first day of school with Young's. What are some of the similarities and some of the differences? How would you have managed in her situation? When there are new students in your school, how can you make them feel welcome?

5. Uhmma is disappointed when they move into the rented house. What does she think they should have done? How does Apa react? How does Young feel about his violence? How would you feel seeing a member of your family being abused?

6. How does Apa feel about the birth of his son? What does he say and do that saddens Young? How does she feel about her new brother? How does she express her feelings? What are some things that her parents could have done differently to make Young happier about Joon?

7. Why does Young tell her second grade class that her brother is dead? Can you understand her motive? What does she do at home to cover herself? Is lying a good way to solve problem?

8. Why does Young wish that she could have Joon's balloon instead of her pink elephant? What does she do when the balloon breaks? What does this tell you about her?
9. When they are washing the car, Apa tells Young to speak Korean. Why do you think he does this? Why does this cause confusion for Young? Can you understand both of their feelings?
10. What happens when Apa becomes the Blob? Does this show a side of Apa that we have not seen? What do Young and Joon feel about the Blob?
11. Apa slaps Joon for whining. Why is Joon embarrassed? Why do you think Apa acts as he does? What does Apa expect from Joon? How does Joon react to Young's attempt at kindness? Is this a matter of "like father like son"?
12. When Halmoni dies in Korea, Apa is devastated. Why? How does Young console him?
13. Why does Apa return to Korea? Do you think he will be happier there? Why is it easier for the Park family to be more content in America without Apa?

Projects
1. The Park family is Christian, but this is not a major religion in Korea. Investigate the religions practiced by the Korean people. Create a graph showing the number of people who practice each religion.
2. *A Step from Heaven* is filled with beautiful imagery. Select a favorite passage, and illustrate it in a medium of your choosing.
3. Study the agencies in your community that can be of assistance to battered wives and abused children. Prepare a handout listing the addresses and phone numbers of each and the services provided.
4. Using a Korean-American dictionary, discover the meaning of the Korean terms used in the book. Prepare a chart to illustrate your findings.

Vocabulary
Each of the following quotations chosen from *A Step from Heaven* includes one or more vocabulary words in **bold print**.
1. "I am so **embarrassed**."
2. "No need to **apologize**, the ahjimma says."
3. "What is **fermenting**?"
4. "She **cautiously** approaches the Blob."
5. "the **humiliation** of being punished in public, in front of his friend."
6. "I forgot, Joon **drones**."
7. "The mask of glass explodes into fine **shards** of pain, **etching** his face **unrecognizable**, old."
8. "Uhmma takes it from me, presses it to her eye, and **grimaces**."
9. "More and more like a **demure** young lady."
10. "Uhmma **discreetly** wets her fingers with spit and reaches up, pressing the lock of hair back down."
11. "pretends to become interested in his **crumpled** program."

12. "'They're just doing one of those **sobriety** checks.'"
13. "I smile even though I know Amanda thinks her parents are way too **dorky**."
14. "She shakes her head and **laments** . . ."
15. "Uhmma places my **certificate** in the middle of the coffee table . . ."
16. "She does not want to **inconvenience** Mrs. Song more than she believes we already do."
17. "Apa asks with a **squinty** eye."
18. "He says through **clenched** teeth, I saw you."
19. "You are no better than a common **hoodlum**."
20. "What if I stand out like an **alien**?"

About the Author

Like Young Ju, An Na is a Korean who immigrated to the United States as a small child. While many of the incidents are memories, the story is not autobiographical. An Na's family prospered and adjusted well to America. Finishing her Master of Fine Arts, she knew she wanted to be a writer but thought it would be children's literature. *A Step from Heaven* was written in pieces with no audience in mind. The result is a poetic first novel in which every character lives and breathes evoking the deep hurts and the small victories felt by new immigrants in this country. There will be no sequel, but future books will deal with new Americans. An Na perhaps hopes to fill the void she felt in literature as a child.

From the Author

"*A Step from Heaven* grew from a need to express some of the longings and frustrations that I felt as an immigrant growing up in America. Many people ask me if this novel is autobiographical, and I always respond by saying yes and no. As with all writing, the novel draws on past emotions, but the story is not my life. What the protagonist and I do share are some of the same feelings of yearning, of joy, and shame that come with trying to negotiate a foreign culture.

For all the reading I did when I was growing up, I never ran across books that dealt with the feelings of isolation and duality that I experienced as an immigrant. My hope is that this novel will speak to the readers who find themselves lost between cultures, between worlds. Help them to know that they are not alone. That they must dream, must be strong, and have faith in themselves."

Taking Sides
Author: Gary Soto
Publication date: 1991

Awards
NYPL Book for the Teenage

Characters
Lincoln Mendoza, "Linc"
Tony Contreras
Mrs. Mendoza
Roy
James Kaehler
Monica Torres
Coach Yesutis

Character Traits
Dependability
Fairness
Integrity
Loyalty
Self-control
Self-respect
Tolerance
Trustworthiness

Setting
Modern day—San Francisco

Plot
Following a break-in to their apartment in the poor but ethnically mixed Mission District of San Francisco, Lincoln and his mother move to a largely white, affluent suburb. Linc, a tall, well-built eighth grade basketball player, feels the physical and cultural differences between his new neighborhood and his old; gone are the littered streets, the graffiti-filled walls, the staggering drunks, and the loud cars, replaced with green lawns, tree-lined streets, colorful flowerbeds, and quiet nights. Also, gone are his friends, especially Tony, his best friend, and Vicki, his girl. Instead of his patient and understanding coach, Mr. Ramos, he has Coach Yesutis, who does not seem to like Lincoln.

Lincoln's new school, Columbus, is to play Franklin, his former school, for the league championship. This situation is a dilemma to Linc, for how can he play his best since he feels more loyalty to Franklin than he does to Columbus?

This is not his only problem because, to Linc's chagrin, his mother is dating Roy, a white man, rather than a brown one like him. In a visit to his old neighborhood, he disagrees with Tony who accuses him of getting soft just like the white folks in his new neighborhood. At school, his grades are slipping, and he has a fight with Monica, the girl he would like for his own. While playing basketball with her, he injures his knee, giving Coach Yesutis the excuse to bench him for the game. With Columbus behind, the coach finally puts Lincoln in the game and Lincoln learns something about himself, his family, and his friends.

Questions for Discussion

1. Why did the Mendoza's move from the Mission District to the affluent suburbs? What does this tell you about Mrs. Mendoza? Why is Lincoln not happy about the move? How would you feel about moving to a neighborhood in which you were an ethnic minority?

2. Lincoln is disappointed when his mother is not sure she can make the game. As a single parent, do you think it might be hard for her to find the time? How do you feel in this situation?

3. Franklin is a school diverse in the ethnic backgrounds of its students while Columbus is mostly white. Why do you think this is so? What benefits to society does Franklin offer that Columbus does not?

4. Why does Monica impress Linc? How do you feel when you meet someone who has a similar background to you?

5. Coach Yesutis singles Lincoln out for ridicule. Why does he do this? What do you think of him as a person? Would you like him to coach your team?

6. What reasons does Lincoln have for not liking Roy, his mother's friend? Are they valid reasons? Why does Linc lie to his mother about basketball practice?

7. What do Linc and Tony argue about? Why do you think Tony feels this way? How does Linc respond? Do you agree with Linc that people don't change? Would this be healthy for society?

8. At breakfast time, Linc and his mother have an argument. Do their words and actions sound familiar to you? Why do you think Linc and his mother had words on this particular morning? Do you find that stress and fatigue are often the cause of family disagreements? What do you suggest that might lessen tension in the home?

9. What makes Lincoln have second thoughts about Roy? What does Roy's story about the game between Franklin and Columbus in his day tell you about Coach Yesutis and about Roy? What is Mrs. Mendoza's attitude toward Coach Yesutis? Is this a fair assumption about all coaches?

10. Linc tells one of his teammates that they are going to lose to Franklin. How would you feel if one of your teammates said this to you? Why did Lincoln make the comment? Have you ever made a statement that you regretted? How can this be avoided?

11. Why do you think Coach Yesutis benched Lincoln? Was his decision a fair one for the team? Do you often let personal prejudice sway your judgment? How can you correct this problem?
12. What has Lincoln learned about himself when he finally plays in the game? What has he learned about others? What have you learned about prejudice?
13. How does Lincoln show that he is proud of his heritage? What have you learned about the Hispanic-American culture from reading *Taking Sides*? How do you show that you are proud of your heritage?

Projects
1. The Mission District of San Francisco has a long and varied history. Research its place in the history of San Francisco, and write a paper of your findings.
2. Murals, which embrace Hispanic heritage, transform the walls in the Mission District. Get permission from your school or community to paint a mural that depicts an important facet of your community's history or culture.
3. *Taking Sides* mentions many ethnic groups. Select one culture and research it using the library, the Internet, and other resources. Present your findings in an illustrated magazine article.
4. Talk to a person in your community who is of a culture different from your own. Ask if you can interview this person on video tape about the differences between his or her society and the one in which he or she now lives. Ask this person to express his of her likes and dislikes about each culture. Show the tape to your class and lead a discussion of findings.
5. Lincoln is a new student at school. Talk to your class about ways to make a new student comfortable and accepted.

Vocabulary
Each of the following quotations chosen from *Taking Sides* includes one or more vocabulary words in **bold print**.
1. "an **urban barrio**."
2. "Tired of the Number 43 bus leaving shreds of black smoke **hovering** in the **dank** city air."
3. "The sun leaked through the neighbor's **eucalyptus** tree, whose top swayed with the wind that seldom reached the ground."
4. "His mother searching **frantically** for the keys in her purse . . ."
5. "His mother **harangued** him about his clothes, but he wore jeans busted at the knees, and his coat was a hand-me-down from an uncle."
6. "He stopped for a moment, **grimacing**, then **hobbled** after the players, a spark of pain flashing in his foot."
7. "The cheerleaders **oblivious** to the game, raised their arms and screamed."
8. "The A-team should be **clobbering** the second-stringers."
9. "Lincoln couldn't **concentrate** on algebra."
10. "It began to sprinkle, shining the black **asphalt** court."
11. "biting her apple **furtively** because no food was allowed in the library."
12. "his mother **mimicked** playfully."

About the Author
A native Californian, Gary Soto grew up poor as the son of working-class, Mexican-American parents. He learned the value of hard work early, but reading and the writing of poetry and prose was a later experience. He did not write his first poem until he was attending college at California State University at Fresno. After receiving his Master of Fine Arts, he became a writer-in-residence, an associate professor, and a lecturer at several locations of the University of California. His interests and his experiences as a Hispanic American are reflected in his work.

True Believer
Author: Virginia Euwer Wolff
Publication date: 2001

Awards
> National Book Award
> Michael L. Printz Honor Book
> YALSA Best Books for Young Adults
> Jane Addams Children's Honor Book

Characters
> LaVaughn
> LaVaughn's mother
> Myrtle
> Annie
> Jody
> Dr. Rose
> Patrick
> Lester
> Ronell, Doug, and Artrille (Doc)

Character Traits
> Dependability
> Integrity
> Optimism
> Perseverance
> Resilience
> Responsibility
> Self-respect
> Tolerance

Setting
> Present day—a city

Plot

Fifteen-year-old LaVaughn tells the story in free verse of her life with her widowed mother in a poor and crime-ridden neighborhood. On the ceiling of her bedroom, LaVaughn has painted a tree with birds and bird nests; she is proud of this special space. Her mother has rules that LaVaughn must follow—about working in school, having a job, and making good decisions. They cherish the dream that LaVaughn's intelligence and hard work will lead her to college and ultimately a better life.

Myrtle and Annie are LaVaughn's life-long friends. They have supported each other when LaVaughn's father was killed, when Annie's parents divorced, and when Myrtle's father became a drug addict. However, when Myrtle and Annie join the Joyful Universal Church of Jesus, they drift apart. LaVaughn does not go to their meetings, having a difficult time understanding how their God could have let her father die and how he could punish all those who do not believe in this church. At home, LaVaughan's mother has a boyfriend; her father's pictures are gone, and the best china is out; soon they begin to talk about buying a house and moving out of the city. LaVaughn has difficulty accepting Lester in their lives and doesn't want to leave her friends and school. This relationship ends when LaVaughn's mother finds out that Lester has been lying to her about his finances and when he asks to borrow money from LaVaughn's college fund.

An old friend moves back into their building. Jody and his mother tried to live in a better neighborhood, but their financial situation got worse and worse. Jody's mother and LaVaughn's mother were close friends, even trading apartment keys so the children would always have a safe place to go. Jody is very handsome, and LaVaughn is attracted to him. She asks him to a dance and he accepts. She suggests that they kiss at the end of the evening; the kiss is a quick brush, after which Jody laughs. LaVaughn is hurt and disappointed; a nice evening has been ruined for her.

In school, LaVaughn continues to do well. A teacher recommends that she sign up for an after-school tutorial class, Grammar Build-Up. LaVaughn is in a study group with Ronell, Doug, and Artrille. Along with the grammar they learn, they develop a camaraderie based upon their shared hope for their future. At one point, Dr. Rose leads them in the recitation, "We will rise to the occasion which is life." When her ability in science is recognized, LaVaughn is switched to a biology class. There she is partnered with Patrick, another new student who is friendly and smart. She lies to him about having a date for the dance, and eventually, Patrick confronts her for treating him in many ways with disdain.

When Jody is sick, LaVaughn bakes him cookies and takes them to his apartment, letting herself in with the key. She finds Jody kissing another boy. Devastated, she slashes the dress she wore to the dance and wants to stay home from school. Her mother will not allow this, however. Her grades suffer, but her job in a hospital laundry inspires her to tell her guidance counselor that she wants to be a nurse.

As the end of the school year approaches, LaVaughn, along with Patrick and other friends from the grammar class are invited to be part of a special summer science program. Her mother suggests that they celebrate LaVaughn's sixteenth birthday with a party. Myrtle and Annie, her friends from the grammar class, and Patrick are all there. Jody crashes the party and gives LaVaughn a book about Michaelangelo, another artist who painted on a ceiling. She accepts Jody as he is and reaches a new peace: "I think I can live with my life the way it is."

Questions for Discussion

1. What is LaVaughn's attitude toward school? How has her environment affected this attitude? What positive character traits does she exhibit in her attitude toward learning? How does her mother support her? How is she supported by teachers?

2. Describe the friendship of LaVaughn, Annie, and Myrtle. How does their friendship change when Myrtle and Annie become members of the Joyful Universal Church of Jesus? Have you ever been part of a friendship that changed? How did you feel?

3. What do you think about the beliefs of the Joyful Universal Church of Jesus? How do Myrtle and Annie change when they are members? Is theirs a change for the good? How do the beliefs of this church differ from those of the minister to whom LaVaughn talks?

4. What kind of woman is LaVaughn's mother? What admirable character traits does she possess? What do you think of her parenting skills? Why does she end the relationship with Lester? What does she do after she tells Lester to leave? What does this tell you about her?

5. How does LaVaughn feel about Jody when he returns? Does he encourage her feelings? Do you think that LaVaughn misreads his actions? Describe LaVaughn's reaction and feelings when she discovers Jody kissing another boy. Do you think that her reactions are understandable?

6. When LaVaughn finds Jody, she understands how a person's life can change in an instant. Have you ever shared this experience? What does this teach you about life and living life to the fullest?

7. Foreshadowing is a literary technique by which situations are predicted by what characters say and do. Does anything in this book lead you to predict that LaVaughn would find Jody kissing another boy?

8. LaVaughn's lab partner, Patrick, has had a difficult life. Describe his life. Do you agree with Patrick that LaVaughn has disrespected him? Does she do the right thing in apologizing to him?

9. LaVaughn gets a job is a hospital laundry. Many of the children in the hospital are critically ill. Although her job might seem a small one, LaVaughn sees herself as doing good. What mark of character does she exhibit? Can you think of any other workers who do not have jobs that might be considered important, yet their jobs are very important in a community?

10. How does the Grammar Build-Up class play an important role in the lives of the students? What goals do the students have? How does the teacher try to motivate and inspire the students?

11. How is the birthday party a fitting end for this novel?

12. By the end of the novel, LaVaughn says "I believe in possibility. In the possibility of possibility. . . . I'm a true believer." How is the title of this book a meaningful one? What are the things in which you truly believe?

Projects

1. LaVaughn is asked to write a character sketch of the most important person in her life, and she chooses her mother. In LaVaughn's voice, write a de-

scription based upon the words and actions of her mother. Explain why and how she is the most important person in LaVaughn's life.

2. Artrille (Doc), Patrick, Ronell, and LaVaughn have all been selected for the special summer science program in chemistry and microbiology. Investigate summer programs like this in your area. Make a catalog of these programs offered in local Ys, schools, colleges, and libraries.

3. Everyone going to the Food and Flashlight Formal had to bring a can of food for the poor. Organize a food drive for your local food pantry, selecting a theme and a method of collection.

4. LaVaughn has decorated the ceiling of her bedroom with trees, birds, and bird nests. Based upon her description, draw the ceiling as you visualize it.

5. Jody buys LaVaughn a book about Michaelangelo. Research the life of the artist, and include in your report the reason why Jody selected this artist.

Vocabulary
Each of the following quotations chosen from *True Believer* includes one or more vocabulary words in **bold print**.

1. "Me and Annie are **sympathetic**. But **sympathy** won't make her life different."
2. "the alleys **reek** and they are full of deadly events that could happen any minute."
3. "birds and beasts are going **extinct**, the rivers are poison, the fish are dying, . . ."
4. "The set has six different greens and enough odd **hues** and shades to do branches and a good tree trunk."
5. "I keep my eyes on the back of Annie's head, **bisecting** her hair **precisely**."
6. "Some little thing makes me **queasy**."
7. "he built the funniest Lego **contraptions** I ever saw"
8. "'You will find other **endeavors** that are more immediately **gratifying**. The rest of you will struggle and be **exalted** in your learning'."
9. "The interviewing woman asked me if I'm **responsible** and **punctual**"
10. "Everything we do is **crucial**."
11. "and hanging plants in the corners, soaking up the steam and **growing immense** with their **privileged** lives."
12. "I **thrash** around and he disappears and the next thing I know he's behind me, hooking both arms under my arms, . . ."
13. "and that makes me feel double bad about getting distracted by my life"
14. "Ick. It makes me **queasy**."

About the Author
Born in Oregon, Virginia Euwer Wolff grew up near Mt. Hood. She was admitted into Smith College, she says, because she was from the West Coast and because she played the violin. After graduating, she became an elementary school teacher, and returned to teaching as an English teacher when her children were grown. She left teaching to become a full-time writer. For relaxation, she swims, hikes, gardens, skis travels, and plays the violin.

From the Author

"I was quite impressionable at the time that Dr. Martin Luther King, Jr. made his 'I Have a Dream' speech. When he spoke of a time when children would be judged 'not by the color of their skin but by the content of their character,' we as a nation were moved. We continue to *say* we believe in this goal, but in practice we're not moving very swiftly or feelingly toward it. Quite simply, I wanted to do my part."

The Watsons Go to Birmingham—1963
Author: Christopher Paul Curtis
Publication date: 1995

Awards
Coretta Scott King Award
Newbery Honor Book

Characters
Kenny Watson
Wilona and Daniel, Kenny's parents
Byron, Kenny's brother
Joetta (Joey), Kenny's sister
Rufus
Grandma Sands

Character Traits
Compassion
Kindness
Perseverance
Respect
Self-control
Tolerance

Setting
1963—Flint, Michigan, and Birmingham, Alabama

Plot
Ten-year-old Kenny narrates the story of his family, whom, he says, the neighbors call the weird Watsons. In fact, the Watson family, consisting of Kenny's parents, Kenny, his brother Byron, and his sister Joey, are a loving, caring, and funny family. Kenny, who is in the fourth grade, is smart but is picked on by other kids for his intelligence and for the lazy eye that gets him nicknamed Cockeye Kenny. He is a sensitive boy, feeling sorry for the victims of bullying. His compassion extends even to bullies who are victimized by bigger bullies; for example, when Byron gets Kenny's gloves back from the boy who stole them, he goes beyond defending his brother and is mean to the point that Kenny cannot stand it and has to leave.

Thirteen-year-old Byron is well on his way to becoming a juvenile delinquent. He charges food on the family's tab, lights fires, takes money from his mother's purse, joins a gang, and has his hair chemically straightened. But he also is sensitive, crying and vomiting when he accidentally kills a bird and comforting

Kenny after the church bombing. He saves Kenny from drowning in a whirl-pool, but doesn't want anyone to know.

When Mrs. and Mrs. Watson believe that extreme measures are necessary to straighten Byron out, they decide to take him to Grandma Sands in Birmingham, Alabama, at least for the summer, and maybe for a year. The family embarks on their trip in the Brown Bomber with Momma's notebook, titled "The Watsons Go to Birmingham—1963," as their guide for everything from where they will stop to what they will eat. The children know that life for Blacks is not the same in the South as it is in Flint, but no one is prepared for the church bombing that physically and emotionally shakes the city. Joey is in the church at the time of the bombing, and the rest of the Watsons run to the church. Kenny is surprised that no one stops him from walking right up to the church. The horrific sights he sees terrify him, and he quickly walks back to his grandma's house.

The family leaves Birmingham the night of the bombing. Back in Flint, Kenny finds a hiding place in back of the couch where he can sit by himself and feel safe. His parents are worried about him, and it takes Byron to coax him out with the truth. Joey left the church to escape the heat, saw Kenny waving at her, and followed him back to Grandma's. Byron tells him how brave he was and ex-plains the unfairness of what has happened. He convinced Kenny that he was going to be all right.

Questions for Discussion

1. Why is Kenny the victim of bullies? Do you know kids who are bullied for similar reasons? What advice would you give Kenny or other children who are victimized in this way?

2. Why is Kenny happy to see the new boy Rufus come to his school? How does their friendship develop? What does Kenny do to jeopardize the friendship? Can you excuse what he did? Have you ever acted as Kenny did?

3. How does Byron deal with the bully who steals Kenny's gloves? How might he have handled the situation in a better way? Why does Kenny have to leave? What does this tell you about him?

4. What kind of boy is Kenny? How does he treat others? Would you like him for a friend? Why?

5. Why does Byron do the things he does? Does he ever surprise you? Can you think of any other ways his parents could have disciplined him that would have been more effective? How does he change as the book progresses?

6. What is the relationship between Kenny and Byron? How do they support each other?

7. Describe the relationships among the members of the Watson family. Do you think they are weird? What does Kenny mean when he says that magic, angels, and genies exist at times when your family is being kind and loyal?

8. Do you think Christopher Paul Curtis does an effective job of showing the horror of the church bombing? How does his description of Joey all dressed up for church add to the horror?

Projects

1. memory.loc.gov/ammem/aaohtml/exhibit/aopart9.html is one of the websites that gives information on the history of the Civil Rights Movement in the United States. Draw a timeline, placing these events in the proper order.
2. In spite of the tragic scene of the church bombing, this novel is full of hilarious scenes of family life. Select one scene, and rewrite it as a one-act play.
3. When Joey gets a white angel as a gift, she wants to hide it because it doesn't look like her. Watch twenty advertisements on television. Make a chart including the product advertised and its appeal to minority groups.
4. Draw a map of the Watson's trip from Flint to Birmingham.
5. Locate information on a person or event of the Civil Rights Movement, for example, Rosa Parks, sit-ins, freedom riders, Martin Luther King, and the March on Washington. Organize your information into a report.
6. Dr. Martin Luther King followed the strategies of Mohandas Gandhi in using nonviolent resistance to bring about change. Make a poster that demonstrates visually the work of both men.

Vocabulary

Each of the following quotations chosen from *The Watsons Go to Birmingham—1963* includes one or more vocabulary words in **bold print**.

1. "Dad said this would **generate** a little heat but he didn't have to tell us this, it seemed like the cold **automatically** made us want to get together and **huddle** up."
2. " 'I've often told you that as Negroes the world is many times a **hostile** place for us.' "
3. "I saw Mr. Alums walking back and forth **whacking** a yardstick in his hand."
4. " 'If, instead of trying to **intimidate** your young brother, you would **emulate** him and use that mind of yours, perhaps you'd find things much easier.' "
5. "This guy was real **desperate** for a friend because even though I wouldn't say much back to him he kept **jabbering** away at me all through class."
6. "Then she **scrunched** her face up like she was eating something sour"
7. "Momma **flicked** some more of Byron's hair back up porcupine-style—"
8. "Momma and Dad just didn't **tolerate** mumbling."
9. " 'The **ultimate** in American knowledge!' "
10. " 'It's the **pinnacle** of Western civilization.' "
11. " 'you have grasped that that speaker is not placed in the rear deck **haphazardly**, . . .' "
12. " 'we've done all we can and it seems the **temptations** are just too much for By here in Flint.' "
13. " 'And you won't believe this, but if you listen to any kind of music long enough, first you get **accustomed** to it and then you learn to like it.' "
14. "He thought I was the **snitch** but it was Joey."

15. "Grandma Sands thought Momma was **hilarious** and cracked up every time Momma got upset or worried about something that she didn't remember or didn't like."

About the Author
Christopher Paul Curtis was born and raised in Flint, Michigan. He worked on an automobile body assembly line and attended the University of Michigan in Flint. While there, he received prizes for his essays and an early version of *The Watsons Go to Birmingham—1963* that became his first published novel. He lives with his wife and children in Michigan.

Zazoo
Author: Richard Mosher
Publication date: 2001

Awards
YALSA Best Books for Young Adults
Association for Library Services to Children Notable Children's Book

Characters
Zazoo
Grand-Pierre
Marius
Monsieur Klein
Juliette LeMiel

Character Traits
Compassion
Courage
Dependability
Kindness
Loyalty
Patience
Resilience
Respect
Respect for the environment
Tolerance

Setting
Present day—France

Plot
Zazoo is almost fourteen years old. Born in Vietnam, she was brought to France by her adoptive grandfather, Grand-Pierre, when she was two, after her parents were killed by a land mine. Zazoo and Grand-Pierre live in an old stone mill between a river and a canal, for which Grand-Pierre is the lockkeeper. Zazoo loves to row her boat on the canal in the warm days and skate with Grand-Pierre in the cold months.

Seventy-eight-year-old Grand-Pierre is becoming increasingly feeble and forgetful. He shuffles when he walks, has difficulty cooking, and can sit for hours knitting socks that could not be worn by anyone. Zazoo learns from the villagers that her grandfather had been a true hero during World War II, which he calls the Awful Time, but he dismisses this thought saying, "Heroes *save* lives." He does not answer Zazoo's questions about the war and tells her to ask the pharmacist, Monsieur Klein.

Monsieur Klein tells her that his was the only Jewish family in their village. His sister Isabelle and Grand-Pierre were in love, but their parents did not want them to marry. The family considered themselves French, first and foremost, and even after they had to wear the Star of David, they refused Grand-Pierre's suggestion to leave the village. Isabelle and her parents were all killed by the Gestapo, and Grand-Pierre led the then fourteen-year-old Klein to safety in the Cévennes Mountains. He tells her that when Grand-Pierre killed soldiers, the Nazis responded by killing the innocent. Later Grand-Pierre tells her that he was blamed for shooting a German lieutenant, and when he didn't turn himself in, Isabelle and her parents were hanged. Monsieur Klein and Grand-Pierre have not spoken for forty-eight years.

Through these days of learning the truth about her grandfather and living with his decline, Zazoo and her friend, Juliette, have a falling out. When Zazoo overhears that Juliette is adopted, she tells her friend the truth, not maliciously but believing that knowledge will strengthen the bond between them. However, Juliette is angry, and they do not speak for months. Zazoo fills the void from this lost friendship with two new friends, Marius and Monsieur Klein. Zazoo is excited about the friendship she has made with the boy Marius, who surprises Zazoo when he asks if Monsieur Klein is married. He visits periodically, but their bond grows through the postcards and messages they mail to each other. Zazoo eventually learns that Marius's grandmother, Simone, and Klein met in the Cévennes Mountains when her family sheltered him. They fell in love, but her family would not allow them to marry because he was Jewish and she was a Protestant Huguenot. Marius wants to reunite them. Through her visits to his pharmacy, Zazoo becomes increasingly friendly with Monsieur Klein. He wants her to call him Félix, and Grand-Pierre suggests she call him Uncle Félix.

At Zazoo's urging, Monsieur Klein comes to the mill, ostensibly to help Zazoo with her boat, but mostly to see Grand-Pierre. He brings with him a picture of Grand-Pierre and Isabelle dancing the tango. Grand-Pierre is overcome with emotion. He looks at it first in the morning and last at night, and talks to the figures in the photograph. Grand-Pierre and Klein are finally at peace with each other. Then, Marius leads his grandmother to a reunion with Félix, and Zazoo and Juliette renew their friendship.

Questions for Discussion

1. From his recollections of Monsieur Klein and his own memories, what qualities did Grand-Pierre possess as a young man? Why does Monsieur Klein tell Zazoo to ask Grand-Pierre about his owl eyes and steady hand? How was Grand-Pierre changed by his experiences and his losses? Why did he adopt Zazoo? What does this tell you about him? Do you think that Grand-Pierre is a coward for not telling Zazoo about his early life as Monsieur Klein claims?

2. What kind of man is Monsieur Klein? How has he been affected by his losses? Do you understand his feelings for Grand-Pierre? Do you agree with Zazoo that he is a brave man?

3. Monsieur Klein and Grand-Pierre have not spoken for forty-eight years. Do you think this is understandable? Is one of them more responsible than the other for this long period of silence?

4. Zazoo tells Marius that her life is complicated. What are the complications in her life? How does she cope with them? Is she a stronger or weaker person because of them?

5. Does Zazoo have any qualities that you admire? Would you like her for a friend?

6. Zazoo is a Vietnamese girl in France. What special problems exist for a minority child in any culture? How would you help Zazoo to feel comfortable if she came to your school?

7. Why does Zazoo tell Juliette that she is adopted? Would you have told Juliette? Do you understand Juliette's reaction? How would you have reacted to similar news?

8. Have you ever had a long period when you did not speak to a good friend? Do you share the feelings Zazoo has about not talking to Juliette? What is important about having a true friend? What does it take to be a good friend?

9. Monsieur Klein and Simone and Grand-Pierre and Isabelle are two couples kept apart by their families because of differences in religion. Do you think the families were right to object to the unions? Are there other circumstances that cause families to object not just to marriages, but also to friendships? Do you agree with this thinking?

10. People call Grand-Pierre a hero, but he disputes this. Do you think he is a hero? Do you think that individuals popular in the media are always true heroes? What qualities do you look for in a hero? Who are your heroes?

Projects

1. In his old age, Grand-Pierre is becoming feeble mentally and physically. Locate information on the elderly and the conditions that commonly afflict them. What has modern medicine discovered that will help in the aging process? Organize your information into a written report.

2. Zazoo and Grand-Pierre live on a canal and operate the locks. Locate information on how locks work in bodies of water. Draw a series of diagrams that show the operation of locks.

3. Zazoo's parents die from an explosion of a land mine. Use the Internet to locate information on the efforts to ban land mines. Organize your information into either a persuasive letter addressed to the President of the United States or a poster.

4. Grand-Pierre and Zazoo both write poetry. Select one, such as the poem about the old grey cat that he started and she finished, or another from the novel. Illustrate the poem with your own drawing, a collage, or a piece of art.

Vocabulary

Each of the following quotations chosen from *Zazoo* includes one or more vocabulary words in **bold print**.

1. "I **peered** down at my feet on the floorboards."
2. "I **clenched** my lip in my teeth to stop it from **quivering**."
3. "A poster showing off a **flawless** blond woman **mocked** me from across the aisle."
4. "He glanced behind me as if to be sure no one **eavesdropped** from the next aisle, . . ."
5. "His smile was so sad, I felt like a **brute**. How could people call him a **finicky** old snob, as if he had no heart?"
6. "I listened to the river **lapping** over the dam where a millstone had once turned to grind the village wheat."
7. "Grand-Pierre **nestled** between us on the bench."
8. "The **clamor** was too loud not to hear."
9. "Through one class and another, I spent my day staring at the ragged flakes and **brooding** about his behavior."
10. "His chair, when he leaned onto it, creaked so loudly it made him **flinch**."
11. "It was more **tolerable** to hear such things if I didn't have to look into his eyes."
12. "He held them out, palms down; they **quivered** and jumped and wouldn't hold still."
13. "It was hard to **traipse** through Monsieur Klein's door as if the world were the same as it had been a few days earlier."
14. "Breathing **plumes** of frost, I **trudged** away from the pharmacy."
15. "while my bones urged me to **burrow** deeper into my bed,"
16. "Grand-Pierre used the arms of his chair to **hoist** himself upright,"

About the Author

Richard Mosher was born in India and grew up in upstate New York. He graduated from Antioch College. He was a cab driver in New York City and a railroad worker in the Midwest. While living in Costa Rica, Ireland, and the Dominican Republic, he worked on his writing. He now lives in Minnesota.

Cultures and Religions Represented in the Novels

African
  Beyond Safe Boundaries
  The Other Side of Truth
  The Return

African-Americans
  Bronx Masquerade
  Miracle's Boys
  Scorpions
  True Believer
  The Watsons Go to Birmingham

Asian
  First Apple
  Sadako . . . Thousand Paper Cranes
  A Single Shard

Asian-American
  Dragonwings
  Journey Home
  A Step from Heaven

Australian
  The Bamboo Flute
  Playing Beattie Bow

Buddhism
  Sadako ... Thousand Paper Cranes
  A Single Shard

Canadian
  Alone at Ninety Foot
  The Maestro

Christianity
  Before We Were Free
  A Hand Full of Stars
  Journey Home
  The Real Plato Jones
  A Step from Heaven

European
  Adem's Cross
  Cat Herself
  Crispin
  Kit's Wilderness
  The Night Journey
  Nory's Song
  The Real Plato Jones
  Zazoo

European Americans
  How I Became an American
  The Night Journey

Hispanic-Americans
  The Circuit
  Esperanza Rising
  The House on Mango Street
  Parrot in the Oven
  Taking Sides

Islam
  Breadwinner
  Homeless Bird
  Shabanu
  A Hand Full of Stars

Judaism
  Beyond Safe Boundaries
  The Night Journey
  The Return
  Samir and Yonatan

Latin American
  Before We Were Free
  Going Home
  Taste of Salt

Middle Eastern
  Habibi

225

A Hand Full of Stars
Samir and Yonatan

Native American
Bearstone
The Heart of a Chief
The Sign of the Beaver
Sing Down the Moon

Southeast Asian
Breadwinner
Clay Marble
Homeless Bird
Shabanu

Interesting and Useful Websites

In doing the research for this book, numerous websites, which might be of great use to those working with the novels, were discovered. Several of the authors cited in this book have created their own home pages, offering a personal contact with the authors and their works. Though the websites differ, biographical information about the author, insights into the writing of the novels, ideas for teaching the novel in the classroom and future projects of the author are usually included.

In addition to these home pages, some publishers of children's novels offer websites that allow you to find data about the authors and their novels as well as ideas for teaching; they also comment on the novels or other sections of the website. Universities and other sources have also provided thought-provoking websites. The following is a list of those we found to be themost interesting and useful; the list does not purport to be all-inclusive.

Author s' Home Pages
Avi: Books, Bios: Bulletin Boards
 www.avi-writer.com
Beverly Naidoo Award Winning Author
 www.beverlynaidoo.com
Ching Yeung Russell Website
 www.ching yeung.homestead.com
David Almond Home page
 www.davidalmond.com
Gloria Whelan Home Page
 www.gloriawhelan.com
Jacqueline Woodson Home Page
 www.jacquelinewoodson.com
Joseph Bruchac Home Page
 www.josephbruchac.com
Linda Sue Park Home Page
 www.lspark.com
Nikki Grimes—Poet—Author
 www.nikigrimes.com
Nina Bawden Home Page
 www.ninabawden.net
Official Gary Soto Website
 www.garysoto.com
Official Website of Award-Winning Children's Book Author, Will Hobbs
 www.willhobbsauthor.com
Pam Munoz Ryan

www.pammunozryan.com
Sonia Levitin Home Page
    www.bol.ucla.edu/~slevitin.com
Suzanne Francis Staples Home Page
    www.suzannefisherstaples.com

Publishers' Websites
Harper Children's
    www.harperchildren's.com
Houghton Mifflin Education Place
    www.eduplace.com
Puffin Books
    www.puffin.co.uk
Random House
    www.randomhouse.com/features/garypaulsen/
    randomhouse.com/teachersbdd/
Scholastic
    www.scholastic.com
Simon Says Kids
    simonandschuster.com/kids
Young Readers Penguin Putnam, Inc.
    www. penguinputnam.com/yreaders/index.htm

Miscellaneous Websites
ALA Website Site Map
    www.ala.org/sitemap.html
Carol Hurst's Children's Literature Site
    www.carolhurst.com/index.html
Children of the World—NYPL
    www.nypl.org/branch/kids/world.html
Children's Book Council Online
    www.cbcbooks.org/index.htm
Children's Literature Web Guide
    www.acs.ucalgary.ca/~dkbrown/authors.html
Education Place
    www.eduplace.com/kids/
ERIC Clearinghouse on Reading, English, & Communication
    www.indiana.edu/~eric_ rec/
The Internet Public Library Youth Division
    www.ipl.org/youth/HomePage.html
Kay E. Vandergrift's Special Interest Page
    www.scils.rutgers.edu~Kvander/
A Multicultural Literature Bibliography
    scholar.lib.vt.edu/ejournals/ALAN
Multicultural Resources for Children
    falcon.jmu.edu/~ramseyil/authormulasia/htm.

The Reading Corner
   www.car.lib.md.us/read/index.htm
Reading Plans from the Teacher's Desk
   www.knownet.net/users/Ackley/reading_plans.html
Voices from the Gap
   voices.cla.umn.edu/authors
Yahoo Author Series
   www.promotions.yahoo.com.promotions/authors
Yahooligans
   www.yahooligans.com

Bibliography

Novels

Almond, David. *Kit's Wilderness*. New York: Delacorte Press, 2000.

Alvarez, Julia. *Before We Were Free*. New York: Alfred A. Knopf, 2002.

Auch, Mary Jane. *Ashes of Roses*. New York: Henry Holt, 2002.

Avi. *Crispin*. New York: Hyperion Books for Children, 2002.

Bawden, Nina. *The Real Plato Jones*. New York: Clarion Books, 1993.

Bruchac, Joseph. *The Heart of a Chief*. New York: Puffin Book, 1998.

Carmi, Daniella. *Samir and Yonatan*. Trans. Yael Lotan. New York: Arthur A. Levine Books, 2000.

Cisneros, Sandra. *The House on Mango Street*. Houston: Arte Publico Press, 1984.

Coerr, Eleanor. *Sadako and the Thousand Paper Cranes*. Illus. Ronald Himles. New York: Puffin Books, 1999.

Creech, Sharon. *Bloomability*. New York: HarperTrophy, 1999.

Curtis, Christopher Paul. *The Watsons Go to Birmingham—1963*. New York: Delacorte Press, 1995.

Cushman, Karen. *Rodzina*. New York: Clarion Books, 2003.

Disher, Garry. *The Bamboo Flute*. New York: Tichnor & Fields, 1993.

Ellis, Deborah. *The Breadwinner*. Buffalo: Douglas & McIntyre, 2000.

Fritz, Jean. *Homesick: My Own Story*. New York: Dell, 1982.

Giff, Patricia Reilly. *Nory Ryan's Song*. New York: Delacorte Press, 2000.

Grimes, Nikki. *Bronx Masquerade*. New York: Dial Books, 2002.

Gündisch, Karin. *How I Became an American*. Trans. James Skofield. Chicago: Cricket Books, 2001.

Ho, Minfong. *The Clay Marble*. New York: Farrar, Strauss, Giroux, 1991.

Hobbs, Will. *Bearstone*. New York: Atheneum, 1989.

Holubitsky, Katherine. *Alone at Ninety Foot*. Victoria, B.C.: Orca Book Publishers, 1999.

Hunter, Molly. *Cat Herself*. New York: Harper & Row Publishers, 1985.

Jiménez, Francisco. The *Circuit: Stories from the Life of a Migrant Child*. Boston: Houghton Mifflin, 1997.

Lasky, Kathryn. *The Night Journey*. New York: Frederick Warne & Co., 1981.

Lawrence, Iain. *Ghost Boy*. New York: Random House, 2000.

Levitin, Sonia. *The Return*. New York: Ballantine Books, 1987.

Martinez, Victor. *Parrot in the Oven: Mi Vida*. New York: HarperCollins, 1996.

Mead, Alice. *Adem's Cross*. New York: Bantam Doubleday Dell, 1996.

Mosher, Richard. *Zazoo*. New York: Clarion Books, 2001.

Myers, Walter Dean. *Scorpions*. New York: Harper & Row, 1988.

Nye, Naomi Shihab. *Habibi*. New York: Simon & Schuster, 1997.

Na, An. *A Step from Heaven*. Asheville: Front Street, 2001.
Naidoo, Beverly. *The Other Side of Truth*. New York: HarperCollins, 2001.
O'Dell, Scott. *Sing down the Moon*. Boston: Houghton Mifflin, 1970.
Park, Ruth. *Playing Beatie Bow*. New York: Atheneum, 1982.
Park, Linda Sue. *A Single Shard*. New York: Clarion Books, 2001.
Russell, Ching Yeung. *First Apple*. Illus. Christopher Zhong-Yuan Zhang. Honesdale: Boyd Mills Press, 1994.
Ryan, Pam Muñoz. *Esperanza Rising*. New York: Scholastic Press, 2000.
Sacks, Margaret. *Beyond Safe Boundaries*. New York: Lodestar Books, 1989.
Schami, Rafik. *A Hand Full of Stars*. Trans. Rika Lesser. New York: Dutton, 1990.
Soto, Gary. *Taking Sides*. New York: Simon & Schuster, 1997.
Speare, Elizabeth George. *The Sign of the Beaver*. Boston: Houghton Mifflin, 1983.
Staples, Suzanne Fisher. *Shabanu, Daughter of the Wind*. New York: Alfred A. Knopf, 1989.
Temple, Frances. *Grab Hands and Run*. New York: HarperCollins, 1993.
Ucheda, Yoshiko. Journey Home. Illus. Charles Robinson. New York: Atheneum, 1978.
Whelan, Gloria. *Homeless Bird*. New York: HarperCollins, 2000.
Wolff, Virginia Euwer. *True Believer*. New York: Atheneum Books for Young Readers, 2001.
Woodson, Jacqueline. *Miracle's Boys*. New York: G.P. Putnam's Sons, 2000.
Wynne Jones, Tim.*The Maestro*. New York: Orchard Books, !995.
Yep, Laurence. *Dragonwings*. New York: Harper & Row Publishers, 1975.

Sources

The Alan Review. scholar.lib.vt.edu/ejournals/ALAN.
Authors & Artists for Young Adults. Detroit: Gale Research, Inc. Multiple volumes.
Biography Resource Center. Gale Group. infotrac.galegroup.com. Jan. 2002–July 2003.
The Children's Literature Web Guide. www.ucalgary.ca/~dkbrown/ Jan. 2002–July 2003.
Gallo, Donald R., ed. *Speaking for Ourselves*. Urbana: National Council of Teachers of English, 1990.
Gallo, Donald R., ed. *Speaking for Ourselves Too*. Urbana: National Council of Teachers of English, 1990.
Junior Book of Authors series. New York: H.W. Wilson. Multiple volumes.
Major Authors and Illustrators for Children and Young Adults. Detroit: Gale Research, Inc. Multiple volumes.
Pam Munoz Ryan. www.pammunozryan.com. Sept. 5, 2003.
Petrescu, Ioana. Garry Disher Website. ehlt.flinders.edu.au/English/Garry Disher/GarryDisher.html. Aug. 10,2003.
Something about the Author series. New York: Gale Group. Multiple volumes.

Index

Fictional characters are found in italic.

About the Authors

Rosann Jweid has received her degrees from the State University of New York with a Bachelor of Science from Oswego and a Master of Library Science from Albany. She spent twenty-five years as a high school and junior high school librarian. For ten years of this time, she was also the library department chairman for her school district. Presently, she is a self-employed consultant. In this capacity, she has set up a textbook purchasing procedure for the area Board of Cooperative Educational Services, and has organized and prepared a private school library for automation.

Margaret Rizzo received a bachelor's degree in English from the College of Saint Rose, a master's degree in English from Siena College, and a master's degree in library science from the State University of New York at Albany. She has been a middle school library media specialist in a suburban school in upstate New York for more than thirty years, and is now the K-12 district department head for libraries. She is very active in school programs that promote positive character traits; for example, she is an organizer for a community service day for students. She is presently working on a book, *Building Character through Service Learning*, to be published by Scarecrow Press.

Both authors spent several years as classroom teachers before entering the library field. As such, they learned the value of collaboration between the library media specialist and the classroom teacher. They coauthored two editions of *The Library Classroom Partnership*, and have presented several programs on reading enrichment and library/subject area collaboration at professional conferences. Their last book, *Building Character through Literature*, introduced novels that show strength of character, with guidance for discussions that can raise character issues.